AN ILLUSTRATED GUIDE TO
MODERN
TRAINS

a Salamander book

Published by Arco Publishing, Inc.
NEW YORK

AN ILLUSTRATED GUIDE TO
MODERN
TRAINS

Brian Hollingsworth

A Salamander Book

Published by
Arco Publishing, Inc.,
215 Park Avenue South,
New York, N.Y. 10003,
United States of America.

© 1985 by Salamander Books Ltd.,
27 Old Gloucester Street,
London WC1N 3AF,
United Kingdom.
All rights reserved.

Library of Congress Cataloging in Publication Data

Hollingsworth, J. B. (John Brian)
     An illustrated guide to modern trains.
     "A Salamander book."
     1. Railroads.   I. Title.
TF145.H7526   1985   625.2'0973   85-6005
ISBN 0-668-06495-1

Credits

Editor: Ray Bonds

Designer: Philip Gorton.

Artwork: David Palmer, Clifford and
Wendy Meadway, Terry Hadler and
Dick Eastland.

Filmset: Modern Text Ltd.
**Color and monochrome
reproduction:** Melbourne Graphics
and Rodney Howe Ltd.
Printed in Belgium by
Proost International Book Production,
Turnhout.

The Author

Brian Hollingsworth, M.A., M.I.C.E., is a former civil engineer with Britain's Great Western Railway. He was also heavily involved with British Rail's computers and the TOPS wagon and train control system. He is a director of the Romney, Hythe and Dymchurch Railway, and civil engineering advisor to the Festiniog Railway. He has a fleet of one-fifth full size locomotives which run in his own "back garden" (on a Welsh mountain!), and he owns the full size LMS "Black Five" Class 4-6-0 No. 5428 *Eric Treacy,* which operates for tourists and rail enthusiasts on the North Yorkshire Moors Railway. Mr. Hollingsworth is the author of more than a dozen books on various aspects of the world's railways and locomotives, besides being a contributor to technical railway periodicals.

The publishers wish to thank **Arthur Cook,** who was responsible for many of the American locomotive entries and who, with his sons, helped with several others; **Christopher Bushell,** who checked the manuscript and made many valuable suggestions; and, for tracking down the beautiful photographs, **Diane** and **John Moore.**

Contents

Introduction

This book describes what has happened to railway motive power during the last 40 momentous years. It tells the story of how at the end of World War II a period of fundamental change began to take place in the sort of locomotive used on the world's railways and how quickly the scene altered beyond recognition.

Only 40 years ago steam still ruled on most railways, just as it had done for more than a century; the star of diesel-electric had still to rise. Electric traction had been with us for a long time but was then an economic proposition in only rather special circumstances. Both electrification and dieselisation still had a long way to go.

Today steam locomotion has in general gone the way of the stage coach and the sailing ship. But happily it has not moved into oblivion. Instead it has become a new kind of showbiz, with steam trains in most parts of the world operated purely for our enjoy-ment. Other forms of power have become the norm for practical use on railways.

Perhaps one sad aspect of this move away from steam is that we can no longer see for ourselves how a locomotive works just by looking at it. Whereas the simple works of a steam locomotive are mostly exposed in full view, the sophisticated technical features of modern traction are completely hidden away. Often the bits that make a modern train go can be tucked away inside the carriages, so no locomotive is needed. No longer does the rail traveller go up to the front "to look at the engine"—if often doesn't have one!

However, the complexities of modern diesels and electrics are nonetheless fascinating and, indeed, the criterion for selection of locomotives in this book has been the presence of some particularly interesting technical features. We have made a point of including a few of those rare machines which manage to survive

whilst swimming against the tide by being neither diesel-electric nor straight electric. Included, then, are samples of diesel-hydraulic, diesel-mechanical, electro-diesel and gas turbine traction.

But it must be said that—with the occasional honourable exception—the degree of success of most locomotive designs depends not on how much technical innovation is included in them but on how little. So the solid reliable work-horses that bear the brunt of the day-by-day burdens of the world's railway systems are given their fair and well-deserved share of attention.

Another change has taken place since the demise of steam. In the old days even quite small and agricultural countries used to design and build their own steam loco-motives. Nowadays, however, not only is the variety much less but most countries of the world outside the Communist bloc buy their locomotives off-the-shelf (or assemble them under licence) from one firm in the USA, so that railway motive power is very much the same from Anchorage, Alaska, to Christchurch, New Zealand.

Coming events cast their shadows before them and signs are beginning to be seen —to be found towards the end of this book—that big changes are again on the way. These have been engendered by the rising cost of oil compared with coal and other sources of energy. Whilst the prophets of doom in this area seem generally to have got their time-scales a little wrong, it seems quite certain that before another 40 years has passed something other than oil-consuming diesel-electric locomotives will have taken prime position in the motive power stakes of the world's railways.

Below: Tilting trains are intended to improve speeds without the need to build new railways. Here an LRC train of Via Rail Canada speeds past.

F3 Model B₀-B₀

Origin: Electro-Motive Division, General Motors Corporation (EMD), USA. **Type:** All-purpose diesel-electric locomotive, "A" units with cab, "B" units without. **Gauge:** 4ft 8½in (1,435mm). **Propulsion:** One EMD 567B 1,500hp (1,120kW) 16-cylinder pressure-charged two-stoke Vee engine and generator supplying current to four nose-suspended traction motors geared to the axles. **Weight:** 230,000lb (104.4t) (minimum without train heating steam generator). **Axleload:** 57,500lb (26.1t). **Overall length:** "A" unit 50ft 8in (15,443mm), "B" unit 50ft 0in (15,240mm). **Tractive effort:** 57,500lb (256kN). **Max speed:** Between 50mph (80km/h) and 120mph (192km/h) according to which of eight possible gear ratios fitted. **Service entry:** 1945.

The railway locomotive leads a rugged existence, and only the fittest survive. Evolution has thus tended to move in moderate steps, and few successful developments have been sufficiently dramatic to merit the term "revolutionary". One such step was the pioneer four-unit freight diesel, No. 103, produced by the Electro-Motive Division of General Motors in 1939. When that unit embarked on a 83,764 mile (134,776km) demonstration tour of 20 major American railroads, few people, other than EMD's Chief Engineer Richard M. Dilworth, ever imagined that it would be possible for the country to be paying its last respects to steam

Below: A pair of "F3" units as supplied to the Baltimore & Ohio Railroad. The left-hand one is a "cab" or "A" unit while the right-hand one with no driving cab is a "booster" or "B" unit.

Above: A short Gulf, Mobile & Ohio Railroad suburban train leaves Chicago behind a single "F"-series diesel-electric locomotive.

Left: "F"-series cab and booster units of the Canadian Pacific Railway on a passenger train at London, Ontario, in January 1983.

only 20 years later.

By 1939 EMD had some six years' experience of powering high-speed passenger trains by diesel locomotives tailored to suit the customer's requirements. Their ability to outrun the best steam locomotives had gained them acceptance in many parts of the USA, but this was a specialised activity, and even the most diesel-minded motive power officer did not regard the diesels an alternative to the ten, twelve or sixteen coupled steam locomotive for the heavy grind of freight haulage.

Dilworth had faith in the diesel, and his company shared his faith to the tune of a four-unit demonstrator weighing 912,000lb (414t) and 193ft (58,830mm) in length. Most of the passenger diesels built so far incorporated the lightweight Winton 201 engine, which EMD had acquired, but in 1938 EMD produced its own 567 series of two-stroke Vee engines (numbered from the cubic capacity of the cylinder in cubic inches). The 16-cylinder version was rated at 1,350hp (1,010kW), and this fitted conveniently into a four-axle Bo-Bo layout, with the whole weight thus available for adhesion. ▶

▶   Two such units were permanently coupled, an "A" unit with cab and a "B" or booster unit without; two of these pairs were coupled back-to-back by normal couplings. Multiple-unit control enabled one driver to control all four units, but they could easily be separated into pairs, or, with a little more work, into 1 plus 3. Dilworth reckoned that a 2,700hp pair was the equal of a typical steam 2-8-2 or 2-10-2, and that the full 5,400hp (4,030kW) set could equal any of the largest articulated steam locomotives. As the combined starting tractive effort of his four units was almost double that of the largest steam engine, his claim had some substance. They were geared for a maximum speed of 75mph (120km/h) but could be re-geared for 102mph (164km/h), thereby producing a true mixed-traffic locomotive.

The units were built on the "carbody" principle, that is, the bodyshell was stressed and formed part of the load-bearing structure of the locomotive. The smooth streamlined casing was in sharp contrast to the Christmas-tree appearance of most large American steam engines, festooned as they were with gadgets. But this was one of the revolutionary ideas demonstrated by No. 103. Bright liveries on the passenger stream-liners had attracted great publicity; now there was the possibility of giving the freight locomotive a similar image.

Despite the scepticism of steam locomotive engineers, 20 railroads

**Above: A single "F" cab unit heads a short train on the Denver &
Rio Grande Railroad's steeply graded Moffat Tunnel route.**

spread over 35 states responded to EMD's invitation to give No. 103 a
trial, and everywhere it went it improved on the best steam performance
by a handsome margin. From sea level to 10,240ft (3,120m), from 40°F
below zero (−40°C) to 115°F (46°C), the story was the same. Typical
figures were an average speed of 26mph (42km/h) over 98 miles (158km)
of 1-in-250 grade with 5,400t, compared with 10mph (16km/h) by a
modern 4-6-6-4, or an increase in load from 3,800t with a 2-8-4 to
5,100t. The booster units were equipped with steam generators for train
heating, and this enabled No. 103 to show its paces on passenger trains.
The impression it made on motive power men was profound.

Not least amongst the startling qualities of No. 103 was its reliability.
Throughout the 11-month tour no failure occurred, and even when
allowance is made for the close attention given by accompanying EMD
staff, this was a remarkable achievement.

Production locomotives, designated "FT", followed closely on the heels
of the demonstrator, and orders were soon received from all parts of the
country. EMD's La Grange Works was tooled-up for quantity production,
and over a period of six years 1,096 "FT" units were built, Santa Fe being ▶

13

▶ the biggest customer with 320 units. The War Production Board was sufficiently impressed by the contribution which these locomotives could make to the war effort to allow manufacture to continue with only a short break, despite the use of scarce alloys.

By the end of the war the freight diesel was fully accepted on many railroads, and total dieselisation was already in the minds of some motive power chiefs. The first post-war development was production of the 567B engine rated at 1,500hp (1,120kW) to replace the 1,350hp 567A model. After 104 interim units designated "F2", there came a four-unit demonstrator of the "F3" model, with a larger generator to suit the 1,500hp engine, and a number of other improvements based on six year's experience with the "FTs". Amongst these were automatically-operated cooling fans; the fans fitted to the "FTs" were mechanically-driven through clutches, and had manually-worked shutters. The fireman had a frantic rush to de-clutch the fans and close the shutters when the engine was shut down, particulary in severe cold when the radiators would freeze very quickly.

EMD proclaimed the "F3" as "the widest range locomotive in history", and the railroads seemed to agree, for new sales records were set with a total of 1,807 units sold in little more than two years up to 1949. Railroads took advantage of the scope which the smooth curved shape offered for imaginative colour schemes, and an EMD pamphlet showed 40 different liveries in which these locomotives had been supplied.

Simplicity of maintenance, and improvements in the engine to reduce fuel consumption, were two of EMD's claims for the "F3", and these same claims were repeated for the next model, the "F7", launched in 1949. The main change from the "F3" was in the traction motors and other electrical

equipment. With the same engine power, the new motors enabled 25 per cent more load to be hauled up heavy grades. The model was offered with the usual options, including eight gear ratios.

The "F7" proved to be a bestseller too; 49 US roads bought 3,681 "F7s" and 301 "FP7s", the version with train-heating boiler, whilst Canada and Mexico took 238 and 84 respectively. They handled every type of traffic from the fastest passenger trains to the heaviest freight. Measured by sales, the "F7" was the most successful carbody diesel ever. "F7" production ended in 1953, to be replaced by the "F9". The main change was the 567C engine of 1,750hp (1,305kW). By time the US market for carbody diesels was drying up, as "hood" units gained popularity, and only 175 "F9s" were buit over a period of three years.

By the 1960s steam had been replaced totally, and manufacturers were now selling diesels to replace diesels. Trading-in old models became popular, and bogies in particular could be re-used. Many "Fs" were replaced in this way as the more powerful hood units became increasingly popular, and the decline of passenger traffic helped the process. Nevertheless some units of the "F" series were still to be found at work in 1984, and the Canadian locomotives, in particular, could still be seen on passenger trains.

The "F" series, more than any other model, showed, showed that improvements in performance and economies in operation could be achieved in all types of traffic by dieselisation, despite uncertainties about the life which could be expected from a diesel locomotive.

Below: Four General Motors' "F" series units of the Denver & Rio Grande Western RR head the westbound "Western Zephyr".

Niagara Class 4-8-4

Origin: New York Central Railroad (NYC), USA. **Type:** Express passenger steam locomotive. **Gauge:** 4ft 8½in (1,435mm). **Propulsion:** Coal fire with a grate area of 10sq ft (9.3m²) generating steam at 272psi (19.3kg/m²) in a fire-tube boiler, and supplying it via a superheater to two 25½ x 32in (648 x 813mm) cylinders, driving the main wheels direct by means of connecting and coupling rods. **Weight:** 274,000lb (124t) adhesive, 891,000lb (405t) total. **Axleload:** 70,000lb (32t). **Overall length:** 115ft 5½in (35,192mm). **Tractive effort:** 61,570lb (27,936kg). **Max speed:** 80mph (128km/h). **Service entry:** 1945.

The New York Central Railroad's speedway from New York to Chicago, was in steam days arguably the greatest passenger railway in the world, in terms of speeds run and tonnage moved. By the 1940s these speeds and loads were beginning to be as much as the famous Hudsons could cope with and the Central's chief of motive power, Paul Kiefer, decided to move on a step. He proposed a 4-8-4 with more than 30 per cent greater adhesive weight and tractive effort than the 4-6-4, together with a fire grate 25 per cent bigger. His aim was a locomotive which could develop 6,000hp in the cylinder for hour after hour and could do the New York-Chicago run day after day without respite.

The American Locomotive Company at Schenectady proposed what was to be the last really new design of passenger locomotive to be produced in the USA. It owed something to the Union Pacific's "800" class; dimensionally, the two designs were very close and, in addition, the design of the 14-wheel Centipede or 4-10-0 tender was certainly based on UP's. The NYC engines had something else unusual for North America, in common with the "800s"—a smooth and uncluttered appearance but with no false streamlining or air-smoothing.

Because the NYC structure gauge only allowed rolling stock to be 15ft 2in (4,623mm) high instead of 16ft 2in (4,928mm) as on the UP, the chimney had to be vestigial and the dome little but a manhole cover. There were other differences, such as Baker's valve gear instead of Walschaert's, but in general the adoption of standard American practice led to similarities.

The foundation of the design was a cast steel integral locomotive frame—nothing else could have stood up to the punishment intended for these engines. Also, as one might expect, all axles, coupling rods and connecting rods had roller bearings. Baker's valve gear has the advantage that it has no slides, so all its moving parts could, as in this case, be fitted with needle bearings. While speaking of the valves, an interesting detail was that the edges of the valve-ports were sharp on the steam side, but slightly rounded on the exhaust side. This eased the sharpness of the blast beats, thereby evening out the draught on the fire.

Although fundamentally of the same design as that fitted to the UP locos, the tender had some interesting differences. The fact that the NYC was one of the very few American railroads equipped with water troughs meant that less water could be carried, leaving more capacity for coal.

Above: Heading "The Missourian" from St Louis to New York, "Niagara" No. 6018 leans to the curve at Peekskill, New York State.

This enabled the New York-Chicago run to be done with just one intermediate coaling, while an improved design of power-operated, pick-up scoop reduced delays by allowing water to be taken at 80mph (128km/h). Special extra venting avoided bursting the tenders (there had been cases!) when some 1,600cu ft (45m³) of incompressible fluid entered the tank all in a few seconds. Incidentally, the overhang of the tank at the rear was to allow the engines to be turned on 100ft turntables by reducing the wheelbase.

Allocating the number 6000 to a locomotive whose target was that amount of horsepower as well as that number of miles run per week might seem to be tempting providence, but all was well. The prototype had the sub-class designation "Sla", while the 25 production models (Nos. 6001-6025) were known as "Slb", and there was also a single poppet-valve version known as "Slc" (No. 5500). This greatest of steam locomotives got the class-name "Niagara" and when the word is uttered, no steam man ▶

Below: Regarded by many as The Ultimate Steam Locomotive Of All Time—the vast "Niagara" 4-8-4 of the New York Central Railroad.

▶ worthy of the name ever thinks of a waterfall!. Both targets were achieved —6,700hp on test and an average of 26,000 miles run monthly.

The original idea was that the prototype should be tested and then a production order confirmed, but before work had gone very far instructions were given for all 27 to be put in hand. This was reasonable because in fact the "Niagaras" were very much a standard, if slightly stretched, product of the industry, whereas what really needed attention was the ground organisation to enable the mileage target to be met. And this, of course, could not be tested until a fleet was available.

By an ordinance of the City of New York, steam locomotives were not allowed inside city limits. Trains therefore left Grand Central Station behind third-rail electric locos for Harmon, 32 miles out in the suburbs. It was here, then, and at Chicago that the "Niagaras" were, in their great days, kept in first-class condition for what was without doubt one of the hardest services ever demanded of steam, or for that matter, of any motive power.

World records are not achieved without extreme efforts, but excellent organisation allowed quick and thorough servicing. The power production part of the locomotives had to be just-so to give such a remarkable performance out on the road, and to achieve this the fire was first dropped with the engine in steam. Then a gang of "hot men" in asbestos suits entered the firebox—the size of a room—and cleared tubes and flues, and did repairs to the brick arch and grate. Good water treatment ensured that no scale built up in the heating surface, preventing the heat reaching the water inside the boiler. On many railways steam locomotives were allocated one "shed day" each week for these things to be done, but running the 928 miles (1,493km) from Harmon to Chicago or *vice versa* each night, the "Niagaras" needed to do a week's work in one 24-hour period.

In those days there were 12 daily trains each way just between New York and Chicago—the "Chicagoan", the "Advance Commodore Vanderbilt", the "Commodore Vanderbilt", the "Advance Empire State Express", the "Empire Express", the "Lake Shore Limited", the "Mohawk", the "North Shore Limited", the "Pacemaker", the "Water Level", the "Wolverine" and, the greatest of all, the 16 hour "Twentieth Century Limited".

Even the most fanatical steam enthusiast would admit that other factors

Above: Smoke and steam fill the air as a New York Central "Niagara" takes a westbound passenger train out of Dunkirk, NY.

have contributed, but nevertheless the Day of the "Niagaras" did mark a peak. The best time by diesel traction today on this route between New York and Chicago is 16hr 50min and there is only one train.

The "Niagaras" also demonstrated once again that modern well-maintained steam power could be more economical than diesel. Alas, in those days, coal supplies controlled by miners' leader John L. Lewis were less reliable than oil supplies; moreover, most of New York Central's steam power was neither modern nor well-maintained. So, having run more miles and hauled more tons in their short lives than most locomotives which run out their term to obsolescence, the "Niagaras" went to their long home. None has been preserved.

Below: Able to produce 6,000hp and run 26,000 miles per month, the superb "Niagara" 4-8-4s of the New York Central RR were regarded by many as the Ultimate Steam Locomotive.

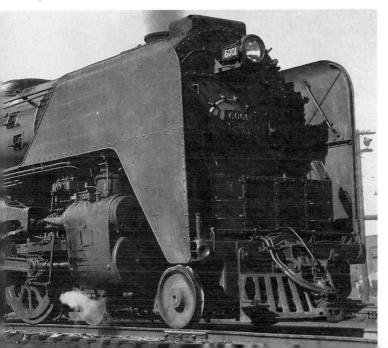

19

E7 Series A1A-A1A

Origin: Electro-Motive Division, General Motors Corporation (EMD), USA. **Type:** Express passenger diesel-electric locomotive; "A" units with driving cab, "B" units without. **Gauge:** 4ft 8½in (1,435mm). **Propulsion:** Two EMD 567A 1,000hp (746kW) 12-cylinder pressure-charged two-stroke Vee engines and generators, each supplying current to two nose-suspended traction motors geared to the end axles of a bogie. **Weight:** "A" unit 212,310lb (96.3t) adhesive, 315,000lb (142.9t) total. "B" units 205,570lb (93.3t) adhesive, 305,000lb (138.4t) total. **Axleload:** "A" 53,080lb (24.1t), "B" 51,390lb (23.3t). **Overall length:** :"A" 71ft 1¼in (21,670mm),"B" 70ft 0in (21,340mm). **Tractive effort:** 53,080lb (236kN). **Max speed:** 85mph (137km/h), 92mph (148km/h), 98mph (157km/h), or 117mph (188km/h) according to gear ratio fitted. **Service entry:** 1945.

In 1930 the General Motors Corporation made two purchases which were to have dramatic effects on the American locomotive scene. The first was the Winton Engine Co, a builder specialising in lightweight diesel engines. The second was Winton's chief customer, the Electro-Motive Corporation, established in 1922 to design and market petrol-electric railcars, which had sold some 500 units in 10 years. With the engine-building facility and the expertise acquired in these purchases, GM's new Electro-Motive Division (EMD) was a major partner in the sensational pioneer streamlined trains introduced in 1934, and in the following year the firm produced its first locomotives. These were four Bo-Bo units with rectangular "Boxcar" bodies, each powered by two 900hp (670kW) Winton 12-cylinder Vee engines. Pending completion of its own plant, EMD had to employ other builders to assemble them.

In 1936 EMD moved into its own purpose-built works at La Grange, Illinois, and work commenced on the next locomotives. These were the first of the "E" series, known also as the "Streamline" series. Like the four earlier locomotives, they had two 900hp Winton engines, but the chassis and body were completely new. The body had its main load-bearing strength in two bridge-type girders which formed the sides. The bogies had three axles to give greater stability at high speeds, but as only four motors were needed, the centre axle of each bogie was an idler, giving the wheel arrangement A1A-A1A. The units were produced in two versions, "A" units with a driver's cab and "B" units without. The Baltimore & Ohio was the first purchaser, taking six of each type to use as 3,600hp (2,690kW) pairs. Santa Fe bought eight "As" and three "Bs", and the "City" streamliner roads bought two "A-B-B" sets for the "City of Los Angeles" and the "City of San Francisco". These latter at 5,400hp were

Above: A model E7 diesel-electric locomotive built to head the streamliners, on a Chicago double-deck commuter train.

the world's most powerful diesel locomotives when they appeared in 1937. The B&O units were classed "EA" and "EB", the Santa Fe were "E1A" and "E1B", and the City units "E2A" and "E2B".

All these locomotives were an immediate success, not only by their performances but also by their reliability. The reliability was a striking tribute to the quality of the design, for there had been no demonstrator subsequent to the "boxcar" Bo-Bos. In multiple-unit working it was possible for some maintenance to be done on the road on the easier stretches, on which one engine could be shut down. With servicing assisted in this way, remarkable feats of endurance could be achieved. One of the B&O "A-B" sets gained national publicity when it completed 365 continuous days of service between Washington and Chicago, covering 282,000 miles (454,000km) at an average scheduled speed of 56mph (90km/h).

Progress at La Grange was rapid. At 900hp the Winton engine was reaching its limit, and an EMD engine was therefore developed. Designated ▶

Below: A 2,000hp E9 diesel-electric cab unit of the Chicago, Rock Island & Pacific RR, specially painted in the stunning livery of that line's prestigious "Rocket" express trains.

Below: A Gulf, Mobile & Ohio passenger train headed by an unusual mixed diesel-electric locomotive set consisting of an "E"-series "cab" unit and an "F"-series "booster" unit.

Above: An "E8A" "cab" unit of the Burlington Northern RR heads a double-deck push-pull Chicago suburban train.

▶ 567 (the capacity of a cylinder in cubic inches), it was available in three sizes with 8, 12, and 16 cylinders, giving 600, 1,000 and 1,350hp (448, 746 and 1,007kW). Simultaneously La Grange began to manufacture its own generators, motors and other electrical equipment.

First all-EMD locomotives were an order from Seaboard Air Line for 14 "A" and five "B" units, which appeared from October 1938 onwards. They had two 1,000hp engines and were operated as 6,000hp three-unit "lash-ups" (in the US jargon). These were the "E4s". "E3" and "E5" followed, the former comprising 18 units for the Santa Fe and the latter 16 for the Burlington.

So far each railroad's order had incorporated some individual variations —hence the different designations—but EMD aimed to gain the maximum benefits from production-line assembly of locomotives, to which end individual variations were to be discouraged. The next series, the "E6", which appeared in the same month in 1939 as the first freight demonstrator (No. 103), was therefore a standard off-the-shelf unit, with the minimum of options. This was the start of real diesel mass production and 118 units had been built by the time the War Production Board terminated building of passenger locomotives in February 1942.

Construction of passenger locomotives was resumed in February 1945 with the first of the "E7" series. These locomotives benefited from the experience gained from both the "E" and the "F" series freight units. Improvements included a new and larger cooling system for the engine. Externally there was a noticeable difference in that the front of the body was sloped at 80° to the horizontal, as in the "F" series, instead of 70°, as in previous "E" series bodies. Apart from this change, there were few differences in external appearance throughout the range of "E" series, and most of them concerned windows and portholes.

With locomotive fleets rundown by wartime traffic, the railroads were even more eager to acquire passenger diesels, and settle down to a steady production of "E7s", averaging 1 per month for four years. During this time 428 "A" units and 82 "B" units were built, so that the "E7" out-numbered the passenger diesels of all other US makers put together. In general, "E7s" were bought by roads with fast passenger services on easy gradients; for mountain work the all-adhesion "F" series was favourite.

Amongst "E7" buyers were the Pennsylvania and the New York Central. With 60 and 50 units respectively they had the largest numbers of any owner. On the NYC the most thorough comparison ever made between steam and diesel was conducted during October 1946. Two twin "E7" locomotives were tested against six of the new "Niagara" 4-8-4 steam engines working between Harmon, New York, and Chicago, 928 miles (1,493km). The "E7s" averaged 28,954 miles in the month and the 4-8-4s 27,221. Average operating costs per mile were $1.11 for the "E7" and $1.22 for the 4-8-4. However, a succession of coal strikes and then some trouble with the alloy steel boilers of the "Niagaras" insured that the NYC did not allow its lingering love of steam to interpret the results in favour of the 4-8-4s. But the tests were still encouraging to steam enthusiasts in showing how small was the improvement when the best of steam locomotives, intensively used and adequately serviced, were replaced by diesels. But on most roads the margin was much wider, and there was a saving from diesels quite sufficient to offset the greater capital cost.

In 1953 the 1,125hp (840kW) 567B engine was available, and this was incorporated in the next series, the "E8". By this time most of the principal passenger services were dieselised, so the impact of the "E8" was less spectacular than that of the "E7". By the time the final version appeared, the "E9" with 1,200hp (900kW) 567C engines, the need for passenger diesels had almost been met, and only 144 units were sold between 1954 and 1963, compared with 457 "E8s".

In the 1960s the American pasenger train declined rapidly in the face of air and coach competition, and many of the later "Es" had short lives, being traded in against the purchase of new general-purpose locomotives.

The "E" series instituted the general conversion of the American passenger train to diesel operation, and they eventually saw many of the most famous trains out. In their heyday the US had an undisputed world lead in passenger train speeds. Geared for up to 117mph (188km/h), although few roads operated them above 100mph (160km/h), the "Es" were the fastest diesel locomotives in the world, and yet their construction was rugged and straightforward. In particular they had nose-suspended traction motors, which the heavy North American rails with their close-spaced sleepers seemed able to accept without distress.

In 1980 Amtrak operated the last run of "E" locomotives in multiple and the ranks were very thin by this time. Fortunately the body of the first B&O unit is preserved.

Below: An early "F"-series "A" or "cab" diesel-electric unit as supplied to the Atchison, Topeka & Santa Fe Railway in 1936.

141R Liberation 2-8-2

Origin: French National Railways (SNCF). **Type:** General-purpose main line steam locomotive. **Gauge:** 4ft 8½in (1,435mm). **Propulsion:** Coal fire with a grate area of 55.5sq ft (5.2m²) generating steam at 200psi (14kg/cm²) in a fire-tube boiler, and supplying it via a superheater to two 23½ x 28in (596 x 711mm) cylinders, driving the main wheels by means of connecting and coupling rods. **Weight:** 176,400lb (80t) adhesive, 413,800lb (187.7t) total. **Axleload:** 48,510lb (22t). **Overall length:** 79ft 3¼in (24,161mm). **Tractive effort:** 44,500lb (20,191kg). **Max speed:** 75mph (120km/h). **Service entry:** 1945.

Of all the different schools of steam locomotive engineering in the world, no two were further apart than the American and the French. Most French main line locomotives were complex four-cylinder compounds of an arrangement developed by Alfred de Glehn (in spite of his name and his place of work, de Glehn was an Englishman) in the early-1900s. Between the wars, when there was no money for new construction, that genius amongst locomotive engineers, André Chapelon, had modernised many of the de Glehn compounds with startling effect, giving both a thermal effeciency and a power-to-ratio unmatched elsewhere at any time.

For such outstanding performance there was, however, a price to pay in high maintenance costs. Furthermore, the men who drove French locomotives were not promoted from firemen but instead had first to qualify as skilled mechanics; in short, French drivers had also to be engineers. Thus they had the understanding to enable them to run compound locomotives with complex controls—two reversers and two throttles, for example.

Towards the end of World War II, even before the Allies had landed in France, the French government took steps to solve the urgent problem of replacing the large number of locomotives destroyed, which would amount to 80 per cent of the fleet. Orders were placed in the USA and Canada for 1,340 2-8-2s based on (but slightly smaller than) the standard USRA light Mikado design.

For use in France the builders fitted buffers and screw couplings, ▶

Top, right: No. 141R 1063, 1043, fitted for oil-firing, pilot a "141C" on a freight train at Angers on the French National Railways in 1967.

Centre, right: Even as late in the steam age as 1968, coal-fired examples of the "141R" fleet were hard at work in north-east France. Here No. 141R611 rolls a freight train near Boulogne.

Below: Few concessions were made to French principles when the "141R" design was on the drawing board in the USA towards the end of the war. But it out-lasted the native product in the end.

squeaky high-pitched whistles, left-hand drive and oil lubrication instead of grease. Lima supplied 280, Baldwin and Alco 460 each, Montreal Loco Works 100 and Canadian Loco Co 40. The number series ran from 141R 1 to 141R 134 and all were shipped between August 1945 and the end of 1947. Seventeen went down with the vessel *Belpamela* which foundered in a mid-Atlantic storm, but the others survived to do great things.

Later examples of the "141Rs" were more up-to-date than the first ones to be delivered. Delta cast rear trucks replaced the built-up Cole pattern, Boxpok wheels replaced spoked ones, cast locomotive beds replaced separate frames and cylinders, and roller bearings were fitted. Many of the later locomotives were delivered as oil burners and others were converted to combat a severe shortage of coal which developed in France as reconstruction progressed.

US principles of design were totally vindicated by the excellent performance and overall economy of *les Americains* and it says enough that the "141Rs" outlasted compound 4-6-2s and 2-8-2s and eventually became the last main line steam locomotives in normal service on SNCF. Several have been preserved and it is the intention that one of these should return to the USA.

Right: Plenty of black smoke as an American-built 141R 2-8-2 of the French National Railways heads a long freight train.

242 A1 4-8-4

Origin: French National Railways (SNCF). **Type:** Express passenger steam locomotive. **Gauge:** 4ft 8½in (1,435mm). **Propulsion:** Coal fire with a grate area of 54sq ft (5m²) generating steam at 290psi (20.4kg/cm²) in a fire-tube boiler, and supplying it via a superheater to three cylinders, one high-pressure 23.6 x 28.3in (600 x 720mm) and two low-pressure 27 x 29.9in (680 x 760mm), the high-pressure cylinder mounted inside and driving the leading main axle, and the two low-pressure cylinders outside driving the second main axle. **Weight:** 185,50lb (84t) adhesive, 496,000lb (225t) total. **Axleload:** 46,500lb (21t). **Overall length:** 58ft 3½in (17,765mm). **Tractive effort:** 65,679lb (29,800kg). **Max speed:** 80mph (130km/h). **Service entry:** 1946.

By every competent authority it is agreed that André Chapelon should be included in the shortest of short lists of candidates to be considered as the greatest locomotive engineer of all. And this magnificent locomotive was his greatest work.

What is now the Western Region of French National Railways had had a bad experience in 1932 with a large 4-8-2 locomotive designed by a government-appointed central design committee. It was a three-cylinder simple, but with poppet valve gear intended to give an expansion ratio

equivalent to a compound. Alas, the mechanism never managed to achieve this, and moreover, there were other defects in the engine which caused bad riding and a tendency to derail. No.241101 was laid aside after tests, an embarassment to all, particularly as it had been announced with a tremendous fanfare as marking a new era in steam locomotive construction.

Chapelon had long wished to get his hands on this machine and to do to it what he had done before to the Paris-Orleans 4-6-2s. Official opposition took some years to overcome, but in 1942 his plans were agreed to, with a view to building a prototype for express passenger locomotives to be constructed when the war was over. The work was put in hand by the Société des Forges et Aciéres de la Marine et d'Homecourt.

The chassis needed substantial strengthening, and the extra weight involved in this and other modifications meant the need for an extra carrying wheel—hence France's first 4-8-4 tender locomotive. The de Glehn arrangement with two low-pressure cylinders inside would have involved a crank axle with two cranks and rather thin webs (since there was no room for thick ones) and it was admitted that this was a source of maintenance problems. So the new engine was to have a single high-pressure cylinder inside driving the leading main axle and two low-pressure ▶

Below: The magnificent 4-8-4 created by Andre Chapelon, the most powerful steam locomotive ever to be used in Europe, but one which irked French rail authorities.

▶ cylinders outside driving the second axle. All were in line between the bogie wheels.

Chapelon also moved away from poppet valves and used double piston-valves to give adequate port openings, as in his last batch of 4-6-2 rebuilds. The outside cranks were set at 90 degrees to one another, as in a two-cylinder engine; the inside crank bisected the obtuse angle between the other two cylinders, being set at 135 degrees to each. The Walschaert's valve gear for the inside cylinder was mounted partly outside—the eccentric rod was attached to a return crank on the second left-hand driving wheel. The bad riding was tackled with a roller centring device for the front bogie, as well as Franklin's automatic wedges to take up wear in the axlebox guides. Both were of US origin.

The boiler had two thermic syphons in the firebox, concentric (Houlet's) superheater elements and a mechanical stoker. A triple Kylchap chimney and exhaust system was provided. When completed in 1946, the rebuilt locomotive (now No.242A1) indicated under test that it was by far the most powerful locomotive existing outside North America—the omission of the word steam is deliberate. It could develop a maximum of 5,500hp in the cylinders, compared with 2,800hp before rebuilding. This power output is similar to that of which a typical US 4-8-4, perhaps 50 per cent heavier than No.242A1, was capable of as a maximum when driven hard.

This sort of power output enabled then unheard-of things to be achieved. A typical performance was to haul a 15-car train of 740 tons up a steady gradient of 1-in-125 (0.8 per cent), at a minimum speed of 71mph (114km/h). A 700-ton train was hauled from Paris to Lille in 140 minutes for the 161 miles (258km), while the electrified line from Paris to Le Mans (131 miles—210km) was covered in 109 minutes with a test train of 810 tons; well under the electric timings even with this huge train. On another occasion a speed of 94mph (150km/h) was reached; this was also on a special test, as there was a 120km/h (75mph) legal speed limit for public trains in France at that time.

Alas for the future of No.242A1, the railway top brass of France were even more embarrassed by its outstanding success than they were by its previous failure. They were engaged in trying to persuade the French government, at a time when resources were at a premium, to underwrite a vast programme of electrification; and here comes a young man (Chapelon was only 58!) with an engine which could outperform any electric loco-motive so far built, and was so economical in fuel consumption as to nullify any potential coal saving through electrification. And *both* of these factors were corner-stones of the railways' case for electrification.

So it is not hard to understand why this great locomotive was never duplicated. In fact it was quietly shunted away to Le Mans depot where, turn and turn-about with lesser engines, it took over express trains arriving from Paris by electric traction. The potential of the 4-8-4 was still appreciated by its crews. When such trains were delayed they could use its great performance in earning themselves large sums in bonus payments for the time regained.

There was another potential question mark standing over a future for a

Left: A view of Chapelon's masterpiece, French National Railways' magnificent three-cylinder compound 4-8-4 242A1, rebuilt from a pre-war 4-8-2.

Below: 4-8-4 No. 242A1, a steam locomotive which could out-perform any electric or diesel engine in existence in 1946, the year it went into service, and for some time afterwards.

production version of 242A1. The rugged American 2-8-2s showed an overall economy over the compounds because low maintenance costs more than balanced the cost of the extra coal burnt. Ironically, some of this was due to Chapelon himself, who had improved the valve events and reduced the cylinder clearances of the 141R so that the amount of this extra coal used was reduced from some 20 per cent to 10.

So it should really be no surprise that, as revealed by Baron Gerard Vuillet in his authoritative *Railway Reminiscences of Three Continents*, there was an alternative proposal in the form of a two-cylinder simple 4-6-4 with cast-steel locomotive frame, roller bearings, mechanical stoker and a grate area of 67sq ft (6.2m²). Vuillet remarks, "this 147-ton locomotive would not have been much more powerful at the drawbar than the best French Pacifics weighing 104 tons, but would have had a higher availability."

Chapelon was countering with proposals for three-cylinder compound 4-6-4s and 4-8-4s for express passenger work. He also had in mind a triple-expansion compound 4-8-4 with four cylinders, using steam at 584psi (41kg/cm²) generated in a boiler with tube firebox. The locomotive was intended to be capable of developing 8,000hp. Confidently with the former, and it was hoped with the latter, Chapelon expected that maintenance costs of these modern compounds could be brought down close to those of simple locomotives. Alas, all this was academic—the great 4-8-4 was withdrawn in 1960 and quietly broken up.

Class WP 4-6-2

Origin: Indian Railways (IR). **Type:** Express passenger steam locomotive. **Gauge:** 5ft 6in (1,676mm). **Propulsion:** Coal fire with a grate area of 46sq ft (4.3m²) generating steam at 210psi (14.7kg/cm²) in a fire-tube boiler, and supplying it via a superheater to two 20¼ x 28in (514 x 511mm) cylinders, driving the main wheels direct by means of connecting and coupling rods. **Weight:** 121,500lb (55t) adhesive, 380,000lb (172.5t) total. **Axleload:** 45,000lb (20.7t). **Overall length:** 78ft 4in (23,876mm). **Tractive effort:** 30,600lb (13,884kg). **Max speed:** 62mph (100km/h). **Service entry:** 1946.

Of only a few classes of steam locomotive amongst those described in this book can it be said (with much pleasure) that many remain in service, doing the job for which they were built. One of them is this massive 5ft 6in (1,676mm) gauge American-style 4-6-2, the standard express passenger locomotive of Indian Railways. Class "WP" comprised 755 locomotives, built between 1947 and 1967, with running numbers 7000 to 7754.

The prototypes were a batch of 16 ordered from Baldwin of Philadelphia in 1946, before Independence, so the decision to go American was not connected with the political changes. It was taken as a result of satisfactory experience with American locomotives supplied to India during the war, coupled with unsatisfactory experience with Indian standard designs of the 1920s and 1930s.

Naturally, the locomotives supplied were built to the usual rugged, simple, basic US standards. Provision of vacuum brakes, standard in India, made them even simpler, because a vacuum ejector is a vastly less complicated device than a steam air-pump. An air-smoothed exterior was provided for aesthetic rather than aerodynamic reasons, giving a solid dependable look to solid dependable locomotives.

The original batch were designated "WP/P" (P for prototypes) and the production version differed in minor details. During the next ten years further members of the class were supplied from foreign countries as follows:

USA—Baldwin	100
Canada—Canadian Locomotive Co	100
Canada—Montreal Locomotive Works	120
Poland—Fabryka Locomotywim, Chrzanow	30
Austria—Vienna Lokomotiv Fabrik	30

Above: One of the standard Class WP 4-6-2 passenger locomotives of Indian Railways at Khurda Road, South Eastern Railway.

There was then a pause until 1963, when India's own new Chitteranjan locomotive building plant began production of the remainder. Some further small modifications to the design were made to facilitate production.

The fleet of "WPs" work on all parts of the broad gauge network and still find full employment on many important express passenger trains, although they have been displaced from the top assignments by diesel and electrics, also Indian-built. Enormous trains, packed with humanity, move steadily across the Indian plains each headed by one of these excellent locomotives. A crew of four is carried (driver, two firemen and a coal-trimmer) but even with two observers on board as well there is ample room in the commodious cab.

Below: A commendably clean Indian Railways 4-6-2 Class WP brings a passenger train into a station on the Eastern Railway system. Note the broad gauge, the 'cow-catcher', the side buffers with screw couplings and the high platforms set at coach-floor level.

West Country Class 4-6-2

Origin: Southern Railway (SR), Great Britain. **Type:** Express passenger steam locomotive. **Gauge:** 4ft 8½in (1,435mm). **Propulsion:** Coal fire with a grate area of 38.25sq ft (3.55m²) generating steam at 280psi (19.7kg/cm²) in a fire-tube boiler, and supplying it via a superheater to three 16⅜ x 24in (416 x 610mm) cylinders, driving the main wheels by means of connecting and coupling rods. **Weight:** 131,000lb (59.5t) adhesive, 304,000lb (138t) total. **Axleload:** 44,500lb (20.2t). **Overall length:** 67ft 4in (20,542mm). **Tractive effort:** 31,046lb (14,083kg). **Max speed:** 100mph (160km/h). **Service entry:** 1945.

When Oliver Bullied from the London & North Eastern Railway was appointed Chief Mechanical Engineer of the Southern Railway in 1937, he affirmed his intention of making a major contribution to the art of steam locomotive design. He was a man of charm, ability, education and integrity, and had never allowed the many years spent working under Sir Nigel Gresley to blunt an extremely keen and original mind. The result so far as express passenger traffic was concerned was the building of 140 4-6-2s, which collectively were some of the most remarkable machines ever to be seen on rails. Bullied's locomotives were amazingly good in some ways yet almost unbelievably bad in others.

He began from the premise (often forgotten by others) that the prime task of the chief mechanical engineer (CME) was to build locomotives which could run the trains to time, regardless of quality of coal, bad weather and the presence on board of the least skilled of qualified engine crews. On the whole he succeeded, except perhaps for the need of a certain specialised expertise on the part of the driver; the fireman, on the other hand, just needed to throw the coal in.

Bullied also went to considerable pains to meet what should be the CME's second objective: that the first objective should be met at minimum cost. Here one must say that despite the very considered and original approach adopted these locomotives were disastrously more expensive than their rivals in first cost, maintenance and fuel consumption.

A third objective was achieved, however. Bullied belied his name by being most considerate towards the men who worked for him. He was an example to many of his peers through the care he took to add a number of far-from-costly features to the locomotives in aid of the convenience and comfort of his crews. The repaid him by doing their very best with the strange and unfamiliar engines he created.

Bullied's 4-6-2s all had three cylinders with three sets of patent chain-driven valve gear inside an oil-filled sump between the frames. Outside-admission piston valves were used, driven from the centre via transverse

Above: "Merchant Navy" class 4-6-2 No. 34002 *Union Castle*. **Note red-and-cream carriages as adopted in early British Railways days.**

oscillating shafts. A large boiler was provided, with a wide firebox tapered on the base line.

The first to be built were called the "Merchant Navy" class; the prototype of the 30 built took to the rails in 1941. With the experience gained, some smaller 4-6-2s known as the "West Country" class were introduced in 1945. Over the next five years 109 were built, making them the most numerous Pacifics in Britain. Southern Railway running numbers were 21C101 upwards; British Railways allocated Nos. 34001 to 341110. Names of west country locations were given to the first 48; most of the remainder were given names associated with the Battle of Britain and were sometimes known as the "Battle of Britain" class—but there was no technical distinction between the two series.

Other features included a multiple-jet blastpipe known as the Lemaître, disc type wheels with holes rather than spokes, and a so-called air-smoothed casing. Innovations (for the SR) appreciated by the crews included rocking grates, power (steam) operated fire-hole door and reverser, rocker grate and electric light. A French system of water treatment known as *Traitment Intégral Armand*—which really kept the boilers free of scale even in chalky SR country—was used later. All ▶

Below: The unusual but impressive Southern Railway "Battle of Britain" class 4-6-2 No. 21C151 *Sir Winston Churchill*. This famous locomotive has been preserved in the National collection.

▶ except six were built at Brighton Works, an establishment that apart from a few locomotives built during the war had not produced a new one for many years. The odd six were built at Eastleigh Works.

The very best features of the 4-6-2s were the boilers. They bristled with innovations so far as the Southern Railway was concerned—they were welded instead of rivetted, fireboxes were made of steel instead of copper and their construction included water ducts called thermic syphons inside the firebox. Yet in spite of these new features the boilers were marvellous steam raisers as well as being light on maintenance, thereby reflecting enormous credit on Bullied and his team.

An elaborate high pressure vessel, holding a mixture of water and steam at 280psi ($19.7kg/cm^2$) had been found easy, but one to hold oil a few inches deep proved to be difficult. The feature that did not work out was the totally enclosed oil filled sump between the frames in which the inside connecting rod and three sets of chain-driven valve gear lashed away. Bullied expected that, as in a motor car, the lubrication drill would consist solely of a regular check of oil level with occasional topping-up. The motion would be protected against dust, dirt and water while wear would be small. Alas, it did not quite work out like this—the sumps leaked and broke and the mechanisms inside also bristled with so many innovations that they were never made trouble-free. The motion also suffered severe corrosion as the oil became contaminated. Hence there were appalling maintenance problems, never properly resolved in spite of many years of unremitting efforts to solve the difficulties.

Stretching of the chains which drove the miniature valve gears, plus the effect of any wear, all of which multiplied when the motion was transferred to the valve spindles through rocking shafts, played havoc with the valve settings. This explained the heavy steam consumption. Oil leaking from the sump went everywhere, making the rails slippery and even adding a fresh hazard to railway working—the danger of a steam locomotive catching fire. This happened several times.

With outside motion in full view, drivers often spotted some defect before it had gone too far and something broke. But on these engines the first sign of trouble was often some extremely expensive noises, followed possibly the puncturing of the oil bath as loose bits forced their way out. Incidentally, the price of all this complexity was very great even when development costs had been paid; the production cost of a "West Country" was £17,000 at a time when even such a complicated loco-motive as a Great Western "Castle" 4-6-0 cost under £10,000.

An unhandy throttle was another handicap and this, combined with the absence of any equalisation between the rear pony wheels and the

Below: Rebuilt "West Country" 4-6-2 No. 34017 *Ilfracombe* at the head end of the "Pines Express" near Shawford, Hants, in June 1964.

Above: The same locomotive as on the opposite page but now in extremely unkempt condition near Weald, Kent, in wintry weather.

drivers, made the locomotives liable to driving wheel slip both at starting and while running. On the other hand the performance which the Bullied Pacifics gave once they got going was superb.

Both classes were good but since the smaller "West Country" class seemed to be able to equal anything the larger "Merchant Navys" could do, one's admiration goes more strongly to the former. During the locomotive exchange trials which took place soon after nationalisation of the railways in 1948, they put up performances equal or superior to any of their larger rivals from other lines. It is clear that the SR people knew their candidates were going to come out bottom in coal consumption anyway, so they determined to show that they could perform instead. Elsewhere than on the SR, punctuality in Britain at that time was dreadful and one cites a run on which No.34006 *Bude* regained 11 minutes of lateness on the level route between Bristol and Taunton (about 40 miles—64km).

On another occasion in the Highlands of Scotland, over 13 minutes time was regained in the famous ascent from Blair Atholl to Dalnaspidal; a drawbar horsepower approaching 2,000 was recorded on this occasion. The coal burnt per mile compared with the normal 4-6-0s on this line was 28 per cent more and the amount burnt per horsepower-hour developed was 22 per cent higher. It is also recorded that the consumption of lubricating oil was not 7 per cent more but *seven times* more; but that was untypical—three times that of a normal engine was more usual! And remember that a normal locomotive was *intended* to be lubricated on a "total loss" system.

On their home territory the "West Country" locomotives were used on almost every Southern steam-hauled main line passenger working from the "Golden Arrow" continental express from Victoria to Dover, down to two and three coach local trains in Cornwall. Their maintenance problems were less apparent because the 140 Bullied 4-6-2s represented a huge over-provision of motive power.

Furthermore, in 1957-60, sixty "West Country" class were rebuilt with new conventional cylinders and motion; in this form, and for the short period left to steam, they were unambiguously amongst the very best locomotives ever to run in Britain. During July 3 to 9, 1967, the last week of steam on the Southern, these rebuilds worked the luxury "Bournemouth Belle" on several days.

Several, both rebuilt and unrebuilt, have been preserved and restored; for example, unrebuilt No.21C123 *Blackmore Vale* on the Bluebell Railway and No.21C192 *City of Wells* on the Keighley & Worth Valley Railway.

Y6b 2-8-8-2

Origin: Norfolk & Western Railway (N&W), USA. **Type:** Steam locomotive for heavy freight haulage. **Gauge:** 4ft 8½in (1,435mm). **Propulsion:** Coal fire with a grate area of 106sq ft (9.8m²) generating steam at 300psi (21.1kg/cm²) in a fire-tube boiler, and supplying it via a superheater to four cylinders, two high-pressure 25 x 32in (635 x 812mm) and two low-pressure 29 x 32in (746 x 812mm), each pair driving the main wheels of its respective unit direct by means of connecting and coupling rods. **Weight:** 548,500lb (248.9t) adhesive, 990,100lb (449.2t) total. **Axleload:** 75,418lb (34.2t).**Overall length:** 114ft 11in (35,026mm). **Tractive effort:** 152,206lb (69,059kg). **Max speed:** not specified **Service entry:** 1948.

"Of all the words of tongue and pen, the saddest are 'it might have been'." In the USA,there was one small (but prosperous) railroad that, on a long-term basis, came near to fighting off the diesel invasion. This was the Norfolk & Western Railway, with headquarters in Roanoke, Virginia, and a main line then stretching 646 miles (1,033km) from ocean piers at Norfolk, Virginia, to Columbus in Ohio. It had branches to collect coal from every mine of importance across one of the world's greatest coalfields. In the end steam lost the battle on the N&W and big-time steam railroading finally vanished from the United States—so dealing a fatal blow all over the world to the morale of those who maintained that dieselisation was wrong. But the Norfolk & Western's superb steam locomotives came close to victory; so let us see how it was done.

The principle adopted was to exploit fully all the virtues of steam while, rather obviously, seeking palliatives for its disadvantages. It was also a principle of N&W management that the maximum economy lay in maintaining the steam fleet in first-class condition, with the aid of premises, tools and equipment to match.

Above: Norfolk & Western Railway "Y6b" Mallet No. 172 hauls a westbound freight at Shaffers Crossing, near Roanoke, Virginia.

During the period when steam and diesel were battling for supremacy on US railroads, it was typically the case that brand new diesel locomotives were being maintained in brand new depots while the steam engines with which they were being compared were worn out and looked after in tumble-down sheds. Often much of the roof would be missing while equipment was also worn out and obsolete. The filth would be indescribable.

On the Norfolk & Western Railroad during the 1950s, steam locomotives were new and depots almost clinically clean, modern, well-equipped and well-arranged. A "J6B" class could be fully serviced, greased, lubricated, cleared of ash, tender filled with thousands of gallons of water and many tons of coal, all in under an hour. The result was efficiency, leading to Norfolk & Western's shareholders receiving 6 per cent on their money, while those of the neighbouring and fully-dieselised and electrified Pennsylvania Railroad had to be content with ½ per cent.

In the end, through, the problems of being the sole United States railroad continuing with steam on any scale began to tell. Even a do-it-yourself concern like N&W normally bought many components from specialists and one by one these firms were going out of business. In 1960 this and other factors necessitated the replacement of steam and the replacement of steam and the "Y6bs" plus all the other wonderful loco- ▶

Left: The most striking feature of this view of a "Y6b" compound Mallet 2-8-8-2 is the huge low-pressure cylinders at the front.

Below: The last in the long line of North American heavy steam motive power, the "Y6b" class of the Norfolk & Western Railway.

► motives of this excellent concern were retired.

After gaining experience—some of it traumatic—with other people's Mallets for its huge coal movement, Norfolk & Western in 1918 had built in its own shops at Roanoke, Virginia, a really successful coal-mover in the form of a 2-8-8-2 compound articulated steam locomotive. This "Y2" class received wholesale recognition because, later the same year, the United States Railroad Administration based its standard 2-8-8-2 on this excellent design. N&W was allocated 50 by USRA, which was then running the nation's railroads. The new locomotives, classified "Y3", came from Alco and Baldwin. In 1923 they were augmented by 30 more, designated "Y3a" and a further 10 in 1927, Class "Y4". The "Y4s" were the last new steam locomotives not to be built by N&W at Roanoke; they came from Alco's Richmond Works.

N&W policy was to move forward slowly, not forgetting to consolidate the gains already made. So the successive improvements made between the "Y2", "Y3", "Y3a" and "Y4" classes were modest. For example, provision of feed-water heaters began with the "Y3as", but earlier locomotives were altered to bring them into line, so that operationally the group of classes could be regarded as one.

In 1930 the first of an enlarged version, Class "Y5", was produced. Thus was founded a dynasty of coal-moving and coal-consuming power which would bring the science of steam locomotive operation to a never-to-be-repeated peak. Over the next 22 years modern developments were successively introduced through classes "Y6", "Y6a" and "Y6b" and, as before, the earlier locomotives were rebuilt to bring them into line so that the fleet was kept uniformly up-to-date. The last "Y6b", completed in 1952, was the last main-line steam locomotive to be built in the USA.

This time, some of the improvements passed on were not so minor. The introduction of cast-steel locomotive beds with integrally-cast cylinders on the "Y6s" was followed by rebuilding of the "Y5s" to match. The old "Y5" frames were then passed on to the "Y3"/"Y4" group, by now relegated to local mine runs. One problem with the older Mallets was that they tended to choke themselves with the large volume of low-pressure steam because of inadequately-sized valves, ports, passageways and pipes. This was corrected in the "Y5" design and these locomotives then had the freedom to run and pull at speeds up to 50mph (80km/h), which can be considered an exceptional figure for a compound Mallet.

Roller bearings came on the "Y6s" of 1936, and with the "Y6bs" of 1948 was booster equipment for extra power, whereby a modicum of live

Above: "Y6b" articulated 2-8-8-2 No. 2185 being assembled in the Roanoke Shops of the Norfolk & Western Railway on May 21, 1949.

steam, controlled by a reducing valve, could be introduced to the low-pressure cylinders while still running as a compound. It was quite separate from the conventional simpling valve used for starting. An interesting feature was the coupling of auxiliary tenders behind locomotives in order to reduce the number of water stops.

It says enough of the efficiency of these engines that following a line relocation they displaced in 1948 N&W's pioneer electrification in the Allegheny Mountains. In due time though, Norfolk & Western became the only railroad which saw a long-term future for steam, and this position became untenable in the later 1950s. With reluctance, then, the Company was forced to follow the crowd and the last "Y6" set out on the last mine run in the month of April 1960. One is preserved in the National Museum of Transportation at St Louis.

Below: The Class "A" articulated simple Mallet 2-6-6-4 here depicted hauling a coal drag, intended for fast freight work.

Class A1 4-6-2

Origin: British Railways (BR). **Type:** Express passenger steam loco-motive. **Gauge:** 4ft 8½in (1,435mm). **Propulsion:** Coal fire with a grate area of 50sq ft (4.6m²) generating steam at 250psi (17.6kg/cm²) in a fire-tube boiler, and supplying it via a superheater to three 19 x 26in (482 x 660mm) cylinders, driving the main wheels by means of connecting and coupling rods. **Weight:** 148,000lb (67t) adhesive, 369,000lb (167t) total. **Axleload:** 49,500lb (22.5t). **Overall length:** 73ft 0in (22,250mm). **Tractive effort:** 37,400lb (16,900kg). **Max speed:** 100mph (160km/h). **Service entry:** 1948.

When Sir Nigel Gresley died suddenly in office in 1941, the London & North Eastern Railway had 115 Pacifics and some 600 other three-cylinder engines of his design, all fitted with his derived motion, in which the inside valve took its drive from the two outside valve gears.

The opportunity to build a Pacific incorporating his ideas arose from the poor availability of Gresley's "P2" class 2-8-2 locomotives, one of whose troubles was heavy wear of axleboxes due to the long rigid wheelbase on the sharp curves of the Edinburgh-Aberdeen line. By rebuilding these as Pacifics he hoped to improve their performance, and also to gain experience for further new construction. Elimination of the Gresley gear involved arranging the inside cylinder to drive the leading axle, and as Thompson insisted on all the connecting rods being of the same length, an awkward layout was arrived at, with the leading bogie ahead of the outside cylinders.

Trouble was experienced with flexing of the frame, and loosening and breakage of steam pipes, but nevertheless the arrangement was applied to the "P2s" and to a further 19 mixed-traffic Pacifics with 74in (1,880mm) driving wheels. Before this programme was completed, Thompson also took in hand Gresley's original Pacific, *Great Northern*, and rebuilt it similarly, with separate valve gears, larger cylinders, and a grate area of 50sq ft (4.6m²), in place of the 41.3sq ft (3.8m²) grate with which all the Gresley Pacifics were fitted.

Before Thompson's retirement, his successor designate, Arthur Peppercorn, put in hand quietly in Doncaster drawing office a further revision of the Pacific layout, in which the outside cylinders were restored to their position above the middle of the bogie, and the inside connecting rod was shortened to make the front of the engine more compact. Fifteen new Pacifics with 74in wheels were built to this design, classified "A2", and then 49 more with 80in (2,032mm) wheels were ordered, classified "A1". The *Great Northern* was absorbed into this class.

These engines were not built until after nationalisation, in 1948-49, Nos. 60114-27/53-62 at Doncaster, and Nos. 60130-52 at Darlington. They all had Kylchap double blastpipes, and five of them had roller bearings to all axles. At first they had stovepipe chimneys, but these were

Above: "A1" class 4-6-2 No. 60161 *Amadis* ready to leave King's Cross, London. Note "express passenger" headlamp position.

replaced by chimneys of the normal Doncaster shape. They had assorted names, including locomotive engineers, the constituent railways of the LNER, some traditional Scottish names, some birds and some racehorses.

The "A1s" proved to be fast and economical engines, and they took a full share in East Coast locomotive workings, except for the King's Cross-Edinburgh non-stops, for which the streamlined "A4s" were preferred. Their maintenance costs were lower than those of other BR Pacifics, and they achieved notable mileages. Over a period of 12 years they averaged 202 miles per calendar day, the highest figure on BR, and the five roller bearing engines exceeded that average, with 228 miles per day. Their riding was somewhat inferior to that of the "A4", as they had a tendency to lateral lurching on straight track, but nevertheless they were timed at 100mph plus (160+km/h) on a number of occasions.

These engines were a worthy climax to Doncaster Pacific design, but unfortunately they came too late in the day to have full economic lives. By the early 1960s dieselisation of the East Coast main line was well advanced, and the "A1s" were all withdrawn between 1962 and 1966.

Below: Class "A1" 4-6-2 *North British* depicted in the experimental blue livery tried in the early days of British Rail.

GP Series B₀-B₀

Origin: Electo-Motive Division, General Motors Corporation (EMD), USA.
Type: Diesel-electric road switcher locomotive. **Gauge:** 4ft 8½in (1,435mm). **Propulsion:** One EMD 567D2 2,000hp (1,490kW) 16-cylinder turbocharged two-stroke Vee engine and generator, supplying current to four nose-suspended traction motors geared to the axles. **Weight** 244,000lb (108.9t) to 260,000lb (116.0t) according to fittings. **Axleload:** 61,000lb (27.2t) to 65,000lb (29.0t) according to fittings. **Overall length:** 56ft 0in (17,120mm), GP20 variant of 1959. **Tractive effort:** 61,000lb (271kN) to 65,000lb (289kN) according to weight. **Max speed:** 65mph (105km/h), 71mph (114km/h), 77mph (124k,/h), 83mph (134km/h) or 89mph (143km/h) according to gear ratio fitted. **Service entry:** 1949.

For the post-war boom in diesel sales EMD offered a range of models based on three main series. First the "E" series of A1A-A1A express passenger locomotives, secondly the "F" series of Bo-Bo locomotives for freight work, but with optional gear ratios covering passenger work to all but the highest speeds, and thirdly a number of switchers (shunters) and transfer locomotives for work within and between marshalling yards. There was an important difference between the switchers and the other models. In the switchers the structural strength was in the underframe, on which rested the engine, generator and other equipment. The casing or "hood" was purely protective and had no structural strength. The "E" and "F" series, on the other hand, had load-bearing bodies, or "carbodies", which provided an "engine-room" in which maintenance work could be carried out whilst the train was in motion, and which were more satisfactory aesthetically than a hood.

With these models EMD captured about 70 per cent of the North American market. Its ability to do so stemmed from a combination of quality of performance and reliability in the locomotive, low maintenance costs, which were helped by the large number of parts which were common to the different types, and competitive prices made possible by assembly line manufacture. Full benefit of assembly line methods could only be achieved by limiting the number of variants offered to customers, and this in turn, helped EMD's competitors to pick on omissions from, or weaknesses in, the EMD range by which to hold on to a share of the market. At first EMD's main theme in its diesel sales talk was the benefit

Above: A 30-year-old GP7 diesel-electric locomotive in service in 1982 on the Canadian line known as the Algoma Central Railway.

accruing from replacing steam by diesel traction, but as its competitors achieved modest success in finding gaps in the EMD range, more and more was that firm concerned with proclaiming the superiority of its products over those of its competitors.

To achieve this superiority some changes were made in the range, of which the most important originated in customer enquiries received before the war for a locomotive which was primarily a switcher, but which could also haul branch line trains, local freights and even local passenger trains. To meet this need a small number of locomotives were built with switcher bodies, elongated to house a steam generator, and mounted on bogies of the "F" series; these were "road switchers". Construction was resumed after the war, still on a small scale, and with the design adapted to meet individual customers' requirements.

By 1948 EMD's competitors, particularly Alco, were achieving success ▶

Below: "GP38-2" standard diesel-electric road-switcher locomotive as supplied to the Canadian Pacific Rly by General Motors (Canada).

▶ with a general purpose hood unit for branch line work. For this application, ability to gain access to the working parts was more important than protection for technicians to work on the equipment on the road, and the hoods also gave the driver much wider field of view. In 1948, therefore, EMD offered a branch line diesel, designated "BL", incorporating the 1,500hp (1,120kW) 567B engine, and other equipment including traction motors from the "F" series. These were accommodated in a small semi-streamlined casing, whose main advantage compared with a carbody was the improved view from the cab. There was, however, a serious snag—the "BL" was too expensive.

EMD then designed a true hood for general purpose duties, designated "GP". Richard Dilworth, EMD's Chief Engineer, said that his aim was to produce a locomotive that was so ugly that railroads would be glad to send it to the remotest corners of the system (where a market for diesels to replace steam still existed!), and to make it so simple that the price would be materially below standard freight locomotives.

Although the "GP" was offered as a radically new design, many parts were common to the contemporary "F7" series. The power plant was the classic 567 engine, which like all EMD engines was a two-stroke Vee design; this was simpler than a four-stroke but slightly less efficient. Much development work was devoted over the years to improving the efficiency of the EMD engines to meet the competition of four-stroke engines. The bogies were of the Blomberg type, a fairly simple design with swing-link bolsters, which were introduced in the "FT" series in 1939 and are still, with changes in the springing system, standard in EMD Bo-Bo models in the 1980s. EMD's success with this long-running design is in contrast to the radical changes which have been made in bogie design in other countries over that period.

The cab afforded a good view in both directions, the hood gave easy access to the equipment, and, despite the designer's intentions, EMD's stylists produced a pleasing outline. Electrical equipment was simplified from the "F" series, but nevertheless it gave the driver tighter control over the tractive effort at starting, and a more comprehensive overall control to suit the wide range of speeds envisaged.

First production series of the new design was the "GP7", launched in 1949. It was an immediate success, and 2,610 units were supplied to US roads between 1949 and 1953, plus 112 to Canada and two to Mexico.

In 1954 the next development of the 567 engine, the C series of

Above: The "GP" series of standard diesel-electric locomotives offered by the Electro-Motive Division of General Motors were used all over North America. Here are two "GP9s" of Canadian National.

1,750hp (1,305kW), was introduced into the range, giving the "GP9". This differed in detail from the "GP7", mainly to bring still further reductions in maintenance. By this time the hood unit was widely accepted, and sales of the "GP" at 4,157 established another record. It was America's (and therefore the world's) best selling diesel locomotive.

So far the EMD engines had been pressure-charged by a Roots blower driven mechanically from the engine, but with its competitors offering engines of higher power, EMD now produced a turbocharged version of the 567 engine, 567D2, giving 2,000hp (1,490kW). For customers for whom the extra power did not justify the expense of the turbo-blower, the 567D1 at 1,800hp (1,340kW) was available. Both these models had a higher compression than their predecessors, which, combined with improvements in the fuel injectors, gave a fuel saving of 5 per cent. These engines were incorporated in the "GP20" and "GP18" series, respectively.

By this time US railroads were fully dieselised, and this , combined with a decline in industrial activity, reduced the demand for diesels. EMD therefore launched its Locomotive Replacement Plan. The company claimed that three "GP20s" could do the work of four "F3s", so it offered terms under which a road traded in four "F3s" against the purchase of three "GP20s", parts being re-used where possible. It was claimed that the cost of the transaction could be recovered in three to four years, and the railroad then had three almost new units in place of four older ones with much higher maintenance costs. Despite this, only 260 "GP20s" and 390 "GP18s" were sold over 4 years.

The final phase of "GP" development with the 567 engine came in 1961 with the 567D3 of 2,250hp (1,680kW) in the "GP30". The designation "30" was a sales gimmick, based on there being 30 improvements in the new model; it was claimed that maintenance was reduced by 60 per cent compared with earlier types. The "GP30" was in turn succeeded by the "GP35" of 2,500hp (1,870kW). With trade reviving, and many more early diesels in need of replacement, these models achieved sales of 2,281. At this stage the 567 engine was replaced by the 645 with which the "GP" series remained in full production in the early 1980s. 1984 saw introduction of the 710 engine in the now "60" series locomotives.

Class YP 4-6-2

Origin: Indian Railways (IR). **Type:** Express passenger steam locomotive. **Gauge:** 3ft 3⅜in (1,000mm). **Propulsion:** Coal fire with a grate area of 28sq ft (2.6m²) generating steam at 210psi (14.8kg/cm²) in a fire-tube boiler, and supplying it via a superheater to two 15¼ x 24in (387 x 610mm) cylinders, driving the main wheels direct by means of connecting and coupling rods. **Weight:** 69,000lb (31.5t) adhesive, 218,500 (99t) total. **Axleload:** 23,500lb (10.7t). **Overall length:** 62ft 7½in (19,088mm). **Tractive effort:** 18,450lb (8,731kg). **Max speed:** 45mph (72km/h). **Service entry:** 1949.

A total of 871 of these beautifully proportioned and capable locomotives were built between 1949 and 1970 for the metre-gauge network of Indian Railways. The newest members of the class were the last express passenger locomotives to be built, and many were still at work in 1984.

It could be said that whilst Britain's principal achievement in India was construction of the railway network, the greatest fault in what was done was the division of the system into broad and metre gauge networks of not far off equal size. Even so, 15,940 miles (25,500km) of metre-gauge railways, including many long-distance lines, had to be worked and power was needed to do it. Strictures rightly applied to the standard "XA", "XB" and "XC" 4-6-2s of the 1920s and 1930s were not deserved by their metre-gauge counterparts, the handsome "YB" 4-6-2s supplied between 1928 and 1950. Nevertheless Indian Railways decided to do what it had

Above: A "YP" 4-6-2 at the head of a Southern Railway express train spreads a pall of black smoke over the Indian countryside.

Below: Indian Railways' metre-gauge Class "YP" 4-6-2, the last steam express locomotive class to built anywhere in the world.

Above: A "YP" class Pacific takes a passenger train across a typical river bridge on the metre-gauge system of Indian Railways.

done on the broad gauge and go American. Jodhpur, one of the princely states, in those days still had its own railway, and it had received ten neat 4-6-2s from Baldwin of Philadelphia in 1948. Baldwin was asked to produce 20 prototypes of Class "YP" similar to those locomotives but slightly enlarged. The new locomotives were also a little simpler, with plain instead of roller bearings and eight-wheel instead of high-capacity 12-wheel tenders.

Production orders for the "YP" were placed overseas. Krauss-Maffei of Munich and North British Locomotive of Glasgow received production orders for 200 and 100 respectively over the next five years, but the remainder were built by the Tata Engineering & Locomotive Co of Jamshedpur, India. Running numbers are 2000 to 2870, but not in chronological order. The engines could be regarded as two-thirds full-size models of a standard USA 4-6-2. If one multiplies linear measurements by 1.5, areas by 1.5^2 or 2.25, weights and volumes by 1.5^3 or 3.375 the correspondence is very close. Non-American features include vacuum brakes, chopper type automatic centre couplers in place of the buckeye type, slatted screens to the cab side openings and the absence of a bell.

With so many available, these locomotives can be found in all areas of the metre gauge system; this stretches far and wide from Trivandrum, almost the southernmost point of the Indian railways, to well north of Delhi, while both the easternmost and westernmost points are served by metre-gauge lines.

Diesel locomotives have now arrived in force on the metre-gauge network of India, but the "YPs" still haul important trains.

Class CC7100 C₀-C₀

Origin: French National Railways (SNCF). **Type:** Electric express passenger locomotive. **Gauge:** 4ft 8½in (1,435mm). **Propulsion:** Direct current at 1,500V from overhead catenary fed to six bogie-mounted traction motors geared to the axles through Alsthom spring drive. **Weight:** 235,830lb (107t). **Axleload:** 39,230lb (17.8t). **Overall length:** 62ft 1in (18,922mm). **Tractive effort:** 50,700lb (225kN). **Max speed:** 100mph (160km/h). **Service entry:** 1952.

French locomotive design has always been distinctive, and much of the distinctiveness has been purely French in origin, but from time to time a foreign influence has been seen. Thus in the development of express passenger locomotives for the main line electrification of the Paris-Orléans Railway (PO), adoption of the Swiss Büchli drive led to a notable series of 2-Do-2 locomotives, which bore an external likeness to contemporary Swiss designs. The last 2-Do-2 type, the "9100", was introduced by SNCF as the principal passenger locomotive for the electrification of the former PLM main line to Lyons. However, before those locomotives had been built in the quantity originally intended, another Swiss influence changed the course of French locomotive design.

Until this time, end bogies or pony trucks had been thought essential for fast passenger work, not only to support part of the weight of the locomotive but also to guide it into curves. All-adhesion Bo-Bo locomotives, which constituted the majority of French electrics, were considered suitable only for medium-speed work. Two notable Swiss designs changed the status of the all-adhesion locomotive. In 1946 Swiss Federal Railways introduced the 56t "Re4/4I" Bo-Bo, designed for speeds up to 78mph (125km/h). This class soon attracted attention by its ability to haul trains of 400t at its maximum permitted speed, while two years earlier the Lötschberg railway had introduced its 80t Bo-Bo, classified "Ae4/4". The success of these classes established the respectability of the double-bogie locomotive for express work, and SNCF commissioned two Bo-Bo machines from Swiss makers, based on the Lötschberg design, together with two Bo-Bo and two Co-Co units from French builders.

The Co-Co was produced by Alsthom to a specification based on the

Above, right: French National Railways' Class CC7100 Co-Co 1,500V dc electric locomotive at Paris (Gare de Lyon) in 1979.

Below: No. CC7107, one of these "CC1500" Co-Co electric locomotives broke the world speed record in 1954 and held it for many years.

requirements of the PLM electrification. This called for speeds up to 100mph (160km/h) on the level with 600t, 87mph (140km/h) on the level with 850t, and the ability to start a 600t train on a 1-in-125 (0.8 per cent) gradient and haul it at 75mph (120km/h) on that gradient.

The locomotive has a motor for each axle mounted in the bogie frame, with Alsthom spring drive. The novelty in the bogie was in the pivoting and in the axle guides. The pivots are of Alsthom design, and comprise two vertical links situated mid-way between the pairs of axles on the centre line of the bogie, with their ends resting in conical rubber seatings. Lateral movement of each link is controlled by two horizontal springs. The springs have two effects: when the body of the locomotive swings outward on curves, they provide a restoring force resisting centrifugal action; and when the bogie rotates, the links swing in opposite directions and exert forces tending to restore the bogie to the straight line. Thus, if the bogie rotates on straight track due to irregularities in the permanent way, the ▶

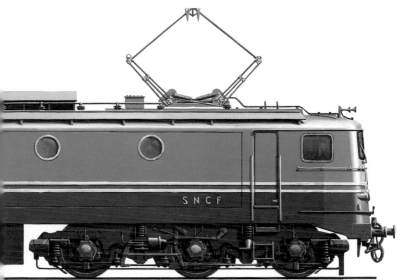

▶ springs tend to damp this motion and discourage the flanges from striking the rails.

Each axlebox is restrained by two horizontal links, which allow vertical movement but not fore-and-aft movement, and they eliminate the wearing surfaces of traditional steam-type axleboxes. End movement of the axles is controlled by stiff springs fitted between the ends of the axles and the axlebox cover plates. These springs reduce the shocks transmitted to the bogie frame when the flanges strike the rails. Extensive use was made of rubber in the pivots of the suspension system.

The electrical equipment was notable for the large number of running notches, made possible by the large amount of field weakening. The external lines were enhanced by the two-tone blue livery, set off by light metal beading of the window frames and of the horizontal flashing.

The two locomotives, Nos. CC7001-2, were delivered in 1949 and were subjected to intensive testing on the Paris-Bordeaux main line, which was then the longest electrified route in France. Early in these tests, No. 7001 hauled a train of 170t from Paris to Bordeaux at an average speed of 81.4mph (131km/h), reaching a maximum of 105.6mph (170km/h), which was a world record performance for an electric locomotive.

After three years of testing, orders were placed for 35 locomotives, differing in detail from Nos. 7001-2. They were delivered in 1952, and numbered from 7101 to 7135. A further order for 23 brought the class to a total of 60. Compared with Nos. 7001-2, the production units had an increase in maximum power from 4,000hp (2,980kW) to 4,740hp (3,540kW), and the weight increased from 96t to 107t. Compared with the "9100" class 2-Do-2, the adhesive weight had increased from 88t to 107t, but the axleload had fallen from 22t to 17.8t, so that the locomotive was much kinder to the track. Six of the locomotives were fitted with collecting shoes for working on the former PLM line from Chambéry to Modane (the Mont Cenis route), which was at that time equipped with third rail current collection.

Electrification from Paris to Lyons was completed in 1952, and the "7100" class then shared with the "9100" 2-Do-2s the heaviest and fastest runs. By the summer of 1954 there were three runs between Paris and Dijon or Paris and Lyons booked at 77.1mph (124km/h) start-to-stop with permissible loads of 650t. Another run from Paris to Dijon was booked at 76.1mph (122.4km/h) with 730t. These were the outstanding speed exploits in Europe at the time—on a railway which 10 years before was devastated by war.

In February 1954, the very first high-speed tests were made with No. CC7121 on a level stretch between Dijon and Beaune. The purpose of the tests was to investigate the effect of high speed on various parameters, including the forces exerted on the rails and the behaviour of the pantograph. With a train of 111t a speed of 151mph (243km/h) was reached, which was a world record for any type of traction, beating the 143mph (230km/h) attained in 1931 in Germany by a propeller-driven railcar.

Testing then moved to the former PO railway, where a long stretch of almost straight line was available south of Bordeaux. First the problem of picking up a very heavy current was investigated with two "7100" class locomotives double-heading. With the line voltage boosted by 25 per cent, these two reached 121mph (195km/h) with 714t and 125mph (201km/h) with 617t.

The next target was a speed of 300km/h (185mph), for which purpose No. CC7107 was fitted with gears of higher ratio than normal. The train comprised three coaches weighing 100t, with a streamlined tail attached to the rear vehicle. The target of 300km/h was reached in 21km (13 miles) from the start, and was maintained for 12km (7½ miles), but, very remarkably, speed rose to 330.8km/h (205.6mph) for 2km (1¼ miles), which required an output of 12,000hp (8,950kW). Equally remarkable, the performance was repeated exactly on the following day by an 81t Bo-Bo, No. BB9004, one of the French-built experimental locomotives mentioned earlier. The two locomotives thus became joint world record holders, and as subsequent developments in very high-speed trains have been with railcars, it is likely that this record for locomotives will stand.

The achievement of No. BB9004 was significant; a locomotive costing little more than half a "7100" had produced the same performance, such was the pace of locomotive development at this time. French activity was then concentrated on four-axle machines, and no more six-axle electric locomotives were built until 1964, by which time design had changed greatly with introduction of the monomotor bogie.

Although the Co-Co locomotives were soon overshadowed by their smaller successors, they took a full share in express work on the former PLM for many years, and in 1982 No. CC7001 became the first French locomotive to cover 8 million km (4.97 million miles), at an overall average of 658km (409 miles) per day.

Below: A CC7000 Co-Co electric locomotive of French National Railways rides the turntable in the roundhouse shed at Avignon.

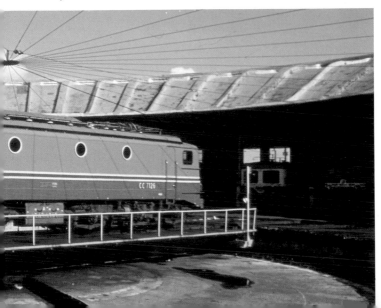

Class 8 4-6-2

Origin: British Railways (BR). **Type:** Express passenger steam locomotive. **Gauge:** 4ft 8½in (1,435mm). **Propulsion:** Coal fire with a grate area of 48.5sq ft (4.5m²) generating steam at 250psi (17.6kg/cm²) in a fire-tube boiler, and supplying it via a superheater to three 18 x 28in (457 x 711mm) cylinders, driving the main wheels by means of connecting and coupling rods. **Weight:** 148,000lb (67.5t) adhesive, 347,000 (157.5t) total. **Axleload:** 49,500lb (22.5t). **Overall length:** 70ft 0in (21,336mm). **Tractive effort:** 39,080lb (17,731kg). **Max speed:** 100mph (160km/h). **Service entry:** 1953.

The railways of Britain became British Railways on January 1, 1948 and naturally there was much speculation concerning the kind of locomotives that would succeed the "Duchess", "King", "Merchant Navy" and "A4" classes of BR's illustrious predecessors. In early 1951 it was announced that none was planned, but instead the first full-size Pacific for any British railway to have only two cylinders was unveiled. This locomotive class was intended to displace such second-eleven power as the "Royal Scot", "Castle" and "West Country" classes rather than the largest types.

"Britannia" was a simple, rugged 4-6-2 with Belpaire firebox and roller bearings on all axles, as well as many other aids to cheap and easy maintenance. It was designated Class "7", and had a capacity to produce some 2,200hp in the cylinders, at a very fair consumption of coal, amounting to some 5,000lb/h (2,270kg/h). This was well above the rate at which a normal man could shovel coal on to the fire but the large firebox enabled a big fire to be built up in advance when some big effort of short duration was required.

A total of 55 "Britannias" were built between 1951 and 1953. They met their designers' goal of a locomotive that was easy to maintain, and also showed that they were master of any express passenger task in Britain at that time. They were allocated to all the regions, but it was the Eastern that made the best use of the new engines. Their "Britannias" were allocated to one line and put to work on a new high-speed train service specifically designed round their abilities. During the 1950s in most of Britain it could be said that 20 years' progress had meant journey times some 20 per cent longer. On the other hand the new 4-6-2s working this improved timetable between London and Norwich meant a 20 per cent *acceleration* on pre-war timings, in terms of the service in general.

In spite of being simple engines in both senses of the world, the "Britannias" displayed economy in the use of steam. In fact they were right in the front rank, yet there was always the nagging thought that the great Chapelon compounds across the Channel could on test do about 16 per cent better. This figure would be diluted in service by various factors but

Above: "Britannia" 4-6-2 No. 70039 *Sir Christopher Wren* hauling a Liverpool-Glasgow express at grips with the climb to Shap in 1965.

even so it was considerable, especially as within almost exactly the same weight limits they could develop nearly 1,500 more cylinder horsepower. There was, however, certain reluctance in Britain to go compound, because for one thing there was no counterpart to the French works-trained *mechanicien* drivers to handle such complex beasts. Past experience had also shown the extra maintenance costs implicit in the complexity to have over-ridden economies due to the saving of fuel.

A point was perhaps missed, though, that since the upper limit of power output was a man shovelling, a more economical machine would also be a more powerful one. And since more power involves faster running times, and faster running times more revenue, a more efficient locomotive might be both a money saver and a money earner. But there is another way to obtaining some of the advantages of compounding and that is to expand the steam to a greater extent in simple cylinders. This in its turn means that the point in the stroke at which the valves close to steam (known as the cut-off and expressed in terms of per cent) must be very early. However, the geometry of normal valve gears precludes cut-offs less than, say, 15 to 20 per cent. This is because, if the opening to steam is limited to less of the stroke than that, the opening to exhaust (the same valve being used for both) is also limited on the return stroke. This means ▶

Below: The solitary Class "8" 4-6-2 No. 71000 *Duke of Gloucester*. Note the shaft which drives the rotary-cam poppet valve gear.

Above: British Railways' one-and-only Class "8" 4-6-2 *Duke of Gloucester* awaits the call to duty in Crewe station in 1961.

▶ steam trapped in the cylinders and loss of power. The solution is to have independent valves for admission and exhaust and the simplest way of doing this is to use poppet valves actuated by a camshaft. Alas, it cannot be too simple because the point of cut-off has to be varied and, moreover, the engine has to be reversed. Both these things are done by sliding the camshaft along its axis, bringing changed cam profiles into action according to the position of the reversing control in the cab.

Permission was obtained in 1953 to build a prototype for future BR top-link express passenger locomotives. As a two-cylinder machine, the cylinder size came out too big to clear platform edges so, in spite of a yen for simplicity, three cylinders had to be used. Now it is a point concerning poppet valves that much of the mechanism is common, however many cylinders there are. So poppet valves of the British-Caprotti pattern were specified for this sole example of the British Railways Class "8" locomotive. On test, No. 71000 *Duke of Gloucester* showed a 9 per cent improvement over the "Britannia" class in steam consumed for a given amount of work done. It was a world record for a simple locomotive.

Alas, although the boiler was of impeccable lineage, being based on the excellent one used on the LMS "Duchess" class, there was some detail of its proportions which interfered with economical steam production at high outputs. It would have been easy to correct the faults with a little investigation. Unfortunately, in the words of E.S. Cox, then Chief Officer (Design) at BR headquarters, "there were some in authority at headquarters, although not in the Chief Mechanical Engineer's department, who were determined that there should be no more development with steam"; so nothing was done and no more Class "8"s were built.

So No. 71000 spent its brief life as an unsatisfactory one-off locomotive. After it was withdrawn, the valve chests and valve gear were removed for preservation, but that has not prevented a more than usually bold preservation society from buying the rest of the remains.

Below: *Mercury* ("Britannia" class 4-6-2 No. 70020) raises the echoes with the Cardiff-London "Capitals United Express" in 1959.

Class 01.¹⁰4-6-2

Origin: German Federal Railway (DB). **Type:** Express passenger steam locomotive. **Gauge:** 4ft 8½in (1,435mm). **Propulsion:** Coal fire with a grate area of 42.6sq ft (3.96m²) generating steam at 227.6psi (16kg/cm²) in a fire-tube boiler, and supplying it via a superheater to three 19.7 x 26in (500 x 600mm) cylinders, driving the main wheels direct by means of connecting and coupling rods. **Weight:** 133,000lb (60.4t) adhesive, 244,000lb (110.8t) without tender. **Axleload:** 44,500lb (20.2t). **Overall length:** 79ft 2in (24,130mm). **Tractive effort:** 37,000lb (16,830kg). **Max speed:** 88mph (140km/h). **Service entry:** 1954.

At the end of World War II in 1945 the railways of Germany were devastated, and a large proportion of the express passenger locomotives were out of service. By the end of the decade services were largely restored, but by that time the partition of Germany had been formalised, and the railway system of the Federal Republic had adopted the name German Federal Railway (DB), whilst that of the German Democratic Republic used the old name German State Railway (DR).

By 1950 it was clear that both systems would extend their electrified networks, and introduce diesel traction on non-electrified lines, but both systems also made plans for limited construction of new steam locomotives for the interim period. In the event, new construction was confined to mixed-traffic and freight locomotives, and only two completely new express passenger engines were built. These were two three cylinder Pacifics completed by DB in 1957, by which time the progress of electrification was so rapid that there was clearly no prospect of the class being extended.

Steam-hauled passenger trains therefore continued to be worked by the pre-war Pacifics. To prolong their lives, many of these on both systems were rebuilt to varying degrees. Although each railway adopted its own scheme of rebuilding, they had much in common.

The first engines to be altered were the 55 three-cylinder Pacifics of Class "01.¹⁰", all of which came into DB ownership. These engines had been built in 1939 and 1940 with full streamlining, but by the end of the war parts of the casing had been removed, and many of the engines lay derelict for up to five years. Between 1949 and 1951 the class was given heavy repairs, in the course of which the streamlined casing was removed, and the engines acquired an appearance in accordance with post-war standards. Compared with the non-streamlined pre-war Pacifics, there was no sloping plate connecting the side running boards with the buffer beam, and the full-depth smoke deflectors were replaced by the small Witte pattern on the upper part of the smokebox. Removal of the casing around the smokebox revealed that the cylinder of the feedwater heater was mounted externally in a recess in the top of the smokebox, instead of

Below: East German Class "01.10" 4-6-2 ready to return through the iron curtain with a Hamburg to Dresden express passenger train.

Above: A standard German coal-burning "01" class 4-6-2 on a passenger train. Many members of this famous class burnt fuel oil.

being buried in the smokebox as in the "01" and "03" engines.

The next rebuilding involved fitting new welded fireboxes with combustion chambers to five of the "01" Pacifics, the existing parallel barrel being retained. The original fireboxes without combustion chambers had been troublesome to maintain, despite the intentions of the designer, Dr R.P. Wagner who was head of the German State Railway's Central Locomotive Design section. The modified boiler could be detected by the extra firebox washout plugs, but even more conspicuous was the fitting of Heinl feedwater heaters, with a raised casing ahead of the chimney.

Deterioration of the alloy-steel fireboxes of the "01.10" and "03.10" Pacifics then led to design of a new all-welded boiler with tapered barrel, suitable for fitting to all the large Pacifics; a smaller version of the same boiler was produced for the "03" and "03.10" classes. This new boiler was fitted to all the "01.10" engines between 1956 and 1958. At the same time new front end systems, with larger chimneys, were fitted, along with a Heinl feedwater heater, with its tank concealed within the smokebox. The outline of the boiler was simplified compared with the pre-war types, as there was only one dome, and the sandboxes were on the running plates. The dimensions given above refer to these rebuilds.

The rebuilt "01.10" engines became the mainstay of heavy steam passenger workings on DB. As electrification spread northwards, they too moved north, and most of them ended their days at Rheine, where they were amongst the last DB steam engines to finish work in 1975. To increase the availability of the engines, 34 of them were converted to burn oil in 1957-58. These engines became class "012" under the 1968 renumbering, whilst the remaining coalburners were "011". In the latter days of steam operation on the Hamburg-Bremen line, these engines were hauling 600-tonne trains at speeds up to 80mph (130km/h), and were achieving monthly mileages of 17,000 (27,000km).

It was planned to fit the same type of boiler to 80 of the "01" Pacifics, but due to the increasing pace of electrification, only 50 were converted.

In East Germany the slower pace of electrification led to extensive rebuilding of 35 "01" Pacifics between 1961 and 1965. New all-welded boilers were fitted, but whereas on DB the new boilers had slightly smaller grates than their predecessors, those on DR had larger grates to cope with inferior coal. The external appearance of engines was changed greatly by fitting a continuous casing over the boiler mountings, and a deep valancing below the footplating (later removed). Eight of the rebuilds were given Boxpok driving wheels, and 28 of them were later converted to burn oil. The rebuild engines were classified "01.5". The rebuilding was so extensive that little of the original engine remained. They took over the heaviest DR steam workings, which included the international trains into West Germany, and they could be seen alongside the DB variants of Class "01" at Hamburg and Bebra.

Eleven of the "01.10" group of Pacifics have been preserved.

P36 Class 4-8-4

Origin: Soviet Railways (SZD). **Type:** Express passenger steam loco-motive. **Gauge:** 5ft 0in (1,524mm). **Propulsion:** Coal fire with a grate area of 73sq ft (6.75m²) generating steam at 213psi (15kg/cm²) in a fire-tube boiler, and supplying it via an external main steam pipe and superheater to two 22½ x 31½in (575 x 800mm) cylinders, driving the main wheels direct by means of connecting and coupling rods. **Weight:** 163,000lb (74t) adhesive, 582,000lb (264t) total. **Axleload:** 41,000lb (18.5t). **Overall length:** 94ft 10in (29,809mm). **Tractive effort:** 39,686lb (18,007kg). **Max speed:** 81mph (130km/h. **Service entry:** 1953.

Having by 1930 established an excellent class of 2-6-2 passenger loco-motives—the "S" class— and built about 3,000 of them, Soviet Railways could sit back and consider the future of long-distance passenger traffic at leisure. Passenger traffic had so far always taken second place to freight, but it was recognised that in due time higher speeds and more comfortable (and therefore heavier) trains would be needed for those whom the Soviet government permitted to travel.

The first prototype came in 1932 and it was a logical enlargement of the 2-6-2 into a 2-8-4, combining an extra driving axle to increase tractive

effort and an extra rear carrying axle to give greater power from a larger firebox. The class was given the designation "JS" (standing for Joseph Stalin) and some 640 were built between 1934 and 1941. None is working today but a freight equivalent with the same boiler, cab, cylinders, tender and other parts was the "FD" class 2-10-2, many of which were still in service in southern China until recently, after conversion from 5ft (1,524mm) gauge to standard.

The episode was typical of a sensible and logical attitude towards the needs of the railway system, in respect of which the new socialist regime hardly differed from the old Czarist one. One small prestige extravagance did follow, however, with the building in 1937-38 of the first three of a class of ten high-speed streamlined 4-6-4s for the "Red Arrow" express between Moscow and Leningrad. It was hoped to raise the average speed for the 404-mile (646km) run from about 40 to 50mph (64 to 80km/h). The first two had coupled wheels of 78¾in (2,000mm) diameter, but the third had them as large as 86½in (2,197mm). The latter machine again had boiler, cylinders and much else standard with the "FD" class. Eventually the war put an end to the project, but not before the first prototype had achieved 106mph (170km/h) on test, still a record for steam traction in Russia. ▶

Below: A "P-36" 4-8-4 of the USSR railway system with Train No. 1 "Rossiya" awaits departure at Skovorodino, Siberia, in 1970.

Above: A Russian Class "P-36" 4-8-4 express passenger locomotive waits "on shed" at an unknown location in the Soviet Union.

Right: The immense height and striking lines of the huge Russian Class "P-36" 4-8-4 are best brought out in this head-on view.

▷   World War II for the Russians may have been shorter than it was for the rest of Europe, but it was also a good deal nastier. So it was not until five years after the war ended that the first of a new class of passenger locomotive appeared from the Kolomna Works near Moscow. This prototype took the form of a tall and handsome 4-8-4, designated class "P36". The new locomotive was similar in size and capacity to the "JS" class, but the extra pair of carrying wheels enabled the axleloading to be reduced from 20 to 18 tons. This gave the engine a much wider availabilty, although this was never needed, as we shall see.

Whilst the class was very much in the final form of the steam locomotive, one feature which it had in common with many modern Russian engines was particularly striking and unusual. This was an external main steam pipe enclosed in a large casing running forward from dome to smokebox along the top of the boiler. This arrangement, excellent from the point of view of accessibility, was only made possible by a loading gauge which allows rolling stock to be 17ft 4in (5,280mm) above rail level. Roller bearings were fitted to all axles—for the first time on any Russian locomotive—and there was a cab totally enclosed against the Russian winter, as well as a mechanical stoker for coal-fired examples of the class. Many of the 4-8-4s, however, were oil-burning, particularly those running in the west of the country.

After a cautious period of testing, production began at Kolomna and between 1954 and 1956 at least 249 were built, making them the world's most numerous class of 4-8-4. Of course, compared with other classes in Russia, which numbered from more than 10,000 examples downward, the size of the class was miniscule.

In contrast, though, their impact upon Western observers was considerable because they were to be found on lines visited by foreigners,

such as Moscow-Leningrad and between Moscow and the Polish frontier. Some of the class were even finished in a blue livery similar to the streamlined 4-6-4s, but most looked smart enough in the light green passenger colours with cream stripes and red wheel centres.

For some 15 years the "P36s" handled the famous Trans-Siberian express, the legendary "Rossiya", after the changeover from electric traction through to the Pacific Ocean shore. The run took 70 hours and there were 19 changes of steam locomotive, so Siberia was paradise to at least one class of humanity. Steam enthusiasts had to show some subtlety in recording the objects of their love on film; the use of miniature cameras was very dangerous, but some success was achieved by people who set up a a huge plate camera on its tripod, marched up to the nearest policeman and demanded that the platform end be cleared.

Steam enthusiasm was not without its dangers for those at home. In 1956 Lazar Kaganovitch, Commisar for Transportation and Heavy Industry, who had long advocated the retention of steam traction with such words as "I am for the steam locomotive and against those who imagine that we will not have any in the future—this machine is sturdy, stubborn and will not give up", was summarily deposed and disappeared. Steam construction immediately came to an end in the Soviet Union. Some twenty years later steam operation of passenger trains also ended and with it the lives of these superb locomotives.

Class 12000 B₀-B₀

Origin: French National Railways (SNCF). **Type:** Mixed-traffic electric locomotive. **Gauge:** 4ft 8½in (1,435mm). **Propulsion:** Alternating current at 25,000V 50Hz passed through transformer and mercury arc rectifier to four 830hp (620kW) bogie-mounted traction motors with flexible drives to axles; axles of each bogie geared together. **Weight:** 188,660lb (85.6t). **Axleload:** 47,170lb (21.4t). **Overall length:** 49ft 10⅜in (15,200mm). **Tractive effort:** 54,000lb (240kN). **Max speed:** 75mph (120km/h). **Service entry:** 1954.

At the end of World War II the standard system for main-line electrification in France was 1,500V dc, but French engineers, like those of a number of other countries, were interested in the possibility of using alternating current at the standard industrial frequency of 50Hz. This offered a number of advantages: 50Hz current could be taken from the public supply at any convenient point and only a small transformer would be needed to reduce the voltage to that required for the overhead wires. As alternating current could be reduced on the locomotives by transformer, the supply could be taken from the overhead at high voltage; the higher the voltage, the smaller the current, and the lighter the overhead wires and their supports. With high voltage, the supply points could be spaced more widely, because voltage drops in the line would be proportionately smaller than with a lower-voltage system.

The second most comprehensive test so far made with electric traction at 50Hz was on the Höllenthal line in West Germany, which happened to be in the French zone of occupation after the war. French engineers thus had an opportunity to study this line closely and the results of ten years' operation of it. They formed a favourable opinion of the system, particularly as a means of electrifying lines with lower traffic densities than had previously been considered economic for electrification. SNCF therefore chose for an experimental ac system the line from Aix-les-Bains to La Roche-sur-Foron in Savoy. This was mainly single track without complicated track layouts, but it had gradients sufficiently severe to test the equipment thoroughly. French and Swiss manufacturers supplied a number of locomotives and motor coaches for this conversion, some to work on ac only and some on both ac and dc.

Success of the Savoy scheme led to a bold step forward—conversion of ▶

Above: A 25,000V ac Class "12000" Bo-Bo electric locomotive moves freight in the province of Alsace-Lorraine. French trains take the left-hand track except here where Germany once ruled.

Below: A central cab, enabling the same control console to be used for both directions of running, was a feature of these SCNF Class "12000" high-voltage industrial-frequency electric locomotives.

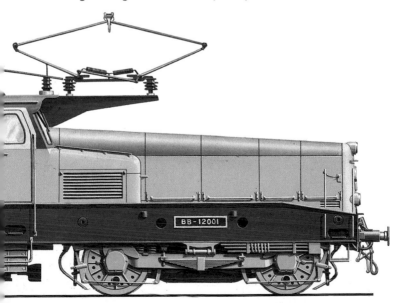

▶ 188 miles (303km) of the Thionville to Valenciennes route in northern France to electric working at 25,000V 50Hz. Although a secondary route, it carried three express passenger trains and up to 100 freight trains in each direction daily, and it had gradients of up to 1-in-90 (1.1 per cent).

The ac traction system in West Germany and Switzerland used current specially generated at $16^2/_3$Hz. A normal type of electric motor as used on dc will operate on ac, but each time the current reverses there are induced effects which tend to upset the working of the commutator. These effects are proportional to the square of the frequency. At $16^2/_3$Hz they can be coped with, but 50Hz is a different proposition, and up to and including the Höllenthal line experiment satisfactory traction motors for this frequency had not been produced, but the target was worth striving for.

Two main alternatives were available in a 50Hz system: to persevere with 50Hz motors or to convert the supply to some other form on the locomotive for supply to the traction motors. In fact SNCF decided to test four arrangements, conversion to dc by static converter, direct use of the 50Hz supply, conversion to dc by rotary converter, and conversion to three-phase by rotary machines.

For this purpose four types of locomotive were designed, two B-Bs for the first two systems and two Co-Cos for the second two. Of these systems the simplest was the second, for as with the $16^2/_3$Hz locomotives in other countries, it involved only a transformer to step down the voltage to a value suitable for the motors, and a tap changer on the transformer to vary the voltage. For the ac to dc conversion by static converter, the ignitron was selected. This was a form of steel-tank mercury-pool rectifier developed by Westinghouse in the United States. The two types of Co-Co locomotive had heavier equipment involving one or more rotating machines. The four classes were designated "12000", "13000", "14100", and "14000" respectively.

Layout of the locomotives was unusual in that they had centre cab, an arrangement normally found only on shunting locomotives. The main reason for this was that SNCF had found that 50 per cent of failures of equipment in electric locomotives on the road were in the control equipment. With cabs at both ends of the locomotive, remote control of equipment was unavoidable, but with a central cab, in which the driver could use the same controls for both directions of travel, some of the equipment could be controlled directly. Further advantages were the good all-round view and more protection for the driver in collisions. A conspicuous feature of the locomotives was the platform mounted on the cab roof, and protruding beyond it, to support the pantographs.

Below: Industrial frequency alternating current electrification became the standard as a result of the success of the Class "12000".

Above: The lightness of the overhead wire system required for high-voltage electrification is clearly shown in this picture.

Bogies of the B-B locomotives were derived from those of the experimental high-speed B-B machines, Nos. 9003-4, with the axles geared together, but as the new locomotives were intended for lower speeds than Nos. 9003-4, the bogie was shortened and the suspension simplified. For the Thionville line it was sufficient for one of the four classes to be capable of express passenger work, so the "12000s" were geared for 75mph (120km/h), the "13000s" for 65mph (105km/h) and the two Co-Co types for 37mph (60km/h).

The first of the "12000" class, No. 12001, was delivered in July 1954 and was put to work immediately on passenger and freight trains ranging from 500t to 1,300t. Control of voltage to the motors was by a tap changer on the high-tension side of the transformer, as is common in ac practice. On test No. 12006 achieved some remarkable results. It started a train of 2,424t on a gradient of 1-in-100 (1 per cent), with a maximum tractive effort of 38t, or 47 per cent of the adhesive weight. At 8.5km/h the tractive effort was still 33.7t. These were outstanding figures, and the ability of the locomotive to sustain this high tractive effort, just on the point of slipping, but without actually "losing its feet", was considered to be a notable achievement of the ignitron control in conjunction with the gearing together of the two axles on each bogie. The other classes performed well, but not so well as the "12000s", and furthermore the "12000s" proved to be the most reliable.

The other classes were not extended beyond the initial orders, but a total of 148 of Class "12000" were eventually built. The success of the Thionville-Valenciennes scheme led to a major policy decision—that future electrification, except for certain extensions of existing dc routes, would be on ac at 25,000V 50Hz. The first scheme to be affected by this decision was the main line of the former Nord Railway, and this scheme met the Thionville route at its northern extremity. The last of the "12000" class were ordered as part of the Nord scheme.

Before construction of the class was complete, there was a major development in electrical equipment with introduction of the silicon diode rectifier. This was a simpler, more compact and more robust piece of equipment than the ignitron, and well suited to the rough life of equipment on a locomotive. The last 15 of the "12000s" were built with silicon rectifiers, and others have been converted over the years. As the most successful and the most numerous of the four types of locomotive for the Thionville electrification programme, these locomotives still dominate traffic on that route.

Experience with these four classes settled finally the type of traction equipment to be used on future ac lines. Once again, the direct 50Hz motors proved unsatisfactory, whilst the simplicity of the silicon rectifier ruled out decisively any system with rotating machinery.

Class 20 2-D-1+1-D-2

Origin: Rhodesia Railways (RR). **Type:** Beyer-Garratt steam freight locomotive. **Gauge:** 3ft 6in (1,067mm). **Propulsion:** Coal fire with a grate area of 63.1sq ft (5.9m²) in a fire-tube boiler generating steam at 200psi (14kg/cm²) which is supplied to two pairs of 20in bore by 26in stroke (508 × 600mm) cylinders, each pair driving the main wheels of its respective unit directly by connecting and coupling rods. **Weight:** 369,170lb (167.5t) total. **Axleload:** 38,019lb (17.25t). **Overall length:** 95ft 0½in (28,969mm). **Tractive effort:** 69,330lb (308kN). **Max speed:** 35mph (56km/h). **Service entry:** 1954.

Most railways in Africa were built to open up newly-developed colonies. Traffic expectations were not great, and the lines were often constructed cheaply to a narrow gauge, with light rails, and with severe curvature. As the colonies developed, and particularly when their mineral resources became important, the railways ·faced the problem of acquiring larger locomotives which would be suited to existing gauge and curvature. The solution for many lay in articulated or hinged locomotives, particularly if there was a limited axleload.

The type of articulated locomotive most popular in Africa was the Garratt, a British design which originated in 1907, and which reached its highest state of development in the 1950s. In this design the boiler is mounted on a frame suspended by pivots from two rigid units which carry the fuel bunker and water tanks. As there are no wheels under the boiler, it can have a large diameter and deep firebox, and the whole boiler unit is more accessible than in a normal rigid locomotive. Each end unit can have as many axles as the curvature of the line permits, six or eight driving axles being the norm.

The largest user of Garratts was South African Railways with 400, but Rhodesia Railways, now the National Railways of Zimbabwe, came second. This system bought 250 of them between 1926 and 1958 from Beyer Peacock of Manchester, 200 of them coming after World War II. They constituted half the total steam locomotives built for the railway. The last and largest were 61 4-8-2 + 2-8-4 machines built between 1954 and 1958. The engines have an axleload of 17t, made possible by installation of heavy rail on parts of the system, and their total weight put them near the top of the Garratt league table. They are equipped with every device ▶

Below: National Railways of Zimbabwe Class "20" Garratt 4-8-2 + 2-8-2 No. 748 at Thomson Junction in 1984.

► for reducing maintenance costs and fuel consumption, and for increasing availability. They are notable in being the only Rhodesian Garratts to be stoker fired.

As with other African railways, Rhodesia Railways succumbed to the charms of the diesel salesmen, who could offer not only machines which were much more economical in fuel than steam engines, but also low-interest loans, which some Western governments would make available to third-world countries to assist their own diesel manufacturers. 1980 was set as the date for the dieselisation of the whole Rhodesian system.

However, the combination of the tremendous increase in the cost of oil from 1973 onwards, with the difficulties caused by imposition of sanctions against Rhodesia following UDI, made the railway authorities review their policy. The country had large supplies of coal but no oil, so that imported oil cost thirty times as much as coal. Even though the diesel had three times the efficiency of a steam engine, this still left fuel costs for the diesel ten times as great as for steam. Furthermore, whereas many wearing parts of the steam engines could be manufactured locally, the diesels required specialised parts which only the makers could supply, and sanctions had cut these supplies. Plans for dieselisation were therefore halted, and replaced by a long-term programme of electrification. In the meantime, in 1978, a scheme was initiated for rehabilitating 87 of the remaining Garratts, many of which had already been laid aside.

Although locomotives had never been built in the country, there was an engineering firm which could undertake major work on locomotive parts,

beyond the capacity of the railway workshops. The work included renewal of fireboxes and, surprisingly, replacement of friction bearings by roller bearings, together with a thorough overhall of all other working parts.

The locomotives concerned were 18 light branch line 2-6-2+2-6-2s of Class "14A", 35 4-6-4+4-6-4s of classes "15" and "15A" (these had been the principal passenger engines before dieselisation), 15 heavy 2-8-2+2-8-2s of Class "16A", and 19 of the largest 4-8-2 I 2-8-4s of classes "20" and "20A". As a symbol of their revivification, many of the locomotives were given names. The first rehabilitated engines emerged in June 1979 and the scheme was completed in 1982.

The locomotives are largely employed in the south-western part of the country near the coalfields, and they work between Gwelo, Bulawayo and Victoria Falls. They are intended to have a life of at least 15 years, but whether electrification will be sufficiently advanced by the mid-1990s for them to be released remains to be seen. The first electrified route, Harare to Dabuka (Bulawayo), 199 miles (320km) was energised in 1984. In the meantime, Zimbabwe has the largest steam locomotives still in operation in the world, many of which are as good as new. There must be other African countries which have coal but no oil wondering if their hasty replacement of steam was really wise.

Below: A Class "16A" 4-8-2+2-8-4 heads a Victoria Falls train in 1976. This class was just as up-to-date as the Class "20s", but considerably lighter, permitting a wider sphere of operation.

Class 59 4-8-2+2-8-4

Origin: East African Railways (EAR). **Type:** Steam locomotive for heavy freight haulage. **Gauge:** 3ft 3⅜in (1,000mm). **Propulsion:** Coal fire with a grate area of 72sq ft (6.7m²) generating steam at 225psi (15.8kg/cm²) in a fire-tube boiler, and supplying it via a superheater to two pairs of 20½ x 28in (521 x 711mm) cylinders, each pair driving the main wheels of its respective unit direct by means of connecting and coupling rods. **Weight:** 357,000lb (164t) adhesive, 564,000lb (256t) total. **Axleload:** 47,000lb (21t). **Overall length:** 104ft 1½in (31,737mm). **Tractive effort:** 83,350lb (38,034kg). **Max speed:** 45mph (72km/h). **Service entry:** 1955.

In discussing locomotive performance, British inclines like Shap and Beattock are often spoken of with awe. Shap has 20 miles (32km) of 1-in-75 (1.3), per cent, but what would one say about a climb of 350 miles (565km) with a ruling grade of 1-in-65 (1.5 per cent)? Such is the ascent from Mombasa to Nairobi, up which every night the legendary "Uganda Mail" makes its way.

Construction of the metre-gauge Uganda Railway, begun in 1892, was a strangely reluctant piece of empire building, violently opposed at home, yet successful. One of its objectives was the suppression of the slave trade, and that was quickly achieved. The second objective was to facilitate trade, and that also was successful to a point where the railway was always struggling to move the traffic offering. By 1926 a fleet of 4-8-0s was overwhelmed by the tonnage, and the Kenya & Uganda Railway (as it then was) went to Beyer Peacock of Manchester for 4-8-2+2-8-4 Beyer-Garratts, with as many mechanical parts as possible standard with the 4-8-0s. It was the answer to mass movement on 50lb/yd (24kg/m) rail.

As the years went by, other Garratt classes followed and the K&UR became East African Railways. In 1954, with the biggest backlog of tonnage ever faced waiting movement, the administration ordered 34 of the greatest Garratt design ever built. Whilst their main role was hauling freight, these giant "59" class locomotives were regarded as sufficiently passenger train oriented to be given the names of East African mountains. Also, of course, they bore the attractive maroon livery of the system.

By British standards their statistics are very impressive—over double the tractive effort of any locomotive ever employed in passenger service back home, coupled with a grate area nearly 50 per cent larger. Oil-firing was used, but provision was made for a mechanical stoker if coal burning ever became economic in East African circumstances. There was also provision for easy conversion from metre gauge to the African standard 3ft 6in (1,067mm) gauge, as well as for fitting vacuum brake equipment, should the class ever be required to operate outside air-brake territory.

All the latest and best Beyer-Garratt features were applied, such as the self-adjusting main pivots, the streamlined ends to the tanks, and those long handsome connecting rods driving on the third coupled axle. Four sets of Walschaert's valve gear were worked by Beyer's patent Hadfield

72

Above: Beyer-Garratt No. 5934 *Nenengai Crater* stands outside Nairobi Works in 1977 after the last steam overhaul done there.

steam reverser with hydraulic locking mechanism. The virtues of the short fat Garratt boiler, with clear space beneath the firebox, made 14 or 15 hours continuous hard steaming no problem. Later, Giesl ejectors were fitted to the class, with results that were controversial operationally, and quite unambiguously awful aesthetically.

One feature which did not work out was the tapered axleloadings, which gave successive axleloads in tons when running forward of 15.4, 15.4, 19.0, 20.9, 20.8, 18.8, 15.3; 15.5, 19.0, 21.0, 21.0, 19.0, 15.3, 15.3. The idea was that the gradual rise in axleload should permit operation on 80lb/yd (38.6kg/m) rail north and west of Nairobi, in addition to the 95lb/yd (45.7kg/m) rail by then general between Nairobi and the coast.

The results of fresh motive power were very impressive, the backlog of traffic was quickly cleared and the new engines soon found themselves the largest and most powerful steam locomotives in the world. That they remained that way for 25 years was due to the economical use of well-maintained steam power long preventing any case being made out for a change to diesel traction.

Even so the diesel did win in the end, displacing the "59s" from the mail trains quite early on and from the freights gradually between 1973 and 1980. In addition a proposed "61" class 4-8-4+4-8-4 with 27-ton axle loading, 115,000lb (52,476kg) tractive effort and 105sq ft (9.8m^2) fire grate was shelved indefinitely. ▶

Below: Oil-fired Beyer-Garratt Class "59" 4-8-2+2-8-4 *Mount Kilimanjaro* depicted in former EAR's superb crimson-lake livery.

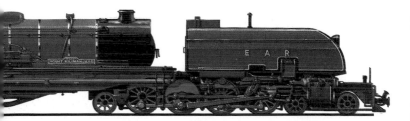

A magnificent Class 59 Beyer-Garratt No. 5917 *Mount Kitumbeine* halts for water en route from Mombasa up to Nairobi.

Nos 111-120 1-E-1

Origin: Rio Turbio Industrial Railway, Argentina. **Type:** Mineral-hauling gas-fired coal-consuming steam locomotive. **Gauge:** 2ft 5½in (750mm). **Propulsion:** Gas-producing firebed 26sq ft (2.43m²) in area, generating steam at 228psi (16kg/cm²), which is supplied to two 16½in x 17⅜in (420 x 400mm) cylinders, each driving the main wheels directly by connecting and coupling rods. **Weight:** 83,700lb (38t) adhesive, 190,529lb (86.5t) locomotive and tender. **Axleload:** 16,740lb (7.6t). **Overall length:** 61ft 7¾in (18,790mm). **Tractive effort:** 12,420lb (55.5kN). **Max speed:** 28mph (45km/h). **Service entry:** 1956.

The many attempts to improve the efficiency of the steam locomotive in the 20th Century fall into two main groups: first, those which involved radical changes in the Stephenson locomotive, such as complex high-pressure boilers or turbine drive; and secondly, those which concentrated on improving the proportions and detailing design of the conventional locomotive. In the second category the work of André Chapelon was outstanding, and his rebuilds developed up to twice the power of the original locomotive, and at the same time used fuel more efficiently.

Amongst disciples of Chapelon were several Argentinian engineers, notably Dante Porta. Under the direction of Porta and his colleagues, and with Chapelon's aid, a number of classes were improved beyond recognition, with increases in power of up to 55 per cent despite limitations imposed by the quality of labour compared with France. These rebuilds followed Chapelon's doctrine—increased cross-section of flow throughout the path of the steam, increased steam temperature by redesigning the superheater, and improved blast to increase the steaming rate without restricting the exhaust from the cylinders.

The designers incorporated a number of advances on Chapelon's work, of which the most notable was the gas-producer firebox. In this the firebed is at a comparatively low temperature, and almost all the combustion takes place in the firebox above the fire, air and steam being blown into the firebox under careful control so that almost perfect combustion can be maintained up to the highest rate of steaming. This remedied a major weakness in the normal locomotive boiler—that combustion deteriorates at high rates of steaming, reducing efficiency.

Porta's most spectacular results were achieved on the world's most southerly railway, the Rio Turbio line in Argentina, a 2ft 5½in (750mm) gauge line which carries coal 160 miles (257km) from the Rio Turbio mines to the port of Rio Gallegos on the Atlantic, with grades of 1-in-333 (0.3 per cent) against loaded trains and winds of up to 100mph (160km/h) to contend with. Light rail limits the axleload to 7½t and the maximum speed is 25 to 28mph (40 to 45km/h).

In 1956, ten 2-10-2 locomotives, based on a design of the Baldwin

Above: Two Porta-Chapelon improved 2-10-2 steam locomotives stand ready to take a train from the port of Rio Gallegos.

Locomotive Company, were built for this line in Japan, and Porta later applied his ideas, including the gas-producer firebox, to three of them. As a result, the sustained drawbar horsepower was increased from 700 to 1,200. Despite the poor quality of the coal, which is small for firing in locomotives and has a high ash content, combustion is almost smokeless. The improvements enabled the locomotives to haul 1,700t regularly, and on test as much as 3,000t was hauled on the level.

In 1964, ten more locomotives were built incorporating Porta's modifications, and one had a circular firebox of his design, arranged to give even more intense combustion by mixing the gases, steam and air in a swirling motion.

Not the least remarkable feature of these engines is that, for a grate area of 22.5sq ft (2.1m²), a mechanical stoker is provided; many European and North American grates of twice that size were hand fired, but the controlled firing which the stoker permitted was of great help to Porta in his modifications to the firebox.

Porta produced a design for a two-cylinder compound 2-8-0 aimed at railways in under-developed countries which had coal but no oil, and in which the railways had difficulty in obtaining skilled labour. However, climbing on the diesel band wagon was already a characteristic of the railways in countries which could have benefited from Porta's work, aided by nations which made cheap loans available to the third world to aid their own diesel locomotive industry. By the time the crisis in oil prices showed the folly of total dependence on oil, dieselisation had proceeded too far in most countries, and no country has built an engine to the Chapelon/Porta design, although, as recorded later, Porta's ideas have been applied in South Africa.

Below: 2-10-2 No. 108 *Andre Chapelon*, a modern steam coal-burning locomotive of the Rio Turbio Industrial Railway.

QJ "Forward" 1-E-1

Origin: Railways of the People's Republic of China (CR). **Type:** Steam freight locomotive. **Gauge:** 4ft 8½in (1,435mm). **Propulsion:** Coal fire burning on a firegrate 73sq ft (6.8m²) in size generating steam at 213psi (15kg/cm²) in a fire-tube boiler and supplying it via a main steam pipe mounted above the boiler and a superheater to two 25⅝ x 31½in (650 x 800mm) cylinders which drive the main wheels directly through connecting and coupling rods. **Weight:** 221,500lb (100.5t) adhesive, 486,080lb (220.5t) total, with small tender holding 15t (16.5US tons) of coal and 7,700gall (35m³—9,620 US gall) of water. With large tender the total weight is increased to 546,592lb (248t), the length to 95ft 9in (29,180mm) and the coal and water capacity to 21.5t (23.7 US tons) and 11,020gall (50m³—13,775 US gall) respectively. **Axleload:** 44,300lb (20.1t). **Overall length:** 86ft 1½in (26,251mm). **Tractive effort:** 63,500lb (282kN). **Max speed:** 50mph (80km/h). **Service entry:** 1956.

China began seriously to build steam locomotives after the rest of the world had stopped. Production still continues at a rate approaching one per working day and, not only that, has recently been reprieved indefinitely. In fact, this "QJ" class is currently, at 4,000-strong, the largest class of locomotives in the world, of whatever type of propulsion; it also comprises about a fifth of all the steam locomotives left active in the world.

The reasons for China being out of step with the rest of mankind are plain. Ample indigenous supplies of coal, modest oil reserves and plenty of people to serve a rather labour-intensive form of traction are three of them. More important, perhaps, is the pressing need to keep the capacity of the railways abreast of the rising demands of a rapid industrial growth. This need is best met by continuing with steam locomotives which can be mass-produced in a purpose-built factory for one seventh of the cost, like-for-like, of diesel-electric ones. In Western money, a Chinese steam 2-10-2 costs some £70,000 ($US105,000), while a diesel of equivalent

Below: A superb spectacle—two "QJ" or "Forward" class 2-10-2 steam locomotives of the Chinese railways double-heading a freight.

Above: The only class of steam locomotive being produced in the world today, a Chinese "Forward" class 2-10-2 near Jilin in 1980.

capacity built in China is priced at £500,000 ($US800,000). Fuel costs are also now lower with steam than with diesel. A last factor is that the Chinese suffer less pressure to follow the example of neighbouring railway administrations than others. No need to "keep up with the Joneses" if you live by yourself.

The first steps in development of the "QJ" began in 1949 when, after 12 years of struggle, Mao's communist government took over a war-torn and ramshackle railway system. To improve the motive power situation in the long-term, Russian assistance was given in setting up a works at Datong in northern China to build large freight locomotives. Delays occured through withdrawal of Russian help and the confusion that resulted, and also because of Mao's "Great Leap Forward", during which embryo locomotive factories were ordered to produce diesel locomotives—Datong's attempt is said to have been called *Sputnik*.

It was 1962 before production of this class (then called *Ho Ping* or "Peace") began at Datong. The design was basically the "Lv" class of 2-10-2 from Russia; some prototypes were built in 1956 at Daliean Works in Manchuria. Certain modifications, principally to the boiler, were made in the version for production, which built up steadily as experience was gained. The 500th "QJ" was built in 1968, the 1,000th in 1970, the 2,000th in 1974 and the 3,000th in 1979, all except the very first at Datong. Even in 1985, Datong was turning out some 325 steam locomotives a year. Datong has also built a number of "JS" or "Construction" class 2-8-2s and a series of mobile diesel-electric generating plants.

The "QJs" are very well-equipped and, apart from having the main steam pipe in trunking above the forward part of the boiler instead of out of sight inside, very much in the North American genre. They have mechanical stokers, exhaust steam injectors, feedwater heaters, electric lighting, and air-horn as well as a dragon-scaring steam whistle, and even cooking facilities and a toilet on board. The standard models (numbered with a few exceptions chronologically from QJ 100 upwards) have eight-wheel tenders, but a few in the QJ60xx series have large 12-wheeled versions for use in dry areas.

Though designated for heavy freight movement, these superb locomotives can often be seen on passenger work on heavily-graded mountain lines. With extensive new railway construction going on, it is possible to travel in China on a 1980s railway behind a 1980s steam locomotive. With 2,980hp (2,223kW) available at the wheel-rim —equivalent to say 3,700hp (2,760kW) developed in the cylinders of a diesel engine—an excellent level of performance is available.

RM Class 4-6-2

Origin: Railways of the People's Republic of China (CR). **Type:** Express passenger steam locomotive. **Gauge:** 4ft 8½in (1,435mm). **Propulsion:** Coal fire with a grate area of 62sq ft (5.75m²) generating steam at 213psi (15kg/cm²) in a fire-tube boiler, and supplying it via a superheater to two 22½ x 26in (570 x 660m) cylinders, driving the main wheels direct by means of connecting and coupling rods. **Weight:** 137,750lb (62.5t) adhesive, 383,600lb (174t) total. **Axleload:** 46,284lb (21t). **Overall length:** 73ft 5½in (22,390mm). **Tractive effort:** 34,597lb (15,698kg). **Max speed:** 69mph (110km/h). **Service entry:** 1958.

This unusual but neat-looking 4-6-2 is thought to be the final design of steam express passenger locomotive in the world, and the country which built it is the last in the world to have steam locomotives in production. Those now being built are basically freight locomotives, but like the "QJs" they are used for express passenger trains on certain mountain lines in the People's Republic.

The "RM"—"Ren Ming" or "People" class—4-6-2s are descended from some passenger locomotives supplied by the Japanese to the railways of their puppet kingdom of Manchukuo, otherwise Manchuria. The older engines in pre-liberation days were known as Class "PF-1" ("PF" stood for "Pacific") but afterwards they became re-designated "SL" standing for "Sheng-Li" or "Victory". Locomotive construction to Chinese design did not begin for several years after the Communist victory of 1949, but by 1958 construction of the "RM" class was under way at the Szufang (Tsingtao) Works. It was an enlarged version of the "SL" class, capable of a power output 12½ per cent greater.

Above: The world's final express passenger steam locomotive design, an "RM" or "People" class 4-6-2 near Jinan, China in 1980.

Below, left: A fine plume of steam is thrown up by "People" class 4-6-2 No. RM1019 as she heads north from Harbin, Manchuria, in 1980.

The main difference between the "RM" and "SL" class—and indeed between the "RM" class and virtually all other steam locomotives outside the USSR—was in the position of the main steam-pipe. This normally ran forward from the dome inside the boiler, but in these engines there was room for it to be situated much more accessibly in well-insulated trunking above the boiler. An interesting detail shared with other Chinese steam power, is the provision of an air horn, in addition to a normal deep-sounding steam chime whistle. In other ways, though, these fine engines followed what had been for many years the final form of the steam locomotive. Thus we find two cylinders only, using outside-admission piston-valves driven by Walschaert's valve gear, coupled with a wide firebox boiler with no frills except a big superheater and a mechanical stoker. Apart from this last feature British readers could reasonably regard the "RM" as what a Class "7" 'Britannia' 4-6-2 might have been if the designers had had similar axleload limitations, but another 3ft (914mm) of vertical height with which to play.

Visitors to China report that these engines can frequently be encountered travelling at speeds around 65mph (105km/h) on level routes hauling 600 ton passenger trains. There is reason to suppose that about 250 were built during the years 1958 to 1964 and that the numbers run from RM1001 to RM1250. Wide variations in the insignia and slogans which decorate present day Chinese steam locomotives introduce some variety into the plain (but always clean) black finish used. An "RM" class, specially painted in green, was used to haul the inaugural train over the great new bridge across the Yangtse River at Nanking.

Class 44 "Peak" 1-C_o-C_o-1

Origin: British Railways (BR). **Type:** Diesel-electric express passenger locomotive. **Gauge:** 4ft 8½in (1,435mm). **Propulsion:** 2,300hp (1,715kW) Sulzer Type 12LDA28 twin-bank turbocharged diesel engine and generator supplying current to six nose-suspended traction motors geared to the axles with resilient gearwheels. **Weight:** 255,360lb (116t) adhesive, 309,120 (140t) total. **Axleload:** 42,560lb (19.5t). **Overall length:** 67ft 11in (20,701mm). **Tractive effort:** 70,000lb (311kN). **Max speed:** 90mph (144km/h). **Service entry:** 1959.

The famous "Peaks" when new were the highest-powered diesel-electric locomotives supplied to British Railways. They were the first of a huge and unprecedented order for 147 express passenger locomotives (later increased to 193) with Sulzer twin-bank engines (with two parallel crankshafts in the same crankcase). Most of the latter were made under licence by Vickers Armstrong of Barrow-in-Furness, England. After the first 10, engines rated 200hp (150kW) higher were provided.

    Running gear was similar to that of the Class "40" locomotives introduced in 1958. This, together with the bodywork, was built at BR's Derby and Crewe works where the locomotives were erected. Electrical equipment for the first 137 engines came from Crompton Parkinson

Above: British Railways' Class "46" Co-Co No. 46042 heads south from Newcastle-upon-Tyne with a relief express to London in 1978.

(CP) and for the remainder from Brush Engineering.

Originally the class was numbered D1 to D193, in the prime position in BR's diesel list. Later, the 10 original 2,300hp Sulzer/CP locomotives became Class "44", the 2,500hp Sulzer/CP batch Class "45" and the 2,500hp Sulzer/Brush batch Class "46". All were provided with such usual equipment as an automatic train-heating steam boiler, a vacuum exhauster for train brakes, straight air brakes for the locomotives, multiple-unit control gear and a toilet. Later the locomotives were fitted for working air-braked trains and (in some cases) heating electrically-heated carriages. The first 10 were named after mountain peaks in Britain; a few others received names of regiments and other military formations.

Although there was 15 per cent more power available than on the Class "40s", the "Peaks" also had very little margin in hand when working to the best steam schedules. But even though one may criticise the design as being unenterprising, with little to offer over and above steam traction, it must be said that this slow, solid approach has paid off in longevity. At the time of writing after more than 20 years, 125 of the original 193 are still in service, while many of their more enterprising successors have taken their brilliant performances with them to the scrapyard.

Left: Class "46" No. 46004 crosses the River Tyne by the King Edward VII Bridge in 1977, with a Newcastle to Liverpool express.

Below: One of the original "Peak" (later "45") class 1-Co-Co-1 diesel-electric locomotives depicted in original colour and style.

FL9 B₀-B₀-A1A

Origin: New York, New Haven & Hartford RR (New Haven). **Type:** Electro-diesel passenger locomotive. **Gauge:** 4ft 8½in (1,435mm). **Propulsion:** General Motors 1,750hp (1,350kW) Type 567C V-16 two stroke diesel engine and generator—or alternatively outside third-rail feeding current to four nose-suspended traction motors geared to both axles of the leading bogie and the outer axles of the trailing one. **Weight:** 231,937lb (105.2t) adhesive, 286,614lb (130t) total. **Axleload:** 57,984lb (26.3t). **Overall length:** 59ft 0in. (17,983mm). **Tractive effort:** 58,000lb (258kN). **Max speed:** 70mph (112km/h). **Service entry:** 1956.

These unusual and interesting machines, like a number of others, were the results of that famous ordinance of the City of New York prohibiting the use therein of locomotives which emitted fumes. It occurred like this: the New Haven railroad was is the 1950s considering abandonment of its path-finding single-phase electrification, which dated from as early as 1905, and changing over to diesel traction. The only problem was how to run into New York.

New Haven trains used both the Grand Central terminal (of the New York Central RR) and the Pennsylvania Station. Both routes were equipped with conductor rails (of different patterns) supplying low-voltage direct current. This corresponded closely to the current produced in the generator of a diesel-electric locomotive and it was suggested that a standard General Motors"FP9" passenger cab unit could be modified easily to work as an electric locomotive when required. The ac electrification could then be dismantled, yet trains could continue to run without breaking the law. In fact axleload restrictions led to one quite substantial change—substitution of a three-axle trailing bogie for the standard two-axle one; hence a unique wheel arrangement. The end product was designated "FL9" and 60 were supplied between 1956 and 1960. The most obvious evidence of their unique arrangement was the two-position retractable collecting shoes mounted on the bogies, to cater for New York Central's bottom-contact conductor rail and Long Island RR's top-contact one. Otherwise the presence of additional low-voltage control gear inside the body was the principal technical difference between an "FP9" and an "FL9" locomotive.

In the event, the New Haven changed its mind over dispensing with the electrification, but the "FL9s" still found employment, surviving long

Above: One of the New Haven's unique Bo-A1A electro-diesel locomotives of Class FL9, still giving good service after more than 30 years hard work and now running under the flag of AMTRAK.

enough to be taken over by the National Railroad Passenger Corporation (Amtrak) in the 1970s. Many locos of what is now a veteran class are still shown on Amtrak's books at the time of writing.

While they exist, the "FL9s" represent a spark of originality in a country whose locomotives were and are much of a muchness (apart from their livery) from Oregon to Florida or Arizona to Maine.

Below: New York, New Haven & Hartford Railroad electro-diesel locomotive. As well as running as a normal diesel-electric, the FL9s could run on current drawn from two types of third rail.

TEP-60 C$_o$-C$_o$

Origin: Soviet Railways (SZD). **Type:** Diesel-electric express passenger locomotive. **Gauge:** 5ft 0in (1,524mm). **Propulsion:** Type D45A 3,000hp (2,240kW) turbocharged 16-cylinder two-stroke diesel engine and generator supplying current to six spring-borne 416hp (310kW) traction motors geared to the axles via flexible drives of the Alsthom floating-ring type. **Weight:** 284,316lb (129t). **Axleload:** 47,390lb (21.5t). **Overall length:** 63ft 2in (19,250mm). **Tractive effort:** 55,750lb (248kN). **Max speed:** 100mph (160km/h). **Service entry:** 1960.

These powerful single-unit machines form one of the Soviet Union's principal diesel-electric passenger locomotive classes, although they have been displaced from the very top assignments by the 4,000hp "TEP-70" class. Production of the "TEP-60" continued for at least 15 years, though the total number built has not been revealed. For many years it has been the only type of Soviet diesel locomotive passed for running at speeds above 140km/h (87mph), although neither the need nor the opportunity for such fast running really exists as yet on the SZD network.

Russian experience with diesel locomotives was minimal (and, as far as

it went, totally unsatisfactory) before World War II. Therefore in 1945 the mechanical engineers began with a clean sheet and the early diesels were based very sensibly on US practice. By 1960, sufficient confidence had been attained so that original ideas could be incorporated.

A serious weakness in early adaptations of freight locomotives for passenger work was bad tracking of the bogies. Having regard to SZD aspirations towards faster passenger trains, some electric locomotives had been ordered from Alsthom of France, maker of the bogies for world rail speed record-breaker, French National Railways' Co-Co No. 7107.

Alsthom features were used in the bogies for the "TEP-60", in particular the flexible drive which enabled the traction motors to be spring-borne, and the prototype reached 118mph (189km/h) on test. This was claimed at the time to be a world record for a diesel locomotive and certainly vindicated the restrained wisdom of those responsible for the design. Other features of note in these locomotives included electric braking and the ability to cope with temperatures both hot and cold considerably more extreme than are found in conjunction on other railways.

Below: The diesel-electric Co-Co locomotives of Soviet Railways' Class TEP-60, depicted here in "ex-works" condition, form the country's principal motive power for passenger expresses.

Class 060DA C_o-C_o

Origin: Romanian State Railways (CFR). **Type:** Mixed-traffic diesel-electric locomotive. **Gauge:** 4ft 8½in (1,435mm). **Propulsion:** Sulzer Type 12LDA28 2,300hp (1,690kW) turbocharged twin-bank 12-cylinder diesel engine and generator supplying direct current to six traction motors driving the axles via resilient gearwheels. **Weight:** 257,870 (117t). **Axleload:** 42,980lb (19.5t). **Overall length:** 55ft 9in (17,000mm). **Tractive effort:** 64,125lb (285kN). **Max speed:** 62mph (100km/h). **Service entry:** 1960.

The bulk of the diesel-electric locomotive fleet used by Romanian State Railways is based on six prototypes constructed in Switzerland during 1959. Mechanical parts were built by the Swiss Locomotive Works, the electrical equipment by Brown Boveri, and the diesel engines supplied by Sulzer. There are of the "twin bank" configuration with two parallel rows of cylinders, each driving a separate crankshaft.

The elegant bodywork is typical of Swiss locomotives and is of welded construction. No train heating equipment is included; separate heating vans are used when required.

A 550t freight train can be started by one of these locomotives on the ruling grade (1-in40—2.5 per cent) of the Brasnov to Bucharest main line and accelerated up to 9mph (14km/h). For heavier loads, the locomotives can be run in multiple. There is no rheostatic or regenerative braking, but the usual straight and automatic air brakes are provided. Automatic detection and correction of wheelslip is a help on these severe grades.

Production of these locomotives has continued in Romania and they are also offered for export.

Right and below: Three views of Romanian State Railways' Class 060DA diesel-electric Co-Co locomotives. These multi-purpose machines are basically of Swiss origin with Sulzer twin-bank diesel engines. They have the elegantly curved bodywork and coil-spring bogies typical of that country's locomotive products. The class has been produced over a long period and its members are used extensively on passenger and freight train workings all over the network. The bright grey and blue livery is an innovation—a drab green more typical of European national railway systems were the rule in Romania for many years.

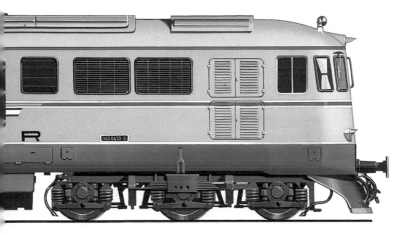

Class Dm3 1-D+D+D-1

Origin: Swedish State Railways (SJ). **Type:** Electric locomotive for heavy mineral traffic. **Gauge:** 4ft 8½in (1,435mm). **Propulsion:** Single-phase low-frequency current at 15,000V 16⅔Hz fed via overhead catenary and step-down transformer to six 1,609hp (1,200kW) motors, driving the wheels by gearing, jackshaft and connecting rods. **Weight:** 528,960lb (240t) adhesive, 595,080lb (270t) total. **Axleload:** 44,080lb (20t). **Overall length:** 115ft 8in (35,250mm). **Tractive effort:** 210,000lb (932kN). **Max speed:** 47mph (75km/h). **Service entry:** 1960.

To exploit the vast deposits of iron ore found in the interior of northern Sweden, a railway was needed. It was comparatively easy work to build from the Baltic port of Lulea to the mining area around Kiruna, but the Baltic at this latitude, near to the Arctic circle, freezes over in the winter. Accordingly, the railway was continued further north still as well as westwards, crossing not only the Ofoten mountains but the Arctic circle itself, and what is now the Norwegian frontier, to reach the sheltered port of Narvik, kept free of ice year-round by the friendly Gulf Stream. The iron ore railway from Lulea to Narvik, which began operations in 1883, extends for a total of 295 miles (473km).

Steam operation was fairly traumatic, especially in winter, because of the heavy loads, the very low temperatures and the mountain gradients, not to speak of continuous darkness. Apart from the mosquitos, in summer things were more pleasant—for example, the lineside tourist hotel at Abisko (with no access except by train!) boasts a north-facing sun verandah to catch the midnight sun!

It is not surprising then that the Lappland iron ore railway was the first important line in Scandinavia to be electrified. Electric working began in 1915 and conversion was completed throughout in 1923. The low-frequency single-phase system was adopted, by then well-proven in Switzerland and elsewhere.

The quality of the iron ore from Kiruna, together with the ease with which it can be won—plus, it must be said, the long-standing neutrality of Sweden, which means that customers are never refused on political grounds—always kept demand high and, in the long term, ever-rising. The problem for the railways, then, has in most years been concerned with the ability to handle the traffic offering. So far, doubling the line has been avoided by increasing the weight of the trains, and for many years they were the heaviest in Europe.

It is typical of the Swedish way of railroading that the motive power there today is a modest adaption of the early standard and essentially simple Class "D" locomotive. The result is this Class "Dm" locomotive of 9,650hp (7,200kW), designed to haul the now legendary ore trains. Loads of up to 5,200t (5,720 US tons) are taken up 1-in-100 (1 per cent) gradients, as well as started in polar temperatures—thereby explaining the need for a tractive effort exceeding 200,000lb (900kN). ▶

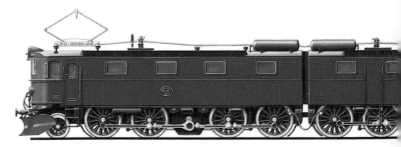

Above: A Class "Dm3" 1-D+D+D-1 electric loco hauls a massive train of iron ore through the arctic forests of Swedish Lapland.

Below: The Swedish rod-drive triple-unit Class "Dm3" electric locomotives can produce more than 200,000lb of tractive effort.

One might be puzzled why Swedish State Railways designates this mighty hauler as a sub-class (the "m" in Dm stands for *malm* or iron) of their modest and ubiquitous Class "D" 1-C-1 standard electric locomotive. The reason was that the original Class "Dm" could be said to be two "Ds" with an additional coupled axle substituted for one pony truck on each unit, which also had a cab at only one end. Two units coupled permanently back-to-back originally formed a Class "Dm" locomotive and these were introduced in the late 1940s. Eventually there were 19 twin locomotives, plus four owned by Norwegian State Railways (the NSB class is "el 12"). Both the brown Swedish engines and the green Norwegian ones operate indiscriminately over the whole line.

In 1960 still more power was required and three cab-less units (also without pantographs) were built and put in the middle of three existing pairs. By 1970 all the Swedish "Dm" pairs had been converted to triples.

Each individual unit bears a separate number although units are not separated in normal operation. The huge tractive effort available caused problems with the traditional screw couplings and so Russian-pattern automatic knuckle couplers have been fitted.

As a rod-drive locomotive the "Dm3" was the last of its line. Since 1970 a need for additional power has been met, and history made to repeat itself, by modifying the current standard Swedish high-power Class "Rc4" express passenger locomotive. The alterations include lower gearing, very sophisticated wheelslip control and addition of 10t (12 US tons) of ballast, all in aid of improving tractive effort, while cabs are insulated against arctic temperatures.

Below: Swedish State Railways' Class "Dm" 1-D + D + D-1 electric locomotive as built in the 1960s for working iron ore traffic.

Above: These mighty haulers are used for bringing iron ore trains from Kiruna in northern Sweden to the ice-free port of Narvik.

U25B B₀-B₀

Origin: General Electric Company (GE), USA. **Type:** Diesel-electric road switcher locomotive. **Gauge:** 4ft 8½in (1,435mm). **Propulsion:** One GE FDL16 2,500hp (1,870kW) four-stroke 16-cylinder Vee engine and generator supplying four nose-suspended traction motors geared to the axles. **Weight:** 260,000lb (118.0t). **Axleload:** 65,000lb (29.5t). **Overall length:** 60ft 2in (18,340mm). **Tractive effort:** 81,000lb (360kN) with 65mph gear ratio. **Max speed:** 65mph (105km/h), 75mph (121km/h), 80mph (129km/h) or 92mph (148km/h) according to gear ratio fitted. **Service entry:** 1960.

If, in the 1920s, one had said to an American locomotive engineer: "The diesel-electric locomotive seems to have great potential; which locomotive manufacturer is capable of exploiting it?" he would almost certainly have said "General Electric", for that company was then building on 30 years' experience of electric traction of all sorts by turning out diesel switchers (shunters) incorporating various makes of engine. However, the prophet would have been wrong, for it was the massive resources of General Motors Corporation thrown into its Electo-Motive Division which sparked off, and largely fuelled, the steam-to-diesel revolution in the United States.

GE was thus destined to take a minor part in the overall process, but within the 25 per cent or so of the market which did not fall to EMD, it has always had a major share. When the American Locomotive Company (Alco) embarked seriously on production of road diesels, it made an agreement with GE to use only GE electrical equipment in its products, in return for which GE agreed not to compete with Alco. From 1940 to 1953 both companies benefited from this agreement; Alco profited from the expertise of the biggest firm in the electrical traction business, and GE acquired an easy market for products which it was well qualified and equipped to supply. A second manufacturer, Fairbanks Morse, likewise offered GE equipment in its models.

By the early-1950s, total dieselisation of US railroads was certain, and although Alco was well established in the market, its sales ran a poor second to EMD and were not improving. GE then took the plunge; it quietly terminated its agreement with Alco and embarked on development of its own range of large diesels. Although most of its previous diesels had been small switchers, it had in fact built a 2,000hp (1,490kW) Sulzer-engined unit in 1936, which for 10 years was North America's most

Above: The Rock Island Railroad is now defunct, but in 1965 one of its "U25C" diesel-electrics headed a consist at Limon, Colorado.

powerful single-engined diesel locomotive, and in the post-war years the company had built up an export market in road locomotives.

The essential requirement for GE to enter the home road-diesel market was a large engine. At this time its switchers were fitted with Cooper-Bessemer 6-cylinder in-line and 8-cylinder Vee engines, so the company acquired the rights to develop this engine. Two versions were made, the 8-cylinder developing 1,200hp (895kW) and the 12-cylinder developing 1,800hp (1,340kW).

First outward sign of GE's new venture was a four-unit locomotive, with "cab" or totally- enclosed bodies, two units fitted with the V8 engines and two with the V12. These units were tested on the Erie Railroad from 1954 to 1959, and based on their successful performance the company launched a new series of export models in 1956, designated the ▶

Below: A four-axle GE "U-boat" road-switcher depicted in the striking and unusual grey livery of the Louisville & Nashville RR.

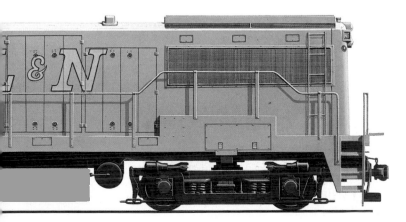

► "Universal" series. With the experience gained from V8 and V12 engines, GE now embarked on a major step forward, a 16-cylinder version developing 2,400hp (1,790kW). Two of these engines were installed in Bo-Bo hood units, and were tested on the Erie, covering 100,000 miles (160,000km) in 11 months. Although masquerading under the designation "XR24", denoting 2,400hp export test units, these were in fact destined to be the demonstrators of a new model for the home market.

In 1960, seven years after ending its partnership with Alco, GE announced a new model, the 2,500hp (1,870kW) "Universal" Bo-Bo, denoted "U25B". Its most obvious sales point was that it had the highest horsepower of any locomotive on the US market, by 100hp (75kW); but to have any chance of breaking into the EMD/Alco markets, it had to have many attractions less obvious, but equally important to customers.

In preparing the design, GE had asked the motive power chiefs of 33 railroads what they liked and disliked in the diesels which they already operated. The costs of operating these units were also analysed, and it was found that repairs accounted for 28.7 per cent of total diesel operating costs. The designers' aim was therefore to improve performance, but at the same time to simplify equipment to make it more reliable and maintenance-free. A major cause of complaint was the air system, both for supplying the engine and for cooling. The incoming air was filtered, and in most contemporary designs the filters needed cleaning at about 2,500 miles (4,000km). Alco designed a self-cleaning mechanical filter.

In contrast to these changes, much of the electrical equipment was well tried, including the traction motors, and roads which operated Alco locomotives would already have many of the parts in stock. However, there was an electrical innovation—use of modular electronic equipment.

Launching of the new model coincided with unfavourable economic conditions on the railroads, and more than a year passed before any orders came in. The first came from Union Pacific, which was always on the lookout for higher-powered locomotives, and other roads which had a specific need for higher power followed. Over a period of six years a total of 478 "U25Bs" were sold, not a great number by EMD standards, but sufficient for GE to displace Alco from second place in the US diesel sales league.

It was already established practice for a US road switcher to be offered both as a four-axle and as a six-axle unit, the latter appealed to railroads which needed more adhesive weight on a slightly lower axleload. The "U25C" therefore appeared in 1963, and added a further 113 units to GE sales. With the spread of the "U" designation, someone referred to "U-boats" and the nickname caught on.

The effect of GE competition on other manufacturers was to spur them

Below: A pair of GE "U25C" Co-Co units belonging to the Lake Superior & Ishpeming RR leased by the Detroit, Toledo & Ironton RR.

Above: A GE "U25B" Bo-Bo diesel-electric locomotive in the colours of the Maine Central RR at Waterville, Maine, in 1984.

to modify their own models. Competition was keen, particularly horse-power competition. GE's 16-cylinder engine and its generator were rated modestly, so that uprating would be possible without major alterations (and more spare parts to stock!), and so in 1966 came the 2,800hp (2,090kW) engine, in the "U28B" and "U28c" models.

UP bought 16 "U25Bs", but then ordered a special model to suit the addiction of its motive power chief, D. S. Neuhart, to very powerful locomotives. Already his road was operating 8,500hp (6,340kW) GE gas turbine locomotives, and the builder now produced a 5,000hp (3,730kW) twin-engined version of the "U25B" mounted on four bogies and weighing 247t; these were the "U50Bs". Later came a simplified Co-Co version of the same power. Neither of these types was entirely successful, and with the coming of standard models of 3,000hp (2,240kW) UP was content to fall into line with other railroads and buy off-the-shelf.

The next landmark in diesel development in the US was the 3,000hp engine, produced by EMD. Alco and GE in 1965-66. The GE models, "U30B" and "U30C", appeared late in 1966, and were followed less than a year later by 3,300hp (2,460kW) versions. In 1969 yet another increase, to 3,600hp (2,690kW), was achieved. The GE decision to use a moderately-rated engine in the first "U-boats" paid good dividends at this time, for whereas GE attained these increases in power by development of the 16-cylinder engine, EMD had to move to 20 cylinders. However, the railroads soon lost their enthusiasm for engines above 3,000hp when they discovered the extra maintenance costs incurred.

In 1976 a further revision of the GE range, known as the "7-series" was accompanied by a change in designation, the 3,000hp Co-Co becoming the "C30-7". These models established GE firmly in the market, to the extent that in 1983, a year of acute depression for US locomotive builders, GE built 324 units compared with EMD's 122.

By this time the railroads were again interested in high-powered loco-motives, whilst increasing fuel prices made fuel economy a strong selling point. In the GE "8-series", introduced in 1983, 3,600hp (2,685kW) 16-cylinder engines were offered, and in 1984 a 3,900hp (2,910kW) "B39-8" was supplied to Santa Fe, the most powerful US four-axle diesel so far. The 12-cylinder engine was also developed to 3,150hp (2,350kW). At the same time, GE exploited the greater inherent efficiency of its four-stroke engines compared with EMD's two-stroke.

Another notable GE development was an order in 1984 for 220 locomotives for China, the biggest order ever placed for US diesels, and the first for China. This was followed by a further 200 ordered in 1985.

Class 55 Deltic C₀-C₀

Origin: British Railways (BR). **Type:** High-speed express passenger diesel-electric locomotive. **Gauge:** 4ft 8½in (1,435mm). **Propulsion:** Two Napier Type 18-25 18-cylinder 1,750hp (1,305kW) "Deltic" two-stroke diesel engines and generators connected in series, feeding current to six nose-suspended traction motors geared to the axles of the two bogies. **Weight:** 222,600lb (101t). **Axleload:** 36,920lb (16.25t). **Overall length:** 69ft 6in (21,180mm). **Tractive effort:** 50,000lb (222kN). **Max speed:** 100mph (160km/h). **Service entry:** 1961.

The sad thing about diesel locomotives is that, unlike steam, all the fascinating mechanism is hidden deep within. That is why it is exceptional for what they are like inside to be reflected in what they are called. But on the "Deltics" the mechanism was so very fascinating that its name spilled out into the lay world. In Greek, the capital letter   or delta is a triangle which, when inverted, exactly describes the layout of some diesel engines of remarkably high power for their weight and size. They were developed by English Electric's subsidiary Napier soon after World War II for fast motor gun-boats for the Royal Navy. They were to replace engines fuelled by petrol, which presented a serious fire hazard, in action and otherwise.

The advantages of an "opposed piston" engine are well known. Instead of having one piston per cylinder, with a massive cylinder head to take the thrust, there are two pushing against one another. It is not quite two for

Below: The "Deltic" Co-Co diesel-electric locomotive shown as built, when it was the world's most powerful single-unit diesel.

Above: A King's Cross to Edinburgh express passes Ouston Junction, County Durham, during 1978, hauled by "Deltic" Co-Co No. 55021.

Left: An East Coast express train rolls southward near Berwick-on-Tweed, hauled by a "Deltic" Co-Co diesel-electric.

the price of one, but part way to it. The only problem is that complications arise in making the two opposed thrusts turn a single shaft. In the "Deltic" engine, three banks of double cylinders, each with a pair of opposed pistons and arranged as three sides of a triangle, are connected to a crankshaft at each apex. Each crankshaft is then geared to the central drive shaft of the engine. The result was specific weight of only 6.2lb per hp (3.8kg/kW), some 2½ times better than contemporary medium-speed conventional diesel engines normally used for traction. There was also perfect balance of the forces generated and of the reciprocating parts.

English Electric's Traction Division was a main supplier of locomotives to British Railways, and EE's chairman Lord Nelson realised that by putting this Napier engine on to an English Electric chassis, he had the means to double the power of a typical diesel-electric locomotive. During ▶

Above: A "Deltic" takes a London to Edinburgh express slowly over the diamond crossings at Newcastle-upon-Tyne in 1975.

▶ 1955, in the teeth of opposition from the Traction Division, and at EE's own expense, a prototype was put in hand. During several years' testing the locomotive did everything that might be expected of a machine that had 3,300hp (2,462kW) available compared with the 2,000hp or so of its competitors. Moreover, it proved unexpectedly reliable.

Under BR's modernisation plan, electrification was envisaged from

London to the north of England both from Euston and from King's Cross. In the event, the former scheme was the only one put in hand at the time and the Eastern/North Eastern/Scottish Region authorities accordingly sought a stop-gap alternative which would give timings similar to those achieved with electric traction for minimal expenditure. The result was an order in 1959 for 22 of these superb locomotives, a class destined to become a legend in their own lifetime. When built they were by a considerable margin the most powerful single-unit diesel locomotives in the world.

Two separate "Deltic" engine-and-generator sets were installed,

Above: A "Deltic" diesel-electric Co-Co No. 55010 *King's Own Scottish Borderer* **under the wires at Kings Cross diesel depot.**

▶ normally connected in series, but in the event of failure the crippled engine could be switched out and the locomotive could continue to pull its full load using the other one, but at reduced speed.

Auxiliary equipment on the "Deltics" included an automatic oil-fired steam generator for heating trains. The water tanks for this equipment were originally arranged so they could be filled from steam-age water cranes and also—amazingly—at speed from water troughs by means of a scoop! Later, windings were added to the generators to provide for electric heating of the train, although this abstracted several hundred horsepower from the output available for traction. Both compressors and vacuum exhauster sets for brake power were provided, as well as cooking facilities and a toilet.

The bogies were standard with the contemporary English Electric 1,750hp Type "3" locomotives (now BR Class "37") and automatic detection and correction of wheelslip was provided. The controls were also generally similar to other English Electric locomotives, although drivers could not run them exactly the same as other locomotives, because the low angular inertia of a "Deltic" engine precluded heavy-handed throttle movements, which were liable to lead to automatic shutdown. Even so, the possibility of climbing the 1-in-200 (0.5 per cent) gradient to Stoke Summit, north of Peterborough, at a minimum speed of 90mph (144km/h) with a heavy East Coast express was something that earned the total respect of footplatemen. In the old LNER tradition, the "Deltics" were all named—some after race horses that had won their races and others after English and Scottish regiments. Originally the class was numbered D9000 to D9021; later Nos. D9001 to 21 became Nos. 55001 to 21 and D9000 became No. 55022.

One of the crucial measures in the scheme to acquire the "Deltics" was that the deal should include maintenance at an inclusive price, with penalties to be incurred if, through faults arising, the locomotives were unable to perform an agreed mileage each year. The task of keeping the "Deltic" fleet in running order was simplified because the engines were maintained on a unit replacement basis. After a few anticipated problems in the first year or so, the "Deltics" settled down to running about 170,000 miles (273,500km) a year, or about 500 miles (800km) a day, with a very low failure rate.

Above: The prototype English Electric "Deltic" Co-Co diesel-electric on trials on the East Coast main line at Markham in 1959.

After some improvements to the route, including major track realignments, the "Deltic"-hauled "Flying Scotsman" ran (for example in 1973) from King's Cross to Newcastle, 271 miles (433km) in 3hr 37min and to Edinburgh, 395 miles (632km), in 5hr 30min, average speeds of 74.9 and 71.8mph (119.8 and 114.5km/h) respectively. Such timings as these were appied not just to one or two 'flag' trains but to the service as a whole; they represented substantial gains—a 1½ hour acceleration compared with 12 years before between London and Edinburgh, for instance. Teesside customers could have as much as 1¾ hours extra time in London for the same time away from home, compared with what was possible in the pre-"Deltic" era. British Rail reaped a reward in the form of a substantial increase in traffic, and this far more than outweighed the fact that the cost of maintenance of these complex engines was admittedly higher than those of lower specific power output.

Fifteen years and 50 million "Deltic" miles later, electrification seemed as far away as ever, and a further stage of development without it became desirable. In the event, a possible "Super-Deltic" based on two "Deltic" engines of increased power was discarded in favour of the self-propelled High-Speed Trains, with more conventional Paxman engines. It might have been hoped that the existing "Deltics" could be moved on to rejuvenate operations on less important lines, where their low axleload would permit usage. In the end, though, because their engines were expensive to maintain, it was not possible to make a case for keeping them, based on the kind of rather uninspiring arithmetic BR's accountants use in such matters.

So on January 2, 1982 the last "Deltic"-hauled train ran into King's Cross. Now all that remains are memories of the monumental labours of these fabled machines. Two at least are preserved—the prototype in the Science Museum, London, and *King's Own Yorkshire Light Infantry* in the National Railway Museum at York.

As a postscript, it is worth mentioning that the plans for electrification of the East Coast route were approved at last in 1984. The irony is that whereas the "Deltics" brought East Coast performance well up to the standard normally expected of electric traction, the new electrics of the late-1980s will barely improve on the best timings achieved by the diesel-powered HSTs.

Class 47 C₀-C₀

Origin: British Railways (BR). **Type:** Diesel-electric mixed-traffic locomotive. **Gauge:** 4ft 8½in (1,435mm). **Propulsion:** Sulzer 2,750hp (2,052kW) 12LDA28C 12-cylinder twin-bank engine and generator supplying direct current to six nose-suspended traction motors geared to the axles. **Weight:** 264,480lb (120t), with variations between different sub-classes. **Axleload:** 44,080lb (20t), with variations. **Overall length:** 63ft 5in (19,329mm). **Tractive effort:** 62,000lb (275kN). **Max speed:** 95mph (152km/h). **Service entry:** 1962.

These useful locomotives are the workhorses of BR's diesel fleet and form almost half the total stock of large diesel locomotives of 2,000hp or over. A total of 528 were built between 1962 and 1967 by Brush Engineering and BR's Crewe Works. All have Brush electrical equipment and use the same Sulzer engine—with modest enhancement of power output—as the "Peak" class, but the overall weight was reduced by careful design to the point where the two outer idle axles of the older type could be dispensed with. The engines were built under licence by Vickers-Armstrong of Barrow, England. Originally the "47s" were numbered D1500 to 99 and from D1100 upwards, but renumbering in 1968 to incorporate the class designation brought them into the 47xxx series.

Details vary; the "47.0" group (243 strong) originally had steam heating boilers and these run on to include the "471xx" and "472xx" number series. There is a "47.3" sub-class (81 in number) which have no train heating equipment either steam or electric, but do include special low-speed control for assisting automatic loading or unloading of merry-go-round coal trains. The 185 "47.4s", which include the "475xx" number series, all have electric heating arrangements (and some steam as well). Lastly there is a group fitted for working push-pull express trains between Edinburgh and Glasgow; these are renumbered and reclassified "47.4". All the "47s"

are equipped for working both air and vacuum-braked trains, and they have automatic wheelslip detectors and correctors as well as an anti-slip brake. The bogies are one-piece steel castings.

It must be said that the electric train heating system absorbs power from the engine and affects the amount of power available to haul the train by a noticable amount—several hundred horsepower in fact. In this case the diminution nicely absorbs the amount of power gained by several years of diesel engine development! When considering these locomotives as express passenger power, then, this loss must normally be taken into account. Of course, it is of lesser importance now that most of the prime diesel express passenger assignments in Britian have been taken over by HST125 sets. However, the "47s" equipped for electric train heating have a device whereby, if the full engine power is temporarily needed for traction, the driver can push his controller handle against a spring return which temporarily interrupts the heating supply.

One noticeable thing missing from the Class "47" armoury is multiple-unit capability and this perhaps underlines BR's general philosophy which is (with some exceptions in special cases) to provide a single locomotive of the power needed to haul any given train. It is in complete contrast to the North American principle that diesel units should be building-blocks from which traction of any desired power can be assembled.

One interesting example of the class, originally No. 47046, has been used as a testbed for a more powerful engine. With a Paxman 3,250hp (2,425kW) 12RK3CT engine fitted in 1975 it became the sole member of sub-class "47.6", later class "47.9" No. 47901.

The following year, this experimental locomotive spawned the BR Class "56". These are a class of Co-Cos similar in size, weight and appearance (apart from the style of painting) to the standard "47s" but given 26 per cent more power by installing the same engine that powers No. 47901.

Below: A Class "47" Co-Co diesel-electric locomotive stands proudly at the head of the royal train, Jamestown, Scotland, 1978.

Class 52 "Western" C-C

Origin: British Railways, Western Region (BR). **Type:** Diesel-hydraulic express passenger locomotive. **Gauge:** 4ft 8½in (1,435mm). **Propulsion:** Two 1,350hp (1,000kW) Bristol-Siddeley/Maybach 12-cylinder Vee-type MD655 "tunnel" engines each driving the three axles of one bogie via a Voith-North British three-stage hydraulic transmission, cardan shaft, intermediate gearbox, further cardan shafts and final-drive gearboxes. **Weight:** 242,440lb (110t). **Axleload:** 40,775lb (18.5t). **Overall length:** 68ft 0in (20,726mm). **Tractive effort:** 72,600lb (323kN). **Max speed:** 90mph (144km/h). **Service entry:** 1962.

The episode of the "Western" class diesel-hydraulics was like a glorious but futile last cavalry charge on the part of some army facing inevitable defeat. Of all the companies absorbed into British Railways on January 1, 1948, the Great Western Railway found nationalisation much the hardest to bear. Its own apparently superior standards evolved over more than a century were largely replaced by those of inferior "foreign" (non-GWR) companies. For some time the regional management at Paddington had largely to content itself with words—the General Manager even issued an instruction to the effect that no locomotive of other than GWR design should be rostered for any train on which he was due to travel!

But after a decade had passed, action became possible. BR's 1950s Modernisation Programme gave Paddington a chance to do its own thing with locomotives which followed the hallowed Great Western tradition of being as different as possible from anyone else's.

At that time the choice of hydraulic transmission as an alternative to electric for high-power diesels was less radical than it is now. BR's central management had plumped (quite correctly, seen with hindsight) for electric transmission in most of the proposed diesel locomotives. But hydraulic transmission had some great attractions, and the GWR, alone amongst the old companies, had no experience with electric traction. Since West Germany was the country in which such motive power had developed furthest, German practice was the basis of what was done. In addition to hydraulic transmission, the German locomotives had high-speed lightweight diesel engines. They revolved at speeds twice those of diesel engines used in other BR locomotives and weighed less than half as much for the same power.

The first class of importance was the 2,000hp B-B "Warship" of 1958, designed to give similar performance to BR's 1-Co-Co-1 Class "40", but weighing 40 per cent less. Sixty-six "Warships" were built, but equality with the rest of BR was not enough. What was wanted was a machine that would run BR's other diesels into the ground.

Above: A "Western" or Class "52" diesel-hydraulic C-C locomotive emerges from Harbury tunnel between Leamington and Banbury.

No. D1000 *Western Enterprise* appeared in late-1961, soon to be followed by 73 more "Western" sisters. The names chosen were mostly evocative and many, like the first, provocative to BR's headquarters at 222 Marylebone Road, London. For example, No. D1001 *Western Pathfinder,* D1019 *Western Challenger,* D1059 *Western Empire.* GWR tradition was also followed in the matter of spelling mistakes—No. D1029 *Western Legionnaire* was at first *Western Legionaire.*

Alas, the locomotives did not cover themselves with Western Glory (D1072). For one thing, the opposition did not allow their lead in power output to be held for long. In the following year came the Brush Class "47" Co-Co (described here), with a fraction more power than the "Westerns", for only just over the some weight, and by 1967 the Class "50" diesel-electrics hired from English Electric also matched the diesel- ▶

Below: "Western" class C-C diesel-hydraulic locomotive in the style originally adopted for these powerful units of motive power.

Above: A "Western" diesel-hydraulic locomotive passes Lostwithiel, Cornwall with the down "Cornish Riviera Express", in October 1974.

▶ hydraulics for power. Moreover, even by 1963, central management had decided that diesel-hydraulics had no real advantage over diesel-electrics, of which it had a growing surplus. So some time before the high-speed HST125 trains took over most long-distance passenger services from Paddington in the late-1970s, the "Westerns" had been taken out of service. Withdrawal began with No. 1019 in mid-1973 and all had gone by early-1977. No less than six have survived in preservation but, in contrast, the rival diesel-electric classes "47" and "50" remain virtually intact in normal service.

The "Westerns" had their own kind of good looks, the unusualness of their appearance being enhanced by inside bearings to the wheels. The Maybach engines were also unusual (but invisibly so) in that they were of the tunnel pattern in which the circular crank webs actually form the bearing journals of the crankshafts. Power was transmitted to the wheels via various hydraulic and mechanical transmission boxes connected by numerous cardan shafts. This mechanical complexity was a source of problems with obscure causes but unfortunate results—substitution of hydraulic fluid and mechanical components for electricity as a medium of transmission tended to lower reliability and efficiency rather than raise them as promised. Also, there were festoons of electrical circuitry serving the control systems and instrumentation, and these gave all the problems to be expected of electrics amongst the oil-mist of a diesel locomotive interior.

The Western Region's mechanical department managed to solve the problems, being especially triumphant when the bad riding which had held down speeds was overcome by altering the bogies (with much simplification) to resemble in principle GWR standard ones dating from Victorian times. Such timings as a 3hr 30min schedule for the 225½ miles (363km) between Paddington and Plymouth then became possible, at last a significant improvement (of 30 minutes) over the best previously achieved with steam.

The reliability problem was eventually solved also by a long and painstaking process of diagnosis, trial and error, and finally by cure of many faults of detail in the design. Alas, by then a decision had already been taken to withdraw the diesel-hydraulic fleet from service prematurely and replace them by the Class "50" diesel-electric locomotives. It then was a case of heaping insult upon injury because (taking 1971 as an example) the "Westerns" were running 15,000 miles per failure while their diesel-electric replacements, the Class "50s", were only managing to achieve an appalling 9,000. At least British Rail gained some self-confidence in overcoming problems with a somewhat imperfect import.

Below: One of the class 52 C-C diesel-hydraulic locomotives of British Railways Western Region brings an express train round a well-ballasted curve laid with steam-age chaired permanent way.

Class 16500 B-B

Origin: French National Railways (SNCF). **Type:** Mixed-traffic electric locomotive. **Gauge:** 4ft 8½in (1,435mm). **Propulsion:** Alternating current at 25,000V 50Hz fed through a rectifier (ignitron, excitron or silicon) to a traction motor mounted on each bogie; motor connected to axles through two-speed gearing. **Weight:** 156,500lb (71t) to 163,100lb (74t) according to fittings. **Axleload:** 39,100lb (17.8t) to 40,800lb (18.5t) according to fittings. **Overall length:** 47ft 3in (14,400mm). **Tractive effort:** Low gear 71,410lb (318kN), high gear 42,320lb (188kN). **Max speed:** Low gear 56mph (90km/h), high gear 93mph (150km/h). **Service entry:** 1962.

The performance of the Class "12000" B-B locomotives on SNCF's Thionville-Valenciennes line established the superiority of the ignitron over other types of rectifier then available, and it also established the advantage of connecting the axles of a bogie by gearing. Wheelslip develops locally, and rarely do both axles of a bogie slip at the same instant. Coupling the axles enables a locomotive to be worked much nearer to the limit of adhesion than with independent axles, and SNCF engineers reckoned that a 60t locomotive with connected axles could maintain as high a tractive effort as an 85t unit with independent axles.

The next electrification after the Thionville-Valenciennes line was the Paris to Lille route of the Northern Region. For this scheme two new types of locomotive were introduced, one of which was a high-speed Bo-Bo geared for 100mph (160km/h). The other was a mixed-traffic B-B machine which introduced another novelty, the monomotor bogie with two-speed gearing. Monomotor bogies had already been tested experimentally and used on two dual-voltage locomotives. As the name implies, each bogie has a single motor mounted above the bogie frame and connected to the axles through gearing and spring drives. Between the small pinion on the motor shaft and the large gear wheel of the reduction gear there is an intermediate gear. Two gear wheels of different sizes are mounted on opposite ends of an arm, and by means of a vertical lever the arm can be rocked to bring one or other of these intermediate gears into mesh; the gear ratio is thereby changed. The changeover can be effected only when

Right and below: The Class 16500 B-B electric locomotives of French National Railways. The bogies of these interesting machines have one motor each driving two axles via gearing. Alternative gearing suitable for passenger or for freight working is provided, thereby increasing the versatility of the class.

the locomotive is stationary. The high-speed gear is the "passenger" gear, and the low-speed is the "freight" setting.

In a monomotor bogie the axles can be brought closer together than in a bogie with two motors situated between the axles, and the whole bogie is more compact. With the motor almost vertically above the centre, the bogie is less susceptible to developing oscillations at speed.

SNCF announced that these locomotives, designated "16500", would weigh only 60t, but in fact they weigh between 71 and 74t. Even so this is low for a locomotive of nearly 3,500hp, capable of developing a starting tractive effort in low gear of 32.4t (318kN). When the class was introduced, the ignitron was the current type of rectifier on SNCF, and with this regenerative braking could be fitted.

Outwardly the most noticeable difference from the Thionville locomotives was reversion to a completely enclosed rectangular body, the advantages of the centre cab having been outweighed by the limited space for equipment in the end bonnets. A total of 294 of the "16500" class were built, and they were divided between the Northern Region and the subsequent Paris-Strasbourg electrification of the Eastern Region. The first 155 had bogie suspension similar to that of the "7100" class C-C locomotives, with two Alsthom spring-loaded conical pivots. The remaining bogies had swing links at the corners.

During construction of the class a new type of rectifier known as the excitron came into use, and these were fitted to Nos. 16656 to 16750 (and a few others). Finally came the silicon rectifier which was fitted to the last 44, and has since been fitted to others.

Class "16500" fulfilled the designers' intentions that they should be a universal locomotive capable of undertaking, singly or in pairs, every type of duty except the fastest expresses. For these a 100mph (160km/h) version was developed the "17000" class, and the "8500" dc class and "25500" dual-voltage class were in turn developed from the "17000".

WDM2 C₀-C₀

Origin: Indian Railways (IR). **Type:** Mixed-traffic diesel-electric loco-·motive. **Gauge:** 5ft 6in (1,676mm). **Propulsion:** Alco 251D 2,600hp (1,940kW) 16-cylinder Vee diesel engine and generator supplying current to six nose-suspended traction motors geared to the axles. **Weight:** 279,910lb (127t). **Axleload:** 47,385lb (21.5t). **Overall length:**58ft 10in (17,932mm). **Tractive effort:** 63,000lb (280kN). **Max speed:** 75mph (120km/h). **Service entry:** 1962.

In spite of India being a country with little oil and much coal, the railway authorities had decided by 1960 that diesel traction would have advantages. Although with hindsight, it was a decision that might prove to be an expensive one, they at least went about implementing it in a way that commands admiration. They ignored the temptation succumbed to by so many other "third world" countries, of ordering a big fleet of ready-made diesels, which would have left India for ever in the power of the suppliers. At the same time they recognised that "do-it-yourself" was not possible without assistance from an overseas manufacturer.

In 1961 then, those entrusted with the project surveyed the field and decided that the United States firm Alco Products Inc had the best deal to offer. The agreement provided for Alco to supply technical help as well as complete designs to Indian Railways and, at the start, finished parts for locomotive production at a diesel locomotive works to be established in Varanasi (Benares), India. When completed, the shops had an area over 20 acres (8Ha) in extent, while the whole factory complex, inclusive of a self-contained township, extended to 550 acres (220Ha).

The first 40 locomotives came over from America early in 1962 in completed form, followed in 1963 by a batch in knocked-down condition. Ten years later production at Varanasi was of the order of 75 units per year and import-content was down from 100 per cent to 25 per cent. The three types which have been or are being produced are the large broad-gauge "WDM2" class (W=broad gauge, D=diesel, M=mixed traffic) described here, a smaller broad-gauge Class "WDM1" and a metre-gauge type, smaller still, Class "YDM4". All three have the Alco 251 engine, the difference being in the number of cylinders— 16, 12 and 6 respectively for the three classes.

Alco's designation for the "WDM2" is "DL560" and in many ways it is similar to locomotives in the "Century" series. The six-wheel bogies have

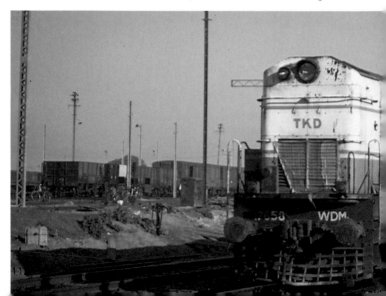

Above: WDM2 No. 18371 takes the "West Coast Express" out of Erode Junction, en route from Mangalore to Madras.

had to be modified to allow for the broad gauge, but they are of the familiar unsymmetrical pattern, taking account of the necessarily unsymmetrical arrangement of three nose-suspended traction motors. One change is the installation of a combined compressor-exhauster, provided to cater for vacuum-braked trains. Axleload is also lower than on models produced for the North American market. Although Alco went out of locomotive manufacture in 1969, its Canadian associate, previously the Montreal Locomotive Works but now known as Bombardier, is still very much in business and giving support to the Indian enterprise.

A scheme to update the "WDM2" design has been proposed, using an alternator in place of a dc generator and replacing the 16-cylinder engine by a 12-cylinder one developing the same horsepower. However, the advantages of building locomotives to the same good design over a long period very often outweigh any advantage accruing from some technical improvement. A factor which occasionally affects sensible judgements is the need on the part of the engineers concerned to be abreast of the latest techniques, but those in charge of locomotive development in India have so far shown a sensible contempt for such motives.

Below: A pair of Indian Railways' home-made Class WDM2 Co-Co diesel-electric locomotives head a long-distance express passenger train. The design is by Alco Products In, USA.

Class 73 B₀-B₀

Origin: British Railways (BR). **Type:** Electro-diesel mixed-traffic loco-motive. **Gauge:** 4ft 8½in (1,435mm). **Propulsion:** Direct current at 675V fed via an outside third rail, or alternatively generated on the locomotive by an English Electric 600hp (448kW) Type 4 SRKT diesel engine, to four 395hp (295kW) nose-suspended traction motors. **Weight:** 168,000lb (76t). **Axleload:** 42,000lb (19t). **Overall length:** 53ft 8in (16,358mm) with buffers extended. **Tractive effort:** 42,000lb (187kN). **Max speed:** 90mph (145km/h). **Service entry:** 1967.

One of the problems of an electrified railway is the need to provide for working over lines which, either permanently or temporarily have no current supply. With third-rail systems this need is accentuated by the impossibility of providing conductor rails uninterruptedly; BR's Southern Region had solved the problem by electric locomotives which could store energy in fly-wheels to pass trains over short gaps.

As the SR's electrification became more widespread, the use of normal diesel locomotives to cover workings over shorter and shorter portions of a journey became less and less satisfactory. So a powerful electric locomotive was conceived which carried a modest (but standard) diesel generating plant for movements away from the conductor rail. The result was this versatile group of locomotives (now designated Class "73") of which 42 were built in 1967 following six prototypes of 1962.

Details of interest include provision for multiple-unit operation not only with other electro-diesels, but also with straight electric and diesel-electric trains and locomotives. The weight of the diesel engine and generator, housed at one end of the locomotive, is balanced by a massive buffer beam at the other. Both screw couplings with buffers (for coupling to freight stock) and automatic buck-eye couplers with central buffing plates (for passenger trains) are provided.

The versatility of Class "73" was demonstrated to the world in July 1981, when Charles and Diana, Prince and Princess of Wales, left London for their honeymoon at Romsey, Hampshire, behind No. 73 142 *Broadlands:* 82 miles (131km) of electrified travel down the main line was followed by 5 miles (8km) under diesel power on a lesser and non-electrified route. The locomotives took on a new role in 1984, when high-speed push-pull trains were introduced between London Victoria and Gatwick Airport. Standard formation is a Class "73" plus up to eight coaches and a driving motor luggage van. Trains run every 15 minutes throughout the day, taking 30 minutes for the 26¾ mile (43km) journey.

Above: Bo-Bo electro-diesel locomotive No. 73142 *Broadlands* with the "Venice-Simplon-Orient Express" in 1983.

Below: A Class "73" electro-diesel locomotive passes Clapham Junction on a Victoria to Gatwick Airport push-pull express, 1984.

Below: British Railways' Southern Region Class "73" No. 73142 *Broadlands*—an electric locomotive with auxiliary diesel power.

Class 68000 A1A-A1A

Origin: French National Railways (SNCF). **Type:** Express passenger diesel-electric locomotive. **Gauge:** 4ft 8½in (1,435mm). **Propulsion:** CCM-Sulzer 2,650hp (1,980kW) 12LVA24 12-cylinder four-stroke Vee-engine and generator supplying current to four semi-sprung traction motors geared to the end axles of the bogies through spring drive. **Weight:** 176,320lb (80t) or 158,690 lb (72t) adhesive, 233,620lb (106t) total. **Axleload:** 44,080lb (20t) or 39,670lb (18t) adjustable. **Overall length:** 58ft 9½in (17,920mm). **Tractive effort:** 66,140lb (294kN). **Max speed:** 83mph (130km/h). **Service entry:** 1963.

During the 1950s, electrification spread rapidly over the busiest main lines in France and many of the most powerful steam engines became available for transfer to non-electrified routes. Until the end of the decade no major steps were taken to introduce large diesel locomotives for ultimate replacement of these steam engines on routes on which the traffic density was insufficient to justify electrification, and in 1962 only 8 per cent of total tonne-km on SNCF were diesel worked.

By 1960 diesel engines were available which made possible design of locomotives to replace even the largest steam engines, and in 1961 orders were placed for four new types of diesel locomotive, 20 B-Bs of 2,000hp (1,500kW), 18 A1A-A1As of 2,650hp (1,980kW), and two each of two twin-engined machines destined ultimately to have a power of 4,800hp (3,580kW).

It was intended that the 2,650hp Class "68000" should take over the heaviest workings on the routes from Paris to Cherbourg and Basle, pending completion of development of the larger units. The engine is of Sulzer design, produced by Sulzer's French associate, CCM. It is a 12-cylinder unit of Vee-formation, in contrast to the 2,750hp Sulzer engine then being built in large numbers for British Railways, which had twin crankshafts. It was Sulzer's first Vee-engine for traction since 1927.

The engine drives a dc generator, which supplies the semi-sprung nose-hung traction motors. The weight of the engine, generator and train

Below: Two French National Railways Class "68000" A1A-A1A diesel-electrics haul an express train near Noyelles in 1968.

Above: "68000" class A1A-A1A diesel-electric No. 68067 brings a passenger train into Angers station, French National Railways.

boiler made it necessary to have six axles, but only four traction motors were required, so the middle axle of each bogie is an idler. A novel system was applied whereby wedges can be inserted above the springs of the intermediate axles to vary the distribution of weight. On routes on which a 20t axleload is allowed, the intermediate axles carry 13t, but on routes with an 18t limit, the intermediate axles carry 17t. In the latter arrangement, a servo-operated mechanism enables the load on the driving wheels to be increased to 20t at starting, until a speed of 18½mph (30km/h) is reached. Maximum speed is 83mph (130km/h).

Control equipment is also novel for a diesel locomotive in that it resembles the "notch-up, notch-down, hold" type of controller, then already in use on electric locomotives. The driver's controller has four positions, "stop", "run", "faster", "slower". Moving the controller from "stop" to "run" energises the motor circuits with the engine running at idling speed, and engine speed is increased by holding the controller at "faster" against the pressure of a spring until the desired engine speed is reached. Similarly holding the controller at "slower" reduces the engine speed. Body sides are finished with a distinctive chevron design, destined to characterise all subsequent large French diesel locomotives, and the livery is blue and white.

The first 18 Class "68000" locomotives were ordered from Cie des Ateliers & Forges de la Loire of St Chamond, and delivery commenced in 1963. A further 18 were ordered in the following year's programme, and eventually the class totalled 82. The first locomotives were put to work between Paris and Mulhouse and Paris and Cherbourg, but it was soon apparent that they could only just equal the everyday work of the "241P" 4-8-2 steam engines on trains of 800t, and then only at the cost of working at full power for a higher proportion of the time than was considered desirable in the interests of reliability.

A second version of the class was introduced late in 1963, fitted with the AGOV 12 engine made by Société Alsacienne de Constructions Mécaniques of Mulhouse. This engine is a smaller version of that used in the "72000" class C-C locomotives. Since the appearance of the "72000", the two series of A1A-A1As have been moved to less-demanding duties.

"Virgin" B-B

Origin: Spanish National Railways (RENFE). **Type:** High-speed diesel hydraulic express passenger locomotive. **Gauge:** 5ft 6in (1,668mm). **Propulsion:** Two Maybach-Mercedes MD6557 12-cylinder Vee diesel engines of 1,200hp (895kW), each driving a Mekydro K1U hydraulic transmission unit and via cardan shafts and gearing, the main axles. **Weight:** 163,000lb (74t). **Axleload:** 40,775lb (18.5t). **Overall length:** 57ft 3in (17,450mm). **Tractive effort:** 54,000lb (240kN). **Max speed:** 87mph (140km/h). **Service entry:** 1964.

Vehicles with fewer than four wheels are rare in the railway world, except in Spain. There the coaches of the famous "Talgo" trains are not only two-wheeled (the wheel-less end being supported by the next car), but so low-slung that the floors are typically only 14in (356mm) above rail level. This compares with 42in (1,067mm) typically for conventional stock. This gives the "Talgos" excellent stability for fast running on heavily-curved routes. The weight per seat is also low, being only about 672lb (305kg) compared with 1,014lb (460kg) of, say, a British Rail MkIII coach.

In 1964, with many "Talgos" running and planned, Spanish National Railways went to Krauss-Maffei of Munich, West Germany, for a batch of five matching low-slung diesel locomotives. These machines, now officialy designated Class "352", were the result. The Spanish share with the British a feeling that locomotives need names, and being a devout nation chose for these names of shrines to the Holy Virgin. Further batches have followed down the years, the next five being virtually identical, except that they were built under licence in Spain by Babcock y Wilcox of Bilbao.

Eight more of a stretched version (Class "353") came from Krauss-Maffei in 1969, offering 25 per cent more power than the originals. In 1982, Krauss-Maffei delivered a further eight, with power output increased to 4,000hp (2,980kW), designated Class "354". The last of the original batch, No. 3005 *Virgen de la Bien Aparecida* is interesting in that it originally ran for a time on standard-gauge bogies. This was to haul the "Catalan Talgo" *Trans-Europ-Express* on the French portion of its journeys between Barcelona and Geneva. The train itself has adjustable axles for a quick change between Spanish broad gauge and French standard gauge.

The locomotives have to have special low drawgear for hauling the

Above: A low-slung "Virgin" B-B diesel-hydraulic locomotive heads a Talgo express at Pancorbo on the Miranda to Burgos main line.

"Talgo" sets and, in addition, must provide power for lighting, heating, air-conditioning and cooking on the train. This is taken care of by two 250hp (187kW) diesel-generator sets. The basis of the design was the German Class "V-200" diesel-hydraulics but modifications were needed to obtain the 'Talgo' height of 10ft 9in (3,277mm) overall, compared with that of 14ft 1in (4,293mm).

The "Talgo" principle has recently been extended to encompass a Paris to Madrid sleeping car express, running the 911 miles (1,458km) in a very creditable 12hr 55min, including gauge change for the carriage units. The most interesting innovation on this and other recent "Talgo" trains is inclusion of a passive tilting system to permit higher speeds on curves.

Below: A Spanish National Railways' "Virgin" class B-B diesel-hydraulic locomotive *Virgen de la Bien Aparecida* runs under the wire with an express train composed of low-slung Talgo cars.

ELD4 Four-car set

Origin: Netherlands Railways (NS). **Type:** Fast electric passenger train. **Gauge:** 4ft 8½in (1,435mm). **Propulsion:** Direct current at 1,500V supplied via catenary with twin contact wires to eight 180hp (134kW) nose-suspended traction motors geared to the axles of the bogies of the two intermediate coaches in the set. **Weight:** 200,564lb (91t) adhesive, 370,270lb (168t) total. **Axleload:** 50,695lb (23t). **Overall length:** 331ft 7in (101,240mm). **Max speed:** 88mph (140km/h). **Service entry:** 1964.

Electrification came early to the Netherlands, for it was as long ago as 1924 that electric traction at 1,500V dc was introduced between Amsterdam, The Hague and Rotterdam. The first streamlined stock came in 1934, various features of which set the pattern for the future. Streamlined ends to the sets precluded through access for passengers when units were coupled, but coupling and uncoupling were made painless with automatic couplers which also made all the brake-pipe and electrical connections needed. Amongst these early units there were sets of varying lengths from two to five cars and, to suit longer runs then becoming possible under the wires, better passenger facilities were provided on the larger units. Matching diesel-electric sets were built too, and there were also travelling post office vans.

The trains were designed to suit a pattern of working appropriate to a small country with a density of population 70 per cent greater than even Britain's, but which has no overwhelming single metropolis such as London. They provided an hourly (or more frequent) pattern of service and gave great emphasis to making journeys possible between all the principal cities without changing trains. Hence those automatic couplers to enable trains to be divided or combined without fuss.

Although the Dutch emerged from World War II facing almost complete destruction of their railways, they quickly set about restoring not just the

status quo, but something very much better, by extending electrification to all important lines in the country. It was decided to continue the use of multiple-unit self-propelled trains, with only a few international and other trains remaining locomotive hauled. This was in order to give employment during the day to motive-power used for freight, which in the Netherlands moves during the night.

New designs of electric and diesel-electric trains put into service during the 1950s followed the lines of their predecessors, except that they were not articulated and only came in two-and four-car form. They also had bulbous extended fronts, provided not for aesthetic reasons but to give protection to the driver. There are also some units with dual voltage capability, used for working through between Amsterdam and Brussels on to Belgium's 3,000V dc system.

In the 1960s, further stock was required and these Class "501" units, whilst in appearance very like their immediate predecessors, represent a considerable step forward. Two prototypes appeared in 1961 and the production version in 1964. By a remarkable feat of design, the overall weight of a four-car unit is 23 per cent less than before, while the rate of acceleration is approximately doubled.

Automatic doors are provided and this, combined with better performance, enabled schedules to be cut. One other major difference is that the two end vehicles of each set are driving-trailer cars, the intermediate carriages being non-driving motor cars. Since the trains were built, denser traffic, higher speeds and a bad accident in 1962 have made it seem prudent to install signalling continuously displayed in the driver's cab, actuated by coded track circuits, for use on the busiest sections.

Below, left: An inter-city express train of Netherlands Railways formed of four-car "ELD4" electric multiple-unit sets.

Below: A Netherlands Railways electric express train formed of two-car multiple-unit sets equipped with automatic couplers.

Class 40100 C-C

Origin: French National Railways (SNCF). **Type:** Express passenger electric locomotive. **Gauge:** 4ft 8½in (1,435mm). **Propulsion:** Current supply from overhead wires at 1,500V dc, 3,000V dc, 15,000V ac 16⅔Hz, or 25,000V ac 50Hz; ac supplies transformed to 1,500V by silicon rectifiers; current then supplied to two bogie-mounted 2,910hp (2,170kW) traction motors with divided armature windings, allowing series, series/parallel and parallel grouping (parallel not used on 3,000V dc); motor geared to all three axles of the bogie through Alsthom flexible drive. **Weight:** 235,830lb (107t). **Axleload:** 39,300lb (17.8t). **Overall length:** 72ft 3¼in (22,030mm). **Tractive effort:** 45,000lb. **Max speed:** 112mph (180km/h). **Service entry:** 1964.

Through locomotive workings from Paris to Brussels were introduced well back in the days of steam, and were later continued with diesel railcars. Electrification of this route by French and Belgian railways permitted through electric working, but as the French part of the route uses ac at 25,000V 50Hz whilst the Belgians use 3,000V dc, a new type of locomotive was required. At this time, in the early 1960s, a network of *Trans-Europ-Express* (TEE) trains had been established, worked by diesel railcars, but SNCF decided to build a small number of locomotives which could work not only into Belgium, but also into other Western European countries, if the TEE trains were ever electrically operated. The requirement was therefore for the locomotives to work on four systems; 1,500V dc (in France and the Netherlands), 3,000V dc (in Belgium and Italy), 15,000V 16⅔Hz (in Austria, West Germany and Switzerland) and 25,000V 50 Hz (in France).

Design of the locomotives, the "40100" class, was entrusted to Alsthom, and they were the first of a new generation of electric and diesel classes incorporating monomotor bogies. So far the principle had been applied only to two-axle bogies, and SNCF had not built any six-axle locomotives since 1952. The specification reflected the prevailing ambitious thinking about TEE trains: to haul 210t at 137mph (220km/h) on the level and at 68mph (110km/h) on the 1-in-37 (2.6 per cent) gradients of the Gotthard and Lötschberg routes; to handle 450t at 100mph (160km/h) on the Paris to Brussels route and at 68 mph (110km/h) on the 1-in-70 (1.4 per cent) gradient between Mons and Quévy in Belgium. These characteristics would enable the locomotive to haul 800t at 100mph (160km/h) between Paris and Aulnoye, and at 77mph (125km/h) on a 1-in-200 (0.5 per cent) gradient.

Below: French Railways' Class CC40100 electric locomotives can run on either 1,500V dc, 3,000V dc, 15,000V ac 16⅔Hz or 25,000V ac 50Hz.

Above: French Railways' C-C tri-current and multi-voltage electric locomotive No. CC40101 heads an international express.

The basis adopted for accommodating the four types of current is that the traction motor windings are designed for 1,500V. From the ac supplies, current is transformed to 1,500V and then rectified by silicon rectifiers. On 3,000V the motor windings are connected in pairs in series, whilst on 1,500V dc the motors take the incoming supply directly. Motor control is through starting resistances and there is provision for rheostatic braking.

The weight of this equipment required six axles. To allow for the regrouping of the motors to accept 3,000V, the armature winding of each motor is in two sections. There are four pantographs to suit the characteristics of the four supply systems, and there are interlocks and "feeler" relays to ensure that the dc supplies are not applied to the transformer and that the correct pantograph is in use. The bogies have provision for changing the gear ratio, but unlike the other French two-speed locomotives, this is a workshop job. The first four locomotives are geared for a maximum speed of 100mph (160km/h) and the second batch of six for 112mph (180km/h).

The first of the class appeared in 1964. They are based at La Chapelle depot, Paris, Brussels and Amsterdam. In the event, the international TEE network did not develop further, and the "40100s" have never worked in countries other France, Belgium and the Netherlands, nor, so far, have the high-speed lines designed for 220km/h running materialised.

Six very similar locomotives were built for Belgian National Railways (SNCB) using French electrical equipment in Belgian bodies.

n-Kansen
Sixteen-car train

Origin: Japanese National Railways (JNR). **Type:** High-speed electric passenger train. **Gauge:** 4ft 8½in (1,435mm). **Propulsion:** Alternating current at 25,000V 50Hz fed via overhead catenary and stepdown transformers and rectifiers to sixty-four 248hp (185kW) motors each driving an axle by means of gearing and flexible drive. **Weight:** 2,031,200lb (922t). **Axleload:** 31,738lb (14.4t). **Overall length:** 1,318ft 6in (401,880mm). **Max speed:** 130mph (210km/h). **Service entry:** 1964.

It took more than 60 years for the promise of high-speed running by electric trainsets implicit in the Zossen trials of 1903 to become reality. Public trains averaging more than 100mph (160km/h) start-to-stop, with normal running speeds 30 per cent above this, appeared first during 1965 when Japanese National Railways put into full service the new *Shin-Kansen* line from Tokyo westwards to Osaka. The line had been opened in 1964, but a preliminary period of operation at more normal speeds had been deemed prudent.

In spite of the impression they give, the *Shin-Kansen* (the words simply mean "New Line") trains are really quite conventional. The high speed is obtained by having plenty of power; a 16-car train has a continuously-rated installed horsepower as high as 15,870 (11,840kW), while high acceleration is achieved by having every axle motored.

No, the interesting thing is to realise how much can be achieved using existing railroad state-of-the-art if you begin with a clean sheet. Until 1964, Japanese National Railways used 3ft 6in (1,067mm) gauge exclusively, but the new line was to be totally separate even to the extent of being of different gauge. The investment involved in building a new standard-gauge (1,435mm) railway connecting some of Japan's major cities was very great, but the courage of those who promoted it was fully justified eventually, mainly by a three-fold increase of traffic up to 1973.

The price of high speed was considerable. Not only are there land costs involved in building new lines into and out of the centres of large cities, but since very flat curves of 125 chain (2,500m) radius are required for this degree of fast running, the engineering works in open country are also

Below: Japanese "Shin-Kansen" high-speed 16-car electric multiple-unit train with snow-capped Mount Fuji seen in the background.

Above: The building of an entirely new 1,435mm gauge high-speed railway was Japan's successful method of cutting journey times.

very heavy. If you cannot turn quickly to avoid natural obstacles, you have to go through them. Of course, with such high power in relation to weight gradients on the heavy side (1-in-66—1.5 per cent) are no obstacle.

The principal innovation is the self-signalling system of the trains. Acceleration and deceleration is not only automatic but is also automatically initiated when required, only the final approach to a stop being directly under the motorman's control. There are no lineside signals and all relevant information about the state of the line is passed to the driving position by coded impulses running in the main conductor wires.

Originally there were 480 cars arranged in 40 12-car sets, each 12-car train being divided electrically into six two-car units, one of which would have a buffet car, with the bullet-shaped ends and driving cabs placed at the outer ends of the train. In 1970, the 12-car trains were strengthened to 16 including two buffet cars, and train frequency increased from 120 to over 200 both ways daily. The fleet of cars had by then become 1,400 arranged in 87 16-car sets.

In 1970, as soon as success was assured, a national plan was prepared to extend the high-speed passenger network from the 320 miles (515km) of the original line by some twenty-fold. So far, four *Shin-Kansen* lines have been built—extending the network from Tokyo to Okayama and Hakata, and from Omiya (outside Tokyo) to Niigata and Morioka, a total of 1,121 miles (1,804km) of standard-gauge line.

The scale of work involved in the mountain regions—not to speak of an 11.6 mile (18.6km) inter-island undersea tunnel—can be seen from the amount of civil engineering work needed. Of the 247 miles (398km) between Okayama and Hakata, 55 per cent is in tunnel, 11 per cent on bridges or viaducts, leaving only 14 per cent as a conventional railway built on the ground. This was partly due to the minimum radius of curvature being increased to 200 chains (4,000m), with a view to raising speed from 130mph (210km/h) to 162mph (260km/h), while at the same time reducing the gradient to 1-in-65 (1.5 per cent). Even though this increase in speed has not yet been realised in public service, the fast hourly *Hikari* trains make the 664-mile (1,069km) overall journey from Tokyo to Hakata in 6hr 40min at an average speed of 99.7mph (160.4km/h). To put this in perspective, a *Shin-Kansen* style journey over the comparable distance between New York and Chicago would more than halve the best current rail time of 18½ hours, to 8¼ hours!

C630 "Century" C₀-C₀

Origin: Alco Products Incorporated (Alco), USA. **Type:** Diesel-electric road-switcher locomotive. **Gauge:** 4ft 8½in (1,435mm). **Propulsion:** One 16-cylinder four-stroke turbocharged 3,000hp (2,240kW) Alco 251E Vee engine and alternator, supplying three-phase current through rectifiers to six nose-suspended traction motors each geared to one axle. **Weight:** 312,000lb (141.5t). **Axleload:** 52,000lb (23.6t), but could be increased to 61,000lb (27.7t) if desired. **Overall length:** 69ft 6in (21,180mm). **Tractive effort:** 103,000lb (458kN). **Max speed:** 80mph (129km/h) according to gear ratio. **Service entry:** 1965.

The old-established American Locomotive Company, long known in the trade as Alco, had pioneered one of the most important types of diesel locomotive, the road switcher, when in 1946 it produced a 1,500hp (1,120kW) A1A+A1A hood unit, the first really successfly American diesel to be equally at home on switching (shunting) or freight duties. It incorporated the Alco 244 engine, which had performed well in switchers, but which revealed weaknesses under the more arduous conditions of road working.

The 244 was therefore replaced by a new engine, the 251, which finally displaced the 244 from the Alco range in 1956. It was available in 6-cylinder in-line and 12-cylinder Vee formation, to which were added V16 and V18. At first it was installed in existing designs of locomotives, but in 1963 a new range of road switchers was launched, the "Century" series.

Despite the success of its new engine, the position of Alco at this time was increasingly difficult. From 1940 to 1953 the company had an agreement with General Electric that only GE electrical equipment would be used in Alco locomotives, in return for which GE agreed not to compete with Alco in the diesel locomotive market. In 1953 GE withdrew from the agreement and began to develop its own range of road switchers, which was launched in 1960. This was formidable competition. With the railroads now fully dieselised, the diesel salesman had to convince potential customers that it would pay them to replace their "first generation" diesels by his latest product.

A very strong selling point in any new model must be reduced maintenance costs, and this point was pressed very strongly in support of the "Century" range. The makers claimed that a saving in maintenance of up to two-thirds could be expected compared with existing designs.

The new series was designated by three figures, of which the first was the number of axles, all powered; the second and third denoted the engine power, in hundreds of horsepower. The first models launched were "C420", "C424" and "C624", of which the two latter were in the range of power which was most popular at this time. The 16-cylinder turbocharged

Below: A line of Alco "Century" Co-Co diesel-electrics of the Atchison, Topeka & Santa Fe Railway pausing between duties.

Above: Northern weather conditions make a snow-plough a necessary addition to this British Columbia Railway "Century".

engine developed 2,600hp (1,940kW), with an output from the generator for traction of 2,400hp (1,790kW); in accordance with US practice it was thus designated a 2,400hp model.

By 1965 there had been two increases in engine speed, raising the power to 3,000hp (2,240kW) for traction. More significantly this model, the "C630", had an alternator generating three-phase ac, which was then rectified for supply to the traction motors. This was the first alternator sold by a US manufacturer, and it led to the general adoption of alternators by other builders.

Finally in 1968 the engine power was raised to 3,600hp (2,690kW), producing the "C636". These increases in power were all achieved with the same 16-cylinder engine. Other variants in the "Century" range were the "C855" for Union Pacific, a massive Bo-Bo-Bo-Bo with two 2,750hp (2,050kW) engines, and the "C430H", a diesel-hydraulic incorporating two 2,150hp (1,600kW) engines and Voith hydraulic transmission. Neither of these was repeated.

Despite this enterprise, Alco was edged steadily out of second place in the US locomotive market by GE. Major improvements at the Schenectady Works could not save the day. Orders declined and in 1969 the works closed. Fortunately for the Alco tradition, the firm's Canadian associate, Montreal Locomotive Works, was in better shape, with continued sales in Canada and Mexico. MLW (now known as Bombardier) took over all Alco designs and patents, and in 1984 was still marketing its own versions of the "Century" series.

Class X C₀-C₀

Origin: Victorian Railways (VicRail). **Type:** Diesel-electric mixed-traffic locomotive. **Gauge:** 5ft 3in (1,600mm) and 4ft 8½in (1,435mm). **Propulsion:** General Motors Type 16-567E 1,950hp (1,455kW) 16-cylinder two-stroke Vee diesel engine and generator supplying current to six nose-suspended traction motors geared to the axles. **Weight:** 255,665lb (116t). **Axleload:** 42,980lb (19.5t). **Overall length:** 60ft 3in (18,364mm). **Tractive effort:** 64,125lb (285kN). **Max speed:** 84mph (134km/h) **Service entry:** 1966.

It is well known that Australia has a serious railway gauge problem, the various states having in the early days gone their own ways in this respect. The state of Victoria and its neighbour South Australia were the two which opted for a 5ft 3in (1,600mm) broad gauge. In steam days this meant different designs of locomotive, but with diesels the differences can be minimal, confined almost wholly to the appropriate wheelsets.

These Class "X" diesels of Victorian Railways (VicRail) are a case in point because, now that standard-gauge has put a tentacle into the state (notably to connect Melbourne to the Trans-Australian railway as well as over the trunk route from Sydney), they provide haulage over both gauges.

The locomotives are a typical General Motors product—like virtually all VicRail's diesel locomotives—and were assembled by GM's Australian licensee, Clyde Engineering Pty of Sydney, New South Wales. This standardisation gives an advantage in that most of the diesel fleet can be run in multiple regardless of class.

Soon after the first six "Xs" had been delivered, Clyde began offering GM's new 645 series engine and this was used for a subsequent batch of 18 supplied in 1970. The power output could thus be increased to 2,600hp (1,940kW) without weight penalty. These were then the most powerful units on the system, but subsequently axleload limits have been raised to 22.5t (24.8 US tons) on certain lines. Hence a further batch of

VL80T B₀-B₀+B₀-B₀

Origin: Soviet Railways (SZD). **Type:** Electric locomotive for heavy freight haulage. **Gauge:** 5ft 0in (1,524mm). **Propulsion:** Alternating current at 25,000V 50Hz fed via overhead catenary, step-down transformer and silicon rectifiers to eight 790hp (590kW) nose-suspended dc traction motors, each geared to one axle. **Weight:** 405,535lb (184t). **Axleload:** 50,695lb (23t). **Overall length:** 107ft 9in (32,840mm). **Tractive effort:** 99,500lb (433kN). **Max speed:** 68mph (110km/h). **Service entry:** 1967.

Soviet Railways' "VL80" series of electric locomotives, one of the most numerous in the world, is the main motive power used for moving heavy freight trains over the USSR's 12,550 mile (20,200km) network of industrial-frequency electrification. The letters VL pay tribute to Vladimir Lenin, no less, whose personal enthusiasm for railway electrification has now, many years after his death, had such impressive results.

The eight-axle locomotive has double-bogie units permanently coupled in pairs, and is a favourite for freight work in the USSR. Some 1,500 of Class "VL8" were built for the 3,000V dc lines from 1953 onwards, followed in 1961 by the start of production of the "VL10" class, also for dc lines. For ac lines, the first "VL80s", externally very similar to the "VL10s" began coming into use in 1963 with the class variant "VL80K".

The first "VL80Ks" had mercury-arc rectifiers, but it is difficult to avoid

Above: Victorian Railways' standard-gauge "X" class Co-Co No. X49 arrives in Melbourne with the "Southern Aurora" from Sydney.

GM Co-Co units (the "C" class) have been supplied with an installed power of 3,300hp (2,460kW).

One requirement for all Victoria's locomotives that possibly defeated General Motors' ability to supply off the shelf was provision of sets of pneumatically-operated token exchange equipment. Under British-style operating rules, some physical token of authority is needed to be on any particular section of single line. The token (or staff) has to be exchanged for another when passing from one block section to the next. The places where this happens often do not coincide with the train's stopping places and the exchange apparatus enables this to be done at speed. Modern electrical methods of signalling are slowly doing away with this picturesque operation, but for the moment it continues and locomotives however modern have to be equipped to cope.

Above: A "VL82mm" class dual-voltage electric locomotive of Soviet Railways. This is an improved version of the "VL80T" class.

problems when (in lay terms) mercury sloshes around under the influence of vibration and traction shocks. Solid-state silicon rectifiers were soon substituted. The "VL80T" was a modification of the "VL80K" which had rheostatic electric braking, and this has been the main production version of the "VL80" class, of which over 2,000 have now been built. After some ▶

▶ years of experiment, "VL80" series-production changed to a version ("VL80R") with thyristor control and—made painlessly possible by the scope of this system—full regenerative electric braking. This is claimed to reduce current consumption by over 10 per cent.

Experiments have been made on a "VL80A" version which uses three-phase asynchronous induction motors supplied with variable-frequency current by a solid-state conversion system. Another interesting development, which is obviously very similar to the "VL80A" arrangement theoretically, but very different practically, is to use thyristors inside each motor as a substitute for the commutator and brushes. In this way

---

Class 72000 C-C

Origin: French National Railways (SNCF). **Type:** Diesel-electric dual-purpose locomotive. **Gauge:** 4ft 8½in (1,435 mm). **Propulsion:** Société Alsacienne de Construcion Mécaniques 3,550hp (2,650kW) 16-cylinder four-stroke diesel engine and alternator supplying current through silicon rectifiers to two traction motors, one on each bogie; motors connected to the axles through two-speed gearing and spring drive. **Weight:** 251,260lb (114t). **Axleload:** 41,880lb (19t). **Overall length:** 66ft 3in (20,190mm). **Tractive effort:** Low gear 81,570lb (363kN), high gear 46,300lb (206kN). **Max speed:** Low gear 53mph (85kh/h), high 87mph (140km/h). **Service entry:** 1967.

When SNCF embarked on construction of large main-line diesel locomotives in 1961, it was recognised that a more powerful unit than the 2,650hp Class "68000" would be needed eventually for the heaviest work. So two pairs of twin-engine experimental locomotives were ordered, which could develop up to 4,800hp (3,580kW). However, enthusiasm for the complications of the twin-engine machines was never great, and development of new diesel engines in the range 3,500 to 4,000hp encouraged SNCF in 1964 to invite manufacturers to submit proposals for a powerful single-engine locomotive. Alsthom made a successful submission of a C-C design, based on the AGO16 engine of 3,600hp (2,700kW). "A" denotes the maker, Société Alsacienne de Constructions Mécaniques of Mulhouse, "G" and "O" denote the designers, Grosshaus and Ollier. This engine was a 16-cylinder version of the 12-cylinder engine already fitted to the "68500" series of A1A+A1A locomotives.

Eighteen of the new design were ordered from Alsthom in 1966, and delivery commenced in the following year, the class being allocated numbers from 72001. SNCF was at this period developing a new family of electric locomotives incorporating monomotor bogies, and the "72000s" incorporated various parts in common with the electric units. The bogies followed closely the design recently introduced in the Class "40100" quadricurrent locomotives, with two gear ratios, the maximum speeds in the two settings being 53mph (85km/h) for freight and 87mph (140km/h) for passenger work. The traction motors are identical electrically with those of the "BB8500", "BB17000" and "BB25500" electric locomotives. SNCF estimated that the monomotor bogie saved 9t in weight compared with conventional bogies with individual axle drive, and it enabled the axleload to be kept within the stipulated limits.

Main innovation in the electrical system was use of an alternator instead of a dc generator. This delivers three-phase current which is rectified by silicon diodes for supply to the dc traction motors. The electrical equipment includes Alsthom's "Superadhesion" system, in which the excitation of the field of the motors is controlled to give an almost direct relationship between motor voltage and current. By this means the tendency for incipient wheelslip to develop is greatly reduced, and it is

the associated problems of mechanical wear and vulnerability to flashover at the commutators can possibly be avoided. A three-unit version ("VL80S") with 13,100hp (9,780kW) available for hauling 10,000t (11,000 US tons) trains has been produced and prototypes have been built of a "VL84" version with increased power.

Also associated with the "VL80s" are the "VL82" series of dual-current locomotives for 3,000V dc and 25,000V 50Hz ac, dating from 1966. Adding together both systems of electrification the overall picture is quite amazing—more electrically-hauled rail freight traffic than the whole of the rest of the world put together, moved on a 29,000 mile (46,800km)

Above: The French National Railways' Class 72000 C-C diesel-electric locomotive as constructed by Alsthom from 1967 onwards.

claimed that the effective starting tractive effort can be increased by 15 to 20 per cent.

The body resembles closely those of the corresponding electric classes but has a higher roof to accommodate the engine. The treatment of the ends incorporates cab windows steeply inclined backwards to reduce glare, as introduced on the "40100" class, but the appearance was much altered by restyling of the ends due to inclusion of massive cellular boxes in front of the cab to protect the driver in case of collision.

They were immediately put to work on the Paris to Brittany and Paris to Basle routes, where they enabled modest increases to be made in train speeds over the "68000" class, but consistent with SNCF's target of not developing full power for more than 60 per cent of the run, compared with 67 per cent recorded with the earlier locomotives, and also consistent with supplying electric train heating from the engine power. The class eventually reached a total of 92, and they took over the heaviest work on most non-electrified routes. Ten had modifications made to enable them to run at 100mph (160km/h).

In 1973 No.72075 was fitted with an SEMT-Pielstick PA 6-280 12-cylinder engine, initially rated at 4,200hp but increased a year later to 4,800hp (3,580kW), making it the most powerful diesel engine in a locomotive (at least in the Western world).

Metroliner Two-car Trainset

Origin: Pennsylvania Railroad (PRR), USA. **Type:** High-speed electric multiple-unit trainset. **Gauge:** 4ft 8½in (1,435mm). **Propulsion:** Alternating current at 11,000V 25Hz fed via overhead catenary, step-down transformer and rectifiers to eight 300hp (224kW) nose-suspended motors, one geared to each pair of wheels. **Weight:** 328,400lb (149t). **Axleload:** 41,880lb (19t). **Overall length:** 170ft 0in (51,816mm). **Max speed:** 160mph (256km/h). **Service entry:** 1967.

In the 1960s, the United States passenger train was at a very low ebb. Most railroads were reporting massive deficits on passenger services as well as a steady loss of traffic. Over long distances the jet airliner had

Right: A "Metroliner" 11,000V 25Hz electric multiple-unit express train speed under the wires on the North-East Corridor main line.

Below: The front end of a "Metroliner" multiple-unit electric two-car set. Note the driving cab window and automatic couplers.

a twenty-fold advantage in time, which hardly affected the time disadvantage between city centre and out-of-town air terminal, compared with rail. Over short distances, though, the opposite was the case and there seemed a possibility of the train continuing to compete, were it not for outdated equipment and image.

One such route was the Pennsylvania Railroad's electrified main line between New York, Philadelphia and Washington, now known as the North East Corridor. It was in order to offer better service on this route that these remarkable trains came into being. Possible prototypes ("MP 85") had been acquired from the Budd Company of Philadelphia in 1958 and in 1963 some cars—the Budd *Silverliners*—were acquired on behalf of Pennsy by the City of Philadelphia.

Later in the decade the railroad received some government assistance towards a $22 million scheme for new high-speed self-propelled trains plus $33 million for improvements to the permanent way, 160mph (256km/h) operation was envisaged.

Orders were placed in 1966 with Budd for 50 (later increased to 61) stainless steel electric cars to be called *Metroliners*. They drove on all wheels, could attain considerably more than the specified speed and had a fantastic short-term power-to-weight ratio of 34hp per tonne. They also had dynamic braking down to 30mph (48km/h), automatic acceleration, deceleration and speed control using new sophisticated techniques. Full air-conditioning, airline-type catering, electrically controlled doors and a public telephone service by radio link were provided. The order included parlour cars and snack-bar coaches as well as ordinary day coaches. All had a driving cab at one end, but access between adjacent sets through a cab not in use was possible. They were marshalled semi-permanently in pairs as two-car units. An over-bold decision was taken to begin production straight from the drawing board. For once, with the Pennsylvania Railroad suffering from a terminal sickness, its officers did not insist on the usual precaution of building and testing prototypes first. As a result, faults galore again and again delayed entry into public service until after ill-fated Penn Central took over in 1968. A single round-trip daily began at the beginning of 1969 and even then a modification programme costing 50 per cent of the original price of the trains was needed to make them suitable for public service.

Amtrak took over the North East Corridor passenger service in May 1971, and a year later 14 daily *Metroliner* trips were being run and start-to-stop average speeds as high as 95mph (152km/h) were scheduled. Speeds as high as the announced 150mph were not run in public service, ▶

although 164mph (262km/h) was achieved on test; the work done on the permanent way was not sufficient for this, 110mph (176km/h) being the normal limit.

Since then a programme of track work has been carried out over the North East Corridor. At a cost of $2,500 million, this was 75 times as much as the original rather naive proposal, but did include the New York to Boston line. At long last this great work has been completed, and autumn 1982 saw introduction of the fastest-ever timings between New York and Washington. However, the *Metroliners*, now nearly 20 years old, have been displaced from New York-Washington services by "AEM7"

E50C C_o-C_o

Origin: Muskingum Electric Railroad (MER), USA. **Type:** Unmanned mineral-hauling electric locomotive. **Gauge:** 4ft 8½in (1,435mm). **Propulsion:** Alternating current at 25,000V 60Hz fed via overhead catenary, stepdown transformer and silicon rectifiers to six 830hp (620kW) dc traction motors geared to the driving axles. Control is by automatically generated radio received continuously at the terminals and at fixed points elsewhere. **Weight:** 390,000lb (177t). **Axleload:** 65,000lb (29.5t). **Overall length:** 65ft 7in (19,989mm). **Tractive effort:** 117,000lb (520kN). **Max speed:** 70mph (112km/h). **Service entry:** 1967.

Railroads are a natural subject for automation but actual automatic railroads hardly exist. There is only one such in the true sense in the whole USA and it feeds the Muskingum River electric power plant near Cumberland, Ohio. Coal is dug about 20 miles (32km) away by a huge dragline excavator known as 'Big Muskie', which has to remove 120ft (36m) of over-burden before the coal seam is reached.

Below: These two electric locomotives form the complete motive power fleet of the Muskingum Electric Railroad, Ohio, USA.

locomotives and trains of Amfleet coaches.

The original *Metroliner* schedule of 2½ hours for the 226 miles (362km) between New York and Washington was never achieved, but 'taking 1978 as an example) hourly trains did the run in a very respectable 3 hours (or a minute or two more) with four intermediate stops, an overall average of 75mph (120km/h). Two years later, when the engineering work was at its peak, this timing had been extended to almost 4 hours. In 1983, however, the locomotive-hauled trains, confusingly also called "Metroliners", were completing the journey in 2hr 49min with four stops, at an average speed of 79.8mph (128.4km/h).

Above: Much like any other locomotive, this Muskingum Electric RR "E50C" even has an engineer's seat—but there's no engineer!

In 1967-68 an electric railroad was built to carry coal from the strip-mine to a point from which a conveyor belt feeds the generating plant. High-voltage industrial frequency alternating current was connected up to a lightweight cantenary and two electric freight trains soon began moving an average of 18,000 tons of coal five days a week. Two Co-Co electric locomotives designated type "E50C" had been supplied by General Electric, rather charmingly numbered 100 and 200 respectively as if the Muskingum Electric Railroad intended to have a huge fleet.

The "E50Cs" were based on the chassis and body of a standard GEC Co-Co diesel-electric road-switcher, with transformer and special control gear replacing the diesel engine and alternator. A cab is provided complete with driver's seat, which is normally vacant. The trains are controlled in the loading and unloading areas by a continuous radio signal modulated to give speed commands ranging from 'stop' and 'creep' to '50'mph. The processes at both ends are entirely automatic although supervised. Air-operated bottom doors on each 100-ton capacity hopper wagon are controlled by a signal received via a shoe mounted on one of its bogies.

Out on the line, the locomotives encounter a fixed control location preceded by a warning marker at approximately one mile intervals. Each one of these presents a fixed coded response to a detector circuit on the locomotive as it goes by, which determines the speed of the train over the next mile. If the time taken from one control location to the next does not correspond within a reasonable margin to the speed set, then the train will make an emergency stop. This will also occur if the train has run further than a mile without encountering a control location.

The locomotives normally run at half the rated maximum speed and the 15 empty wagons of each train are propelled on the return trip. One train is normally loading while the other makes its out-and-back trip to unload, a complete cycle taking 2¼ hours. Six cycles are performed each weekday, making 90,000 tons weekly, hauled almost without human intervention.

Class 581 Twelve-car train

Origin: Japanese National Railways (JNR). **Type:** Electric express sleeping-car train. **Gauge:** 3ft 6in (1,067mm). **Propulsion:** Alternating current at 25,000V 50Hz or 60Hz, or direct current at 3,000V, fed via overhead catenary and conversion and control equipment in two power cars to 24 traction motors of 160hp (100kW) geared to the bogie axles of six of the intermediate sleeping cars in the train. **Weight:** 638,720lb (290t) adhesive, 1,218,812lb (553t) total. **Axleload:** 26,450lb (12t). **Overall length:** 816ft 11in (249,000mm). **Max speed:** 100mph (160km/h). This is the design speed; the maximum permitted speed of the railway is 120km/h (75mph). **Service entry:** 1968.

The worldwide trend in modern forms of motive power towards self-contained multiple-unit trains took a hold of hitherto unconquered (but not unexplored) territory when Japanese National Railways put into service these very fine electric trains. Previous examples of the provision of sleeping cars in self-propelled trains included Union Pacific's M-10001 train, various long-distance interurban electric trains in the USA and a West German set called the *Komet*, which had a brief career in the 1950s. None of these examples led in any way to the idea becoming general practice on the lines concerned.

These handsome trains, however, have taken over many long-distance overnight workings in Japan. They are also available for day use. Their scope is likely to widen considerably when the 33¾-mile (54km) Seikan tunnel connects the railway system of the Japanese main island of Honshu with that of Hokkaido. Intended eventually for high-speed standard-gauge *Shin-Kansen* trains, the new tunnel (nearly twice as long as its nearest existing rival) is likely to carry only narrow-gauge traffic for some years.

All berths are longitudinal and separate accommodation is not provided for "green" (first) and "ordinary" class passengers. Instead, there is a higher charge for lower berths compared to that for middle and upper berths. Berth charges do, however include night attire and washing things, as in Japanese-style hotels. With up to 45 sleeping berths in each narrow-gauge car the designers must be admired for stating that their main objective was to create an impression of spaciousness! The 12-car set includes a dining car seating 40; the remaining 11 cars can sleep 444 or seat 656. The trains are air-conditioned throughout, and it has been said that the sound-proofing is sufficient to reduce noise levels to less than that encounterd in locomotive-hauled sleeping cars.

Right: The end doors of a Class "581" driving-trailer sleeping car can be opened to give communication between adjacent 12-car sets.

Below: A driving trailer car of the Japanese railways' Class "581" sleeping car train coupled to a motor non-driving sleeping car.

Above: A Japanese National Railways narrow-gauge sleeping car express formed of Class "581" electric multiple-unit rolling stock.

Class EF81 B₀-B₀

Origin: Japanese National Railways (JNR). **Type:** Electric mixed-traffic locomotive. **Gauge:** 3ft 6in (1,067mm). **Propulsion:** Direct current at 1,500V or alternating current at 20,000V 50Hz or 60Hz fed via overhead catenary to six 570hp (425kW) nose-suspended traction motors geared direct to the axles of the three bogies. The transformer for the ac current has a fixed ratio and it feeds the normal rheostatic dc control system via solid-state rectifiers. **Weight:** 222,610lb (101t). **Axleload:** 37,470lb (17t). **Overall length:** 61ft 0in (18,600mm). **Tractive effort:** 3,800lb (195kN) on dc, 40,200lb (179kN) on ac. **Max speed:** 72mph (115km/h). **Service entry:** 1968.

In recent years the demands for heavy haulage on Japan's 5,488 miles (8,830km) of electrified 3ft 6in (1,067mm) gauge main lines has been met by building a series of locomotive classes of the B-B-B wheel arrangement. Single-current varieties exist for all three current systems used in Japan, that is dc, ac at 50Hz and ac at 60Hz, and also all the permutations for dual current as well as the tri-current type described here. There are also similar locomotives of the B-2-B wheel arrangement, which include a weight distribution system allowing the weight carried on the two outer motor bogies to be varied according to rail-weight limits and adhesion needs.

Of these other three-bogie electric locomotive classes, EF30, EF63, EF64, EF65, EF66, EF70, EF71, EF80 are B-B-Bs with all axles driven, while EF72, EF76, EF77, EF78 are B-2-Bs. EF63, EF64, EF65, EF66 can run on dc only, EF70, EF72 on 60Hz only and EF71, EF77, EF78 on 50Hz only. Of the remaining three classes two are bi-current, EF30 for dc and 60Hz, EF80 for DC and 50Hz. Class EF76 is for dual frequency.

Class "EF81" is perhaps the most sophisticated design amongst this plethora of fascinating locomotive variety. Complications include automatic control of wheelslip and compensation for load transfer when applying high tractive efforts, but otherwise they are very simple. They have no flexible drive system, neither rheostatic nor regenerative braking, and only the plainest of box-like bodywork. Notable is the relatively high maximum speed for the narrow gauge, although much of Japan's rail passenger traffic is handled by multiple-unit trains—including, as we have

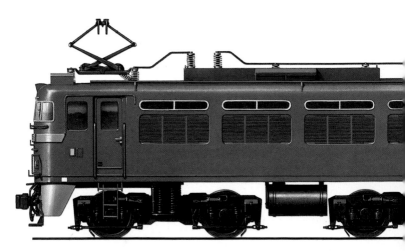

Above: One of the ubiquitous Class EF Bo-Bo-Bo mixed-traffic electric locomotives of the Japanese National Railways at the head of a heavy container train on the Tohoku Line, 1975.

seen, sleeping car expresses. Electric train heating is provided for use when passenger trains are hauled.

A total of 156 "EF81s" are in service, construction being in the hands of such well-known names as Hitachi, Mitsubishi and Toshiba. Four locomotives have stainless-steel bodyshells, as much of their lives will be spent within the corrosive atmosphere of the 11.6-mile (18.7km) undersea tunnel which connects the main island of Honshu with Kyushu.

Below: The Japanese National Railways' bi-current dual frequency Class EF81 standard Bo-Bo-Bo electric locomotive.

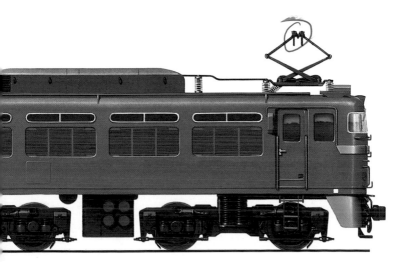

Class DD40AX
"Centennial" D₀-D₀

Origin: Union Pacific Railroad (UP), USA. **Type:** Diesel-electric locomotive for heavy freight duty. **Gauge:** 4ft 8½in (1,435mm). **Propulsion:** Two supercharged two-stroke General Motors 16-cylinder Type 645 engines each of 3,300hp (2,460kW) with integral alternators, feeding eight nose-suspended traction motors. **Weight:** 545,270lb (247.5t). **Axleload:** 68,324lb (31t). **Overall length:** 98ft 5in (29,997mm). **Tractive effort:** 133,766lb (603kN). **Max speed:** 90mph (144km/h). **Service entry:** 1969.

If one were to choose the world's number one rail line, a fairly likely candidate would be the central section of the first United States transcontinental railroad, known now by the same name — Union Pacific — as it was when opened in 1869. In the days of steam, UP had the largest and most powerful locomotives in the world, the legendary "Big Boys", to haul the heavy and constant flow of freight across the continental divide. Going west, this began with the famous Sherman Hill (named after General Sherman who was in charge of building UP) out of Cheyenne, Wyoming; it consists of some 40 miles (64km) of 1-in-66 (1.5 per cent) grade.

When diesel traction took over, the power of a steam 4-8-8-4 could be matched or exceeded by coupling locomotive units in multiple, but UP management consistently made efforts to find a simpler solution by increasing the power of each unit Extensive trials were made with locomotives propelled by gas turbines, giving a much higher power-to-weight ratio; but in the end the ability to buy off-the-shelf from diesel locomotive suppliers proved to have an over-riding advantage.

In the late-1960s, the UP operating authorities once again felt that there should be a better solution than having six or even eight locomotives on one train. General Motors had put together a peculiar 5,000hp (3,730kW) locomotive which they called a "DD35". This was essentially a huge booster unit with the works of two standard "GP35" road-switchers mounted on it. The locomotive ran on two four-axle bogies; these were considered to be hard on the track, but being contained in a mere booster unit could not take the leading position in a train where any bad effects of the running gear would be accentuated. Even so, no one was very keen to put the matter to the test. Only a handful of "DD35s'" were sold and those only to Union Pacific and Southern Pacific. UP's track was (and is) superb, however, and it was suggested to GM that a "DD35" with a normal cab hood would be useful. The result was the "DD35A", of which 27 were supplied to UP. It was not disclosed how much saving in cost, allowing for an element of custom-building, there was between two

Above: Union Pacific No. 6900 heads a "Golden Spike" special celebrating 100 years of rail operation across the continent.

"GP35s" and one "DD35A", but in length at least the former's 112ft 4in (34,240mm) compared with the latter's 88ft 2in (26,873mm).

A centenary in a new country is a great event and when during the late-1960s UP's management considered how to celebrate 100 years of continuous operation, they decided to do it by ordering a class of prime mover which was the most powerful in the world on a single-unit basis. Again, virtually everything except the chassis of the locomotive came off General Motors shelves, but even so the "Centennials" (more prosaically, the "DD40AXs") are a remarkable achievement.

In the same way that the "DD35A" was a double "GP35", the "DD40AX" was a double "GP40". The 16-cylinder engines of the "GP40" (essentially a supercharged version of those fitted to the "GP35") were uprated from 3,000 to 3,300hp (2,240 to 2,460kW), thereby producing a 6,600hp (4,925kW) single-unit locomotive. This was done by permitting an increased rpm. The result was not only the most powerful but also the longest and the largest prime-mover locomotive unit in the world. Forty-seven were built between 1969 and 1971, completion of the first (appropriately No. 6900) being pushed ahead to be ready on centenary day. The locomotives had a full-width cab and incorporated all ▶

Below: Union Pacific class DD40X "Centennial" diesel-electric locomotive. Note the gap between the two engines.

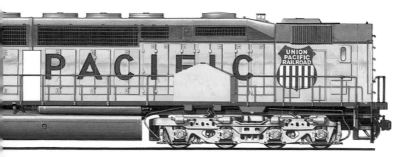

▶ the recent improvements which GM had introduced in the standard range of diesel locomotives. These included the new Type 645 engine, of uniflow two-stroke design like its long-lived predecessor the Type 567. The same cylinder bore and stroke is common to a 1,750hp (750kW) switcher and the 6,600hp (4,925kW) "Centennial". The generator was basically a brushless alternator, but had built-in silicon diode rectifiers to produce direct current suitable for traction motors. Naturally, the control system included dynamic braking and wheelslip correction features.

The complex electrical system common to all diesel-electric locomotives was improved in these machines by being concentrated in a series of modules which could be isolated, tested and easily replaced if found faulty. In this way, repairs, adjustments or an overhaul could be done under factory conditions. Afterwards this arrangement became standard throughout the whole range of GM locomotives, models with it becoming known as "Dash-2", for example "SD40-2" for an "SD40" with modular electrics.

It could be said that this development proved to be self-destructive to the future of monster diesel-electrics, for a principal advantage of combining two "GP40s" on one chassis was the saving of a lot of electrical control gear. So making the electrics less troublesome made inroads into this advantage, and as a result these dinosaurs have not been repeated, even for Union Pacific. Another factor was introduction of the "SD45-2" series with 20-cylinder engines rated at 3,600hp (2,685kW).

After these superb "Centennials", UP once again returned to buying diesel units off-the-shelf like virtually all US railroads and indeed the majority of railways the world over. When a train was called, required power would be calculated on a horsepower per ton basis according to

Above: A pair of "Centennial" diesel-electric units at the head of a freight train at Barstow, California, in 1970.

the severity of the route. The most conveniently available units to make up this total horsepower would then be coupled up to form the motive power: in these circumstances large special indivisible units are more of a hindrance than a help. Thus the "Big Boys" and the turbines have been superseded, and the 'Centennials' submerged by more mundane motive power; even so, the pageant of freight movement up Sherman Hill and across the Divide is still one of the great railway sights of the world.

Below: Brand-new Union Pacific class DD40X "Centennial" diesel-electric locomotive No. 6900, built by General Motors' Electro-motive Division, poses for an official photograph.

DF4 'East Wind IV' C₀-C₀

Origin: Railways of the People's Republic of China (CR). **Type:** General-purpose diesel-electric locomotive. **Gauge:** 4ft 8½in (1,435mm). **Propulsion:** 3,600hp (2,686kW) Type 16-240-Z 16-cylinder Vee-type four-stroke diesel engine and alternator supplying current via solid-state rectifiers to six traction motors geared to the axles. **Weight:** 304,155lb (138t). **Axleload:** 50,695lb (23t). **Overall length:** 62ft 2½in (21,100mm). **Tractive effort:** 76,038lb (338kN). **Max speed:** 75mph (120km/h). **Service entry:** 1969.

Diesel locomotive production in China started off quite incredibly badly in the 1960s when, in response to Chairman Mao's call for a 'Great Leap Forward', the various locomotive works, 'aiming high', set out to design and build their own, unhampered by any previous experience. The result was disaster, but when sanity returned it was rightly felt important not to respond by putting the nation into the hands of some foreign country.

The immediate solution was for steam building to continue and for a slow-but-sure diesel-electric development programme to be put in hand. There were some imports of main line diesel-electric locomotives, notably 50 of 4,000hp (2,985kW) from Alsthom of France during the early-1970s and 20 of 2,100hp (1,567kW) from Electroputere of Romania in 1975, but home-building also began in earnest, and this is the most common type.

The DF4 is a general-purpose locomotive, of which versions exist for both passenger (numbered 2001 upwards) or freight traffic (numbered 0001 upwards). It is not often used in multiple, being the most powerful in China with a single engine and consequently having adequate power to haul trains of the size normally run. Its appearance is neat and there is a cab at both ends. The engine, the ac/dc transmission and the mechanical parts are wholly Chinese-made, and developed from a prototype built in

Above: An "East Wind IV" class diesel-electric Co-Co of the Chinese railways rolls a freight train near Peking in 1980.

1969. Series production is now in hand at the Dalian Works. Incidentally, the type number of the engine, 16240, indicates the number of cylinders (16) followed by their bore in millimetres 240mm-9.45in). It is delightful to note that, with a frankness unmatched amongst the world's railway mechanical departments, the weights are officially specified as being within plus or minus 3 per cent. It is thought that about 450 had been produced by the end of 1981.

Below: A Peking-Shanghai express near Jinan, China, hauled by an "East Wind IV" class Co-Co diesel-electric locomotive.

Class 6E B₀-B₀

Origin: South African Railways (SAR). **Type:** Electric mixed traffic freight locomotive. **Gauge:** 3ft 6in (1,067 mm). **Propulsion:** Direct current at 3,000V fed via overhead catenary and rheostatic controls to four 835hp (623kW) nose-suspended motors geared to the driving axles. **Weight:** 195,935lb (88.9t). **Axleload:** 49,040lb (22.25t). **Overall length:** 50ft 10in (15,494mm). **Tractive effort:** 70,000lb (311kN). **Max speed:** 70mph (112km/h). **Service entry:** 1969.

The first important electrification scheme in South Africa came as early as 1952, when a steeply-graded section of the Durban to Johannesburg main line between Estcourt and Ladysmith was placed under the wires. The Class "1E" locomotives supplied—the original group came from Switzerland—were direct ancestors of Class "6E" with the same wheel arrangement and mechanical configuration. Forty-four years of progress resulted in increases of 77 per cent in tractive effort, 208 per cent in power output, and 180 per cent in maximum permitted speed at a cost of only 31 per cent in weight and 16 per cent in overall length. It is typical of electric traction, though, that many of the "1Es" remain in service on humble but still arduous duties after half-a-century of work.

A country that combines prosperous development and geat mineral riches with non-existent oil supplies is well-suited to electrification. Both the scale of electric operation and its rate of development in South Africa are indicated by the fact that the "6E/6E1" fleet totals 997 units, while 850 of their very similar immediate predecessors, classes "5E" and "5E1", were built between 1955 and 1969. South Africa's growing industrial capability is also shown by the fact that while the 172 "1Es" (and the similar "2Es") were wholly built in Europe, only the earlier examples of Class "5E" and none of the "6Es" were built abroad.

All the classes mentioned, and this is especially impressive for half-a-century ago, are capable not only of regenerative braking but also of working in multiple. This whole concept or railroading, using exclusively tractors with the same two bogies as most other vehicles but coupling up as many of them as are needed to haul the train, was far ahead of its time. Five or six locomotives running in multiple can often be seen.

Below: The class 5E/6E locomotive design of the South African Railways depicted in special "Blue Train" colours.

Above: Matching locomotives and cars make up the "Blue Train".

Above: South African Railways' famous luxury "Blue Train" near Pretoria hauled by two specially painted locomotives.

Class 103.1 C_o-C_o

Origin: German Federal Railway (DB). **Type:** Express passenger electric locomotive. **Gauge:** 4ft 8½in (1,435mm). **Propulsion:** Alternating current at 15,000V 16⅔Hz fed through a transformer to six 1,580hp (1,180kW) traction motors mounted on the bogie frames, connected to the axles through spring drive. **Weight:** 251,260lb (114t). **Axleload:** 41,880lb (19.0t). **Overall length:** 63ft 11½in (19,500mm). **Tractive effort:** 70,000lb (312kN). **Max speed:** 125mph (200km/h). **Service entry:** 1970.

In 1960 the German Federal Railway (DB) began to plan a network of high-speed inter-city trains with which to meet the competition of internal air services. The fast diesel trains in pre-war Germany had operated mainly on routes radiating from Berlin, on which high speeds could be sustained for long distances. In West Germany, however, the principal routes had more frequent stops and speed restrictions, and the ability to reach high speed quickly was thus as important as the ability to sustain it. The specification which was drawn up in 1961 therefore required that a speed of 125mph (200km/h) should be maintained on a gradient of 1-in-200 (0.5 per cent) with 300t, and that the train should be accelerated to this speed in 150 seconds.

In accordance with German practice a number of companies submitted proposals. These included 1-Bo+Bo1 and A1A+A1A schemes with four motors of 1,250kW (1,675hp), but it was considered that six motors should be fitted to keep the motor weight down, and despite some doubts about its riding qualities, the Co-Co arrangement was chosen.

Four prototypes were ordered in 1963 from Siemens Schuckert and Henschel; delivered in 1965 they were numbered E03.001-4. They made a spectacular entry into service, for in connection with an international transport exhibition in Munich that year they worked a special train twice daily from Munich to Augsburg at an average of 88mph (142km/h) with sustained 200km/h running.

The locomotives followed the pattern already established in DB standard designs, with an ac motor mounted above each axle and fully-sprung drive. Control was by tap changers on the high-tension side of the transformer. Automatic speed control was fitted, with increments of 10km/h on the driver's controller. The motors were of light weight for their power, specially designed for high speed. The one-hour rating was

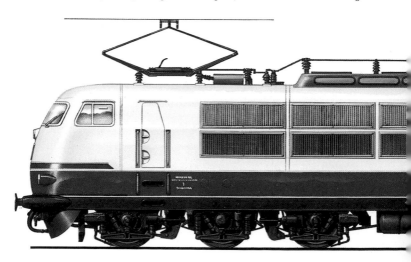

Above: A high-speed inter-city express train of the German Federal Railways hauled by a class 103.1 electric locomotive.

6,420kW (8,600hp) at 200km/h, and the 10-minute rating was no less than 9,000kW (12,000hp). When employed on heavy expresses running at lower speeds, the locos suffered from high transformer temperatures, so larger transformers had to be fitted.

For a time, DB favoured the idea of working the inter-city network by multiple-units, but eventually it was decided that, except for any services which might in the future exceed 125mph (200km/h), locomotives would be used, and 145 more of the Co-Co units were ordered. They were delivered from 1970 onwards; under the computerised numbering system then in use they were designated Nos. 103.101-245. They incorporated various improvements to the motors and control equipment which allowed them to work trains of up to 480t at 200km/h. The earlier locomotives had also developed heavy brush and commutator wear when their high-speed motors were subjected to heavy currents at low speeds, and the new machines had an additional tap-changer on the low-tension side of the transformer which made them suitable for working 600t trains at normal speed.

The body shape of the original locomotives had been determined by wind-tunnel tests, but the resultant curved ends had the effect of making the driver's cab more cramped than in other classes.

Below: German Federal Railways' standard class 103.1 Co-Co electric locomotive, introduced in 1970 for fast expresses.

Class 2130 C₀-C₀

Origin: Queensland Railways (QR). **Type:** Diesel-electric mineral-hauling locomotive. **Gauge:** 3ft 6in (1,067mm).**Propulsion:** General Motors Type 16-645E 2,200hp (1,640kW) 16-cylinder Vee two-stroke diesel engine and alternator feeding via solid-state rectifiers six nose-suspended traction motors geared to the axles. **Weight:** 215,050lb (98t). **Axleload:** 35,850lb (16.3t). **Overall length:** 59ft 3in (18,060mm).**Tractive effort:** 64,500lb (287kN). **Max speed:** 50mph (80km/h). **Service entry:** 1970.

Queensland's railway system has been extended recently to serve various mining operations, and so has rather surprisingly moved into the premier place as regards mileage amongst the Australian state and national administrations. During 1983-84 a further 157 miles (252km) of new route were commissioned, bringing the network to 6,359 miles (10,231km). Furthermore, in spite of being almost entirely laid on narrow-gauge, QR also holds the top place in load hauling. The locomotives that achieve this record are these Class "2130" diesel-electrics. The 11 machines which form the "2130" class are, like more than half the QR fleet, of General Motors design and built (or at any rate, assembled) under licence by Clyde Engineering. They also follow US practice in being used as building blocks to form tractive effort of the power desired.

The most heroic use for these excellent machines is formation as two groups of three on the Goonyella line to haul 148-wagon coal trains weighing 11,140t (12,250 US tons) and carrying 8,700t (9,130 US tons) of coal. As the drawgear of the train is not strong enough to take the tractive effort of all six locomotives, the second group is cut into the centre of the train. These mid-train units are remotely controlled from the lead units without any cable connections between them, by a system of US origin widely-used in North America and known as Locotrol.

The Locotrol system involves a special vehicle marshalled next to the group of units in the centre of the train. This vehicle operates on the principle of sensing the drawbar pull and applying power to the units it controls accordingly. Safety is ensured by having the brakes of the whole train under the control of the driver in the leading unit. Six of the locomotives (Nos. 2135 to 40) are fitted out for use as lead units, with air-conditioned cabs and Locotrol equipment.

The "2130" class is part of a group of generally similar diesel locomotives, 57 in number, all of General Motors origin and numbered in

Above: Note the provision of both automatic "knuckle" couplers and link-and-screw couplings with buffers on these Queensland Railways' class 2130 diesel-electric locomotives.

the 21xx and 22xx series, as befits their rating of 2,000hp-plus. The only non-General Motors units of this order of power on QR are the 16 Class "2350" of 2,350hp (1,735kW) supplied by English Electric and used on lines with an axleload limit of 15t. This high-power fleet is likely to be the summit of diesel development in Queensland because work started in 1984 on QR's first main line electrification scheme. This will eventually see all the heavy coal export routes to ports at Gladstone, Hay Point and Dalrymple Bay come under the wires. A total of 146 25,000V electric locos are on order, and the first is due in service late in 1986.

Below: Queensland Railways' class 2130 diesel-electric Co-Co locomotive, of which 11 were supplied in 1970 to provide for the bulk movement of coal in 11,000-ton 148-wagon trains.

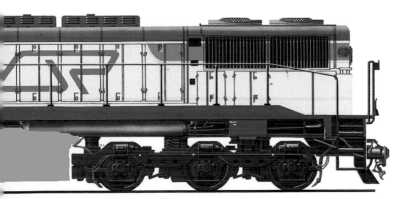

WAM4 C₀-C₀

Origin: Indian Railways (IR). **Type:** Electric mixed-traffic locomotive.
Gauge: 5ft 6in (1,676mm). **Propulsion:** Alternating current at 25,000V
50Hz fed via overhead catenary, step-down transformer and solid-state
rectifiers to six 600hp (448kW) nose-suspended traction motors, each
geared directly to one of the six axles. **Weight:** 249,050lb (113t).
Axleload: 41,876lb (19t). **Overall length:** 62ft 3in (18,974mm).
Tractive effort: 74,600lb (332kN). **Max speed:** 75mph. (120km/h).
Service entry: 1971.

When in the 1950s use of industrial-frequency current combined with
rectifier locomotive became the world norm, India made the change to ac
along with most other countries previously wedded to dc systems. Since
French developments then led the field, the ac locomotives supplied at
first followed that country's practice, whether built in France or in India.
Before long it became apparent that some of their more sophisticated
features such as spring-borne traction motors did not suit Indian
conditions. The result was the first Indian-designed and Indian-built
electric locomotive class, which appeared from the railways' own
Chittaranjan Locomotive Works in 1971.

A feature is the use of the same power bogies as on Indian
diesel-electric locomotives. So many electric and diesel-electric loco
designers pursue separate and divergent courses, those of British Rail
being a notorious example. The fleet of these machines has now reached
over 300, rheostatic electric braking and multiple-unit capability being
provided on all. Silicon-diode rectifiers and tap-changing on the high
tension side of the main transformer are used.

A dual-current series, Class "WCAM1", is also in service, as well as
'WCG2s' for freight traffic on dc lines. Both are similar in appearance to
and have many components in common with the "WAM4s". A small
group of "WAM4s" have been given a lower gearing for heavy iron-ore

Above: Indian Railways' class WAM4 50Hz AC 3600hp Co-Co electric locomotive built "in house" at Chittaranjan Works.

trains ("WAM4B"), while a high-speed version is also reported to be under construction.

Class "WAM4" illustrates how sound thinking and a bold approach to self-help have given Indian Railways an enviable foundation on which to build a sound future.

Below: One of the earlier AC electric locomotives of French design built before standard designs had been developed.

Beijing Class B-B

Origin: Railways of the People's Republic of China (CR).**Type:** Diesel-hydraulic express passenger locomotive. **Gauge:** 4ft 8½in (1,435mm). **Propulsion:** Type 12240Z 3,300hp (2,462kW) 12-cylinder four-stroke Vee diesel engine driving the four axles through a hydraulic torque-converter system. **Weight:** 202,770lb (92t). **Axleload:** 50,695lb (23t). **Overall length:** 54ft 2in (16,505mm).**Tractive effort:** 52,257lb (232kN).**Max speed:** 75mph. **Service entry:** 1971.

In parallel with diesel-electric progress, diesel-hydraulic locomotive development had also been pursued in China. With some experience gained with 30 Class "NY6" 4,300hp (3,208kW) and "NY7" 5,400hp (4,028kW) locomotives imported from Henschel of West Germany, the February 7th Locomotive Works at Peking (Beijing) produced in 1971 some prototypes of a rather smaller locomotive for passenger work. These are known as the "BJ" or "Beijing" class. Full production began in 1975 and by the end of 1981 about 150 were in service, numbered BJ3001 upwards.

These compact-looking locomotives have more haulage capacity than would appear. The powerful engine is matched by high tractive effort, due to the high axleloading. For example, on a really steep gradient of 1-in-30 (3.3 per cent), a load of 600t (660 US tons) can be hauled at the very respectable speed in the circumstances of 15mph (24km/h). A low-level connection to transmit tractive effort from the bogies to the body helps improve performance by reducing weight transfer from one axle to

Below: A "Beijing" diesel-hydraulic locomotive heads the daily tourist train from Peking to the Great Wall of China.

Above: The railways of the People's Republic of China employ many "Beijing" class locomotives for express passenger trains.

another. The hydraulic transmission incorporates two torque converters, one for starting and one for running at normal speeds. Either can be used to drive one or both bogies and the system can also be used as a hydrokinetic brake to give dynamic braking. A twin-engine version has been developed and so highly is the performance and reliability of the "BJ" class regarded that its designers now have sufficient confidence to offer it for export.

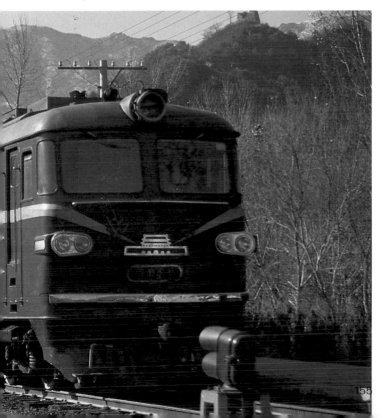

Class 92 1-C₀-C₀-1

Origin: East African Railways (EAR). **Type:** Diesel-electric mixed-traffic locomotive. **Gauge:** 3ft 3⅜in (1,000mm). **Propulsion:** Alco Type 251F 12-cylinder four-stroke 2,550hp (1,902kW) Vee-type diesel engine and generator supplying direct current to six nose suspended traction motors geared to the main axles. **Weight:** 218,200lb (99t) adhesive, 251,255lb (114.5t) total. **Axleload:** 36,370lb (16.5t). **Overall length:** 59ft 1in (18,015mm). **Tractive effort:** 77,000lb (342kN). **Max speed:** 45mph (72km/h). **Service entry:** 1971.

Construction of the so-called Uganda Railway was the start of civilisation in what is now known as Kenya. Little wood-burning steam engines reached the site of Nairobi in 1895, so beginning the history of a line which for most of its existence has had to struggle to move ever-increasing traffic.

Oil-burning took over from wood in the 1930s, and traffic reached a point where articulated locomotives—the legendary Beyer-Garratts—were needed. The efficiency with which traffic was worked by these monsters made East African Railways (the former joint administration of railways in Kenya, Tanzania and Uganda) a very hard nut indeed for diesel traction to crack. Various studies over the years indicated that there was no case for change, apart from "keeping up with the Joneses", but in the

Above: An East African Railways' (later Kenya Railways) class 92 diesel-electric hauls an empty tank train towards Mombasa.

Below: East African class 92 Alco-built diesel-electric locomotive. Note the pony wheels to reduce the axle-loading.

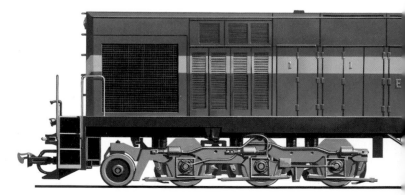

Above: A class 92 1-Co-Co-1 diesel-electric climbs the spiral at Mazeras near Mombasa with a freight for Nairobi.

1960s the administration began to order medium-power units from English Electric of Great Britain.

By 1970 some progress in dieselisation had been made on peripheral routes, but the main trunk route which climbed steadily from sea level at Mombasa to 9,131ft (2,783m) at Timboroa, en route to Uganda, was still a Garratt stronghold. To find a means of working this traffic economically with diesel traction, EAR went shopping outside Britain, almost for the first time. The result was this Class "92" diesel of Alco design, supplied by the Montreal Locomotive Works. It offered 38 per cent more power than the most powerful diesel then in Kenya.

The Class "92"s were based on the standard Alco product adapted for metre-gauge. To reduce the axleload to a value acceptable on the main line west of Nairobi, not only was it necessary to use six-wheel bogies but an idle pony wheel had to be attached to each bogie also. The arrangement was offered by MLW specially for low axleloads as their "African series" and EAR also ordered an even lighter lower-power version on the same chassis (Class "88") for lines with a 12 ton axleload in Tanzania.

In 1976, EAR was divided up among the owning nations, Kenya, Uganda and Tanzania. The Class "92s" went to Kenya, retaining the same classification. Since then a Class "93" Co-Co design of similar power has been imported from General Electric. Advances in design have enabled axleload restrictions to be met without the pony wheels.

Class 15000 B-B

Origin: French National Railways (SNCF).**Type:** Express passenger electric locomotive. **Gauge:** 4ft 8½in (1,435mm). **Propulsion:** Alternating current at 25,000V 50Hz from overhead wires, rectified in diodes and thyristors, supplying two 2,960hp (2,210kW) traction motors, one mounted on each bogie and connected to the axles through gearing and spring drives. **Weight:** 198,395lb (88t). **Axleload:** 49,590lb (22.5t). **Overall length:** 57ft 4⅛in (17,480mm). **Tractive effort:** 64,800lb (288kN). **Max speed:** 112mph (180km/h). **Service entry:** 1971.

Early in its experiments with 25,000V 50Hz ac traction, SNCF recognised that the combination of routes electrified on the new system with its existing network of 1,500V dc lines would make essential the use of dual-voltage locomotives capable of working on both systems. Otherwise the time consumed in changing locomotives, together with the resulting poor utilisation, would nullify much of the economy of the high-voltage system. Dual-voltage machines were therefore included in the batch of experimental ac locomotives, and this was followed by the development of "families" of locomotives, comprising ac, dc and dual-voltage machines incorporating as many common parts as possible. The numbering of these classes was a notable manifestation of Gallic logic, for it was based on the mathematical relationship: $(ac + dc) = (dual\ voltage)$. Thus the "17000" ac class and the "8500" dc class combined to produce the "25500" dual-voltage class.

Successive phases in post-war development of the French electric locomotive produced successive families. Thus one group comprised the first all-adhesion four-axle locomotive with individual-axle drive. The next group, the one mentioned above, incorporated monomotor bogies with two gear ratios,and silicon rectifiers. The third group, "15000" + "7200" = Class "22200", moved into the thyristor era, and at a nominal 5,920hp (4,420kW) they are the most powerful French B-B machines. This group is also notable in reverting to a single gear ratio. Class "15000" was intended primarily for express passenger work, and a low-speed gear was unnecessary, but it was hoped that improvements in various aspects of design since the introduction of the two-speed locomotives would enable the thyristor machines to handle the freight traffic without provision of a special gear ratio.

It is SNCF's practice to apply new technology experimentally to an

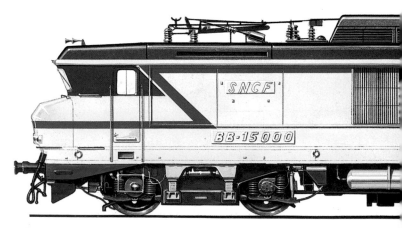

Above: French National Railways' class 15000 50Hz ac locomotives, standard power for express trains in France.

existing locomotive or train, retaining as much as possible of the well-proven equipment, so as to concentrate attention on the special equipment under test. Some of the first thyristor experiments were made with one of the pioneer dual-voltage locomotives, No. 20002, which retained conventional resistance control for dc operation and silicon diodes for ac traction, but had thyristors for ac regenerative braking. The first application of thyristors to control power circuits was on a multiple-unit train, and in 1971 there appeared the first production units equipped throughout with thyristors, a series of multiple-units, and the Class "15000" B-B locomotives.

Up to this time the standard method of controlling power on French ac locomotives had been by tap-changer on the high-tension side of the transformer. The thyristor offered an elegant alternative to the tap-changer, with the possibility of infinitely-variable control of the voltage applied to the traction motors.

▶

Below: The French locomotive design depicted is produced for dc (cl.7200), for 50Hz (cl.15000) and bi-current (cl.22200).

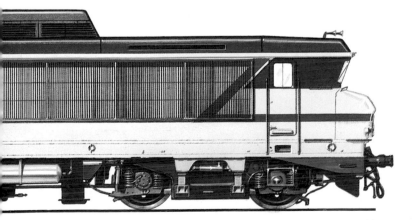

Above: A class 7200 Bo-Bo electric locomotive (the dc version of class 15000) at the Gare du Lyon, Paris, in 1970.

▶ Class "15000"was built to take over principal services on the former Est Railway main line from Paris to Strasbourg, now in the Eastern Region of SNCF. Their introduction followed construction of the "6500" class C-C dc locomotives and the "72000" class C-C diesel-electrics; many parts were common to all three classes, including the main body structure. There is a single traction motor for each bogie, mounted rigidly on top of the bogie frame and connected to the axles through gearing and Alsthom flexible drives. The body rests on four rubber springs, two at each side of the body and close together. The springs are sandwiches of steel and rubber bonded together. They resist the vertical load by compression, whilst lateral oscillations and rotation of the bogie are resisted by shearing action. This is a remarkably simple and effective suspension.

An important innovation in the "15000s" was the control system, made possible by the comparative simplicity of thyristor circuitry. The driver has two normal methods of controlling speed, constant speed or constant current. With the former the driver sets his controller to the speed required, and he also sets up the value of the current which is not to be exceeded. The control circuits accelerate the locomotive to the speed required, and then vary the current to hold it at that speed, provided that the stipulated maximum current is not exceeded. If, due to a change in gradient, the locomotive attempts to accelerate, current is reduced,and finally, if necessary, regenerative braking is set up.Alternatively the driver can isolate the speed control, and the system holds the current to the pre-selected value, observance of speed being the driver's responsibility.

The "15000s" are designed for 112½mph (180km/h), which is somewhat surprising as 124mph (200km/h) had already been permitted on some parts of SNCF when they were built,but so far on the Eastern Region the limit is 100mph (160km/h). Every effort was made to simplify the design to reduce maintenance costs, and with this in mind the traction motor was modified to make it self-ventilating and so eliminate the need for a forced-ventilation system.

They soon established an excellent reputatation,and with 74 in service they dominate the Eastern Region passenger services. Work continued on chopper control for dc locomotives, and for a time C-C locomotive No.20002, with chopper equipment, ran coupled to standard B-B No.9252, No. 20002 serving as a current supply to the motors of No. 9252. Next No. 15007 was converted to a dc machine, numbered 7003, to test the equipment for the "7200" class.

In 1976, delivery of the "7200" class began,followed later in the year by the dual-voltage "22200" locomotives. These classes differ only in that the "22200" has an additional pantograph for ac operation, and a transformer and silicon rectifier for converting the ac supply to 1,500V dc. The current is then fed into the same circuits as the dc supply, so that there is only one control system. Both classes closely resemble the "15000s", but are slightly longer in the body, and they have rheostatic braking instead of regenerative.

The "7200" and "22200" classes are allocated to the South-Eastern Region, and have displaced earlier locomotives from the principal services, apart from those worked by TGVs. Their workings include the ac section from Marseilles to Ventimille, on which "22200s" work through from Paris to Ventimille, 695 miles (1,118km). They also work fast freight trains into northern France, a new departure in inter-regional working, which includes running 696 miles (1,120km) from Marseilles to Lille. These are the longest locomotive workings in France, and the high mileage which the locomotives can thereby build up is held to justify the small extra cost of a "22200" compared with a "7200" or "15000".

Although it had been hoped that Class "7200" would be suitable for heavy low-speed freight work, trouble was encountered with overheating of the motors, and the first 35 locomotives were temporarily fitted with bogies geared for 62mph (100km/h). All later locomotives have force-ventilated motors.

For nine months before its gear ratio was changed, No. 7233 was transferred to the South-Western Region, and worked "L'Etendard" between Paris and Bordeaux with considerable running at 125mph (200km/h). Later No. 22278 was tested similarly, thus proving that the classes were suitable for this speed, although designed for 180km/h.

A total of 210 Class "7200" locomotives and 150 of Class "22200" were built by Alsthom, and in due course the firm received an order for 48 similar locomotives for Netherlands Railways.

In 1982 No. 15056 was fitted with synchronous three-phase motors, and No. 15055 was selected for another series of tests with asynchronous motors. The success of the trials with No. 15055 led to a decision that synchronous motors would power future batches of Bo-Bo locomotives, and in 1984 SNCF ordered 44 dual voltage machines, to be designated Class "26000".

Below: Further development of the class 15000 is in progress in France. Note the laboratory car at the head of the train.

RTG Four-car trainset

Origin: French National Railways (SNCF). **Type:** Five-car express passenger gas turbine set. **Gauge:** 4ft 8½in (1,435mm). **Propulsion:** One Société Française Turboméca Turmo IIIF 1,150 hp (858kW) gas turbine in each end vehicle driving the axles of the outer bogie through Voith hydraulic transmission. **Weight:** 143,040lb (64.9t) adhesive, 570,836lb (259t) total. **Axleload:** 35,760lb (16.2t). **Overall length:** 339ft 6⁵⁄₁₆in (128,990mm). **Tractive effort:** 26,980lb (120kN). **Max speed:** 112mph (180km/h). **Service entry:** 1972.

In 1966 SNCF, with no diesel locomotives able to run at more than 87mph (140km/h), studied the problem of designing railcars for non-electrified lines. The aim was to equal the performance then being achieved by electric traction, that is general running at 100mph (160km/h) with speeds of 124mph (200km/h) on suitable stretches. Non-electrified routes often had a greater number of speed restrictions than the more generously laid-out electric routes, and the performance contemplated would therefore require a much higher power-to-weight ratio than was being achieved in contemporary diesel railcars.

The French aero-engine industry has scored notable successes with small gas turbines for helicopters, and SNCF saw these turbines as a means of providing the high power required without a significant increase in weight over a diesel railcar. The first experiment was started in 1966. A Turmo III F engine manufactured by Société Française Turboméca was fitted to the trailer car of a standard two-car diesel set. The output shaft of this engine was connected through reduction gears to the axles of one bogie. The engine was rated at 1,500hp (1,120kW), but was de-rated to 1,150hp (858kW) for railway use, and it operated on diesel fuel, both for fuel economy and greater safety. The first trial took place on April 25, 1967, and two months later a speed of 147mph (236km/h) was recorded. The train was driven by the diesel engine below a speed of 20mph (30km/h) with the gas turbine shut down. Fuel consumption was considered acceptable.

The next step in 1968 was an order for 10 four-car trains for the Paris-Caen-Cherbourg service. In these a 440hp (330kW) diesel engine was fitted in one end coach and a Turmo III F in the other, as in the "TGS", but the coaches were appointed to main line standard with catering facilites and warm-air ventilation. The difference was that the turbine was connected to the axles through Voith hydraulic transmission, enabling the turbine to be used from rest. These sets are designated "ETG" (*Elément à Turbine à Gaz*).

In 1970 the Paris-Caen and Paris-Cherbourg services were taken over by "ETGs", being the first full inter-city service in the world to be operated by gas turbine traction. Caen was reached in 109 minutes at 81.5mph

Above: "Turbo-train" approaching Chicago. Two sets were supplied from France and several more built in the USA.

(131km/h). Although the sets were designed for 112mph (180km/h) they have always been limited to 100mph (160km/h) in service.

Success of the "ETGs" created a demand for trains with still more and better accommodation. This was met by building units with longer coaches which could be run in four-coach or five-coach sets, with air-conditioning and other appointments as in the latest locomotive-hauled coaches. The diesel engine was omitted, and there was a Turmo III power unit in each end coach. An additional small Astazou turbine was installed in each power car to provide electric power at all times, the main turbines being run only when required for traction. These trains are the "RTGs" (*Rame à Turbine à Gaz*).

"RTGs" took over the Cherbourg services in 1972 and were later introduced on cross-country routes based on Lyons. A total of 41 sets were built, of which two were later sold to Amtrak in the United States.

Gas turbine trains were a notable success for French engineers, for not only do they perform reliably, but they are environmentally acceptable both to the passengers and to those outside the train. However, their operating costs were no longer acceptable after the 1973 oil price rises, and no further extensions have been made to these services. Nevertheless, they rank as the most successful application of gas turbines to railway passenger services.

Below: The power car of an RTG. The power unit is in the small windowless space between the two doors at the front end.

Class Re 6/6 B₀-B₀-B₀

Origin: Swiss Federal Railways (SBB). **Type:** Heavy-duty mixed-traffic mountain locomotive. **Gauge:** 4ft 8½in (1,435mm). **Propulsion:** Low-frequency alternating current at 15,000V 16⅔Hz fed via overhead catenary and step-down transformer to six frame-mounted 1,740hp (1,300kW) motors each driving one axle through a flexible drive system. **Weight:** 26,480lb (120t). **Axleload:** 44,080lb (20t). **Overall length:** 63ft 4½in (19,310mm). **Tractive effort:** 88,700lb (395kN). **Max speed:** 87mph (140km/h). **Service entry:** 1972.

Ten-thousand horsepower plus in a single locomotive! And no cheating either — all is contained in a single indivisible unit. The story of this giant amongst locomotives began with the ever increasing demands of traffic on the St Gotthard main line across the Alps.

The original heavy artillery of the Gotthard line was a famous series of rod-drive 1-C-C-1 articulated 'Crocodile' locomotives, of only one-quarter the power of the "RE 6/6" engines. In all 52 were built and a few lasted into the 1980s. In 1931 two rather amazing experimental "Ae 8/14" 1-Bo-1-Bo-1 + 1-Bo-1-Bo-1 twin units appeared. One of these, built by Oerlikon, brought the power available to 8,800hp (6,560kW), combined with a drawgear-breaking maximum tractive effort of 132,240lb (588kN). The other, by Brown Boveri, was slightly less powerful. These were followed in 1939 by yet another twin locomotive of the same unique wheel arrangement which did offer more than 10,000hp—11,400hp (8,500kW) in fact— as well as 110,200lb l(490kN) of tractive effort. However, it was at the cost of a total weight twice that of the "Re 6/6". Experience with these immense machines was such that they were not repeated.

The "Re 4/4" double-bogie locomotives for express passenger work came to SBB in 1946, following the example of the Bern-Lötschberg-Simplon Railway Class "Ae 4/4" of two years earlier. With hindsight it seems extraordinary that the Swiss did not simply build a lower-geared version of the "Re 4/4" and use it in multiple on the Gotthard. The fact remains, though, that they did not and instead went on seeking a single locomotive unit that would do the job. Hence in 1952 the usual firms—this time in consort—that is Brown Boveri, Oerlikon and the Swiss Locomotive Works, produced a locomotive with six driven axles and all ▶

Above: A Swiss Federal Railways Re6/6 Bo-Bo-Bo climbs up to the Gotthard tunnel with the *Barbarossa Express,* in 1981.

Below: A massive 10,000hp in a single-unit locomotive! The Swiss Federal Railways' Re6/6 Bo-Bo-Bo mixed-traffic design.

▶ but 1,000hp per axle, classified "Ae 6/6". They used all the know-how gained on the "Ae 4/4" and "Re 4/4" units, but adapted the design for six-wheel instead of four-wheel bogies.

The "Ae 6/6s" were rated at 5,750hp (4,290kW) and 120 were built between 1952 and 1966. Regenerative braking was installed and the maximum speed was 88mph (125km/h). The class ushered in the hitherto almost unheard of practice (for SBB) of naming. Naturally they began with the Swiss Cantons, but soon these ran out and it had to be important towns instead; finally, some of the much mightier successors of the "Ae 6/6s" had to make do with the names of some very small places indeed! The extra power of the "Ae 6/6s" came at the right moment, for an explosion of traffic over the line was about to occur. By the late-1960s, three times the tonnage and over twice the number of trains were passing compared with 1950.

Amongst many measures proposed to cope with the situation was provision of still more powerful locomotives. Something was done quickly by converting existing locomotives to work in multiple—a measure that the Swiss were normally reluctant to take. But in 1972, two single-unit super-power prototypes were delivered by the same consortium. There was no point in providing for haulage of trains above 850t (935 US tons) by a single unit because European wagon couplings were not strong enough to pull heavier loads than this up the Gotthard gradients. Larger trains can be hauled, but a second locomotive has then to be cut into the centre of the load.

The first two 'Re 6/6s' were articulated, but later examples and the production version had the single carbody as described. The haulage capacity was nicely balanced, for an 800t (880 US tons) train could be taken up the 1-in-37 (2.7 per cent) at the line limit of 50mph (80km/h). One of the reasons for adopting the Bo-Bo-Bo wheel arrangement in place of Co-Co was that the length of rigid wheelbase is reduced. This is important on a line like the Gotthard, with almost continuous curvature as sharp as 15 chains (300m) radius. On the other hand, having a rigid body to the locomotive greatly simplified and reduced the cost of the centre bogie, which could align itself with the curves by being allowed sideplay.

Above: A class Re6/6 Bo-Bo-Bo electric locomotive at speed with a Swiss Federal Railways' inter-city express train.

All three bogies were pivotless and each one was made to run more easily over small irregularities in track alignment by giving its axles lateral movement centralised with springs.

Now in general use on less taxing parts of the Swiss rail system, the "Ae 6/6s" are still a remarkable design, but the "Re 6/6s" are over 80 per cent more powerful within the same weight limitation. In addition to being an excellent freight-hauler for mountain grades, these versatile machines are also suitable for passenger trains running at the highest speeds permitted in Switzerland.

Below: A freight train is swept through a lowland forest by a Swiss Federal class Re6/6 Bo-Bo-Bo electric locomotive.

-2 C₀-C₀

ro-Motive Division, General Motor Corporation (EMD), ..oad switcher diesel-electric locomotive. **Gauge:** 4ft 8½in ,..435mm). **Propulsion:** One EMD 645E3 3,000hp (2,240kW) 16-cylinder turbocharged two-stroke Vee engine and alternator supplying current through silicon rectifiers to six nose-suspended traction motors. **Weight:** 368,000lb (167t), with variations according to optional fittings. **Axleload:** 61,330lb (27.8t). **Overall length:** 68ft 10in (20,980mm). **Tractive effort:** 83,100lb (370kN). **Max speed:** 65mph (105km/h). **Service entry:** 1972.

For 50 years the Electro-Motive Division of General Motors has dominated the US diesel market, taking 70 to 75 per cent of total orders. The remainder of the market has been shared between the former steam locomotive builders Alco and Baldwin/Lima, a few smaller firms, and latterly GE, but since 1969 only GE has survived. The effect has been that EMD has never had a monopoly, and although the company's success has been due very much to its policy of offering a limited number of off-the-shelf models, it cannot ignore specialist needs of its customers. There has thus been steady development and improvement of the EMD models over the years, directed mainly at increasing power, reducing fuel consumption and maintenance costs, and improving adhesion.

Introduction of the "hood" design "GP7" model in 1949 marked the beginning of the end for the "carbody" unit on which EMD had made its reputation. From then onwards nearly all EMD's road locomotives would be general-purpose machines. There was, however, a variant; the four-axle machines inevitably had a heavy axleload, and EMD therefore offered a six-axle version designated "SD", for "Special Duty". Although the axleload was reduced, the total weight of the locomotive was greater than that of a four-axle machine, and it thus appealed also to roads which had a need for maximum adhesion due to climatic conditions. The pattern thus became established of offering four-axle and six-axle variants of each model.

Up to 1965, the engine used was the 567 of 567in³ capacity, but by the time this engine was pressed to 2,500hp (1,865kW) for traction, it was reaching its limit, and a new engine was produced with the same piston stroke of 10in (245mm), but with the diameter increased from 8½in (216mm) to 9¹/₁₆in (230mm). The cylinder volume became 645in³, thus giving the engine its designation "645". Like the 567 it is a two-stroke engine, and is available with or without turbocharger. A

Above: an SD40-2 diesel-electric road-switcher locomotive heads a line of Burlington Northern units of motive power.

two-stroke engine requires some degree of pressure-charging to give effective scavenging, and if there is no turbocharger, there is a Roots-type blower driven directly from the engine. There have thus been two lines of development: the turbocharged engine pressed to give successive increases in power, and the engines without turbochargers remaining at 2,000hp (1,490kW), but benefiting from mechanical improvements directed at reducing fuel consumption and maintenance costs.

One of the attractions of the diesels which first replaced steam on freight work was that a number of modest-sized units, working in multiple under the control of one crew, could replace the largest steam engine. These diesels were little bigger than some of the diesel switchers which the roads already operated, and their maintenance was easier than that of overworked steam locomotives which were very demanding of attention and needed good quality fuel to give of their best. The diesels could show a reduction in operating costs, even when their higher capital cost was taken into account.

However, when the possible economies from total dieselisation had ▶

Below: The General Motors' Model SD40-2 Co-Co diesel-electric locomotive in the smart blue livery of Conrail.

▶ been achieved, motive power officers looked for other means of effecting savings. With the problems of diesel maintenance now better understood, an attractive idea was to use a smaller number of larger units to achieve the same total power. This was found to save money both in purchase price and in operating costs. EMD's competitors were first in the field with higher horsepower as a selling point, and it was not until 1958 that EMD marketed a 2,400hp (1,790kW) engine in the "SD24" series with which to match the Fairbanks-Morse Trainmaster of 1953. In 1959 EMD produced its 2,000hp (1,490kW) four-axle model, and from then the horsepower race was on.

The 645 engine was launched in 1965 in two versions, the pressure-charged 645E and the turbocharged 645E3. The 645E was made in 8, 12 and 16 cylinder versions, and the 645E3 with 12, 16 and 20 cylinders. These engines were incorporated in a new range of nine locomotives, which included the "GP40" and "SD40" with the 16-cylinder version of the turbocharged engine, giving 3,000hp (2,240kW), and the "SD45" with the 20-cylinder engine giving 3,600hp (2,690kW). This was the first US engine with 20 cylinders, and it brought EMD firmly into the high horsepower stable, some time after Alco and GE had reached 3,000hp. The six-axle types had a new Flexicoil bogie to give improved riding, and the 3,000hp and 3,600hp engines introduced alternators, instead of generators, to the EMD range. The alternators were more compact than generators, and this assisted the designers in finding space for the larger engines.

With the railroads enthusiastic about high-power locomotives, the "SD45" was the most popular model, achieving a total of 1,260 sales in six years. The highest-powered four-axle unit in the range, the 3,000hp "GP40", achieved sales of 12,01, and for roads which required a six-axle layout, 883 of the "SD40" were supplied.

These models remained standard until the beginning of 1972 when, with competition from GE still keen, a revision was made of the whole range, which became known as "Dash-2", from the addition which was made to the class designation, for example, "SD40-2". At this stage no further increase in power was offered, and the alterations were directed at improving fuel consumption and simplifying maintenance. The most important changes were in the electrical control system, which now comprise largely plug-in modules of printed circuits which can be changed quickly from stock.

New high-adhesion bogies were offered in the six-axle models, known as "HT-C" (High Traction, three axle). Adhesion was still a major concern to the railroads, and as orders came in for the "Dash-2" range, two trends

Below: an SD40-2 road-switcher belonging to Southern Pacific, fitted with special high-adhesion type "T" bogies.

Above: Canadian National SD40-2s in multiple at the head of a freight. Note the modified "safety cab" of the second unit.

bccame apparent: first, that the extra maintenance costs of the 20-cylinder engine and its large turbocharger and radiators were not justified for 600hp more than the 16-cylinder engine could give; and secondly, that the 3,000hp four-axle locomotive, the "GP40", had given trouble with wheelslip and excessive maintenance of its highly-rated traction motors. The high-power model to emerge as the most popular in the range was therefore the "SD40-2", with 3,000hp transmitted through six axles. By the late-1970s this was established as virtually the standard high-power diesel in the US, with sales aproaching 4,000 by the end of the decade. The railroad with the largest number was Burlington Northern with about 900, a quarter of its total locomotive stock.

Concurrently the high cost of maintaining a turbocharger compared with a Roots blower had encouraged railroads to purchase large numbers of "GP38-2" units of 2,000hp for duties for which a 3,000hp locomotive was not required, and sales of this model passed 2,000 by 1980.

EMD now tackled the problem of improving adhesion in four-axle locomotives by a wheelslip detector employing Doppler radar, which is sufficiently sensitive to allow an axle to work safely at the limit of adhesion. Engine development made it possible to offer a 3,500hp (2,610kW) 16-cylinder engine, and in 1980 the company launched the "GP50" with the 3,500hp engine on four axles, so that railroads once again had the choice of a high-power locomotive without the expense of six axles. This found little favour, but the corresponding six-axle unit, the "SD50", had reached 300 deliveries by late-1984. By this time also, a new larger engine, the 710, was in production, giving 3,800hp (2,835kW) in its 16-cylinder version. This was used in the "GP60" and "SD60" series, whilst the 12-cylinder version was used in the "GP59". A total of 10 of these locomotives were built in 1984-85 for extended trials.

Class Dx C₀-C₀

Origin: New Zealand Railways (NZR). **Type:** Diesel-electric locomotive for mixed traffic. **Gauge:** 3ft 6in (1,067mm). **Propulsion:** General Electric (USA) 2,750hp (2,050kW) Type 7FDL-12 twelve-cylinder diesel engine and alternator supplying current via solid-state rectifiers to six nose-suspended traction motors. **Weight:** 214, 890lb (97.5t). **Axleload:** 35,925lb (16.3t). **Overall length:** 55ft 6in (16,916mm). **Tractive effort:** 54,225lb (241kN). **Max speed:** 65mph (103km/h). **Service entry:** 1972.

New Zealand may be a country with a small population as well as a small-gauge railway system, but its railwaymen have always believed in big powerful locomotives. For example, the legendary New Zealand-built "K" class 4-8-4s were as powerful as anything that ran in the mother country, in spite of an axleload limit only 71 per cent of that in Britain. Similarly, these big "Dx" diesel-electrics have a power output comparable with Britain's standard Class "47s", again within the limits of axleload in proportion as before.

Class "Dx" was the culmination of a dieselisation programme which began in the 1950s—as regards main-line traction units of, say, 750hp plus—with the 40 Class "Dg" A1A-A1A units of 1955. What was called "Commonwealth Preference" in import duties gave British manufacturers a substantial advantage in those days, and the order went to English Electric. The class was lightweight, able to run over the light rails of the South Island system, where there was an axleload of only 11t (12 US tons).

Between 1955 and 1967, General Motors came in in a very big way with the 74-strong 1,428hp (1,065 kW) Class "Da" as the mainstay of the North Island trunk lines. There were also the 16 lighter GM "Db" class locomotives for North Island branch lines. In 1968 and 1969 the Japanese firm Mitsubishi delivered 60 Class "Dj" Bo-Bo-Bos for the South Island; this class offered 1,045hp (780kW) for an axleload of 10.9t. As a result of these deliveries the last regular steam-hauled train ran in 1972.

It then became apparent that more powerful locomotives could be used to advantage, and the result was this "Dx" class. Very surprisingly NZR went to a fourth source for these magnificent machines. General Electric of USA—not to be confused with GEC Traction of Britain or its subsidiary General Electric (Australia)—supplied 47 of these units during 1972-75. They are used on crack trains on the North Island trunk line between Wellington and Auckland, both passenger and freight. The design is based on General Electric's standard "U26C" export model.

GEC did not capture the market though, because subsequent deliveries were from General Motors with both A1A-A1A and Co-Co versions of a

similar locomotive (classes "Dc" and "Df" of 67 and 30 units respectively). This in spite of a debate then in full cry concerning the need for railways at all in a country with such modest transport requirements. In the end the verdict was favourable to railways but not to diesels—instead New Zealand Railways is going ahead with a programme of electrification which will use indigenous forms of energy, with the first section scheduled for operation in late-1986.

Above: A class Dx diesel-electric locomotives takes a freight across a trestle viaduct typical of New Zealand Railways.

Below: General Electric (USA) supplied the New Zealand Railways with the class Dx Co-Co diesel-electric locomotives for both passenger and freight work on North Island lines.

Class 87 B₀-B₀

Origin: British Railways (BR). **Type:** Mixed-traffic electric locomotive. **Gauge:** 4ft 8½in (1,435mm). **Propulsion:** Alternating current at 25,000V 50Hz fed via overhead catenary, step-down transformer and solid-state rectifiers to four 1,250hp (923kW) fully spring-borne traction motors, driving the axles by gearing and ASEA hollow-axle flexible drives. **Weight:** 182,930lb (83t). **Axleload:** 45,735lb (20.75t). **Overall length:** 58ft 6in (17,830mm). **Tractive effort:** 58,000lb (258kN). **Max speed:** 100mph (160km/h). **Service entry:** 1973.

Although both began almost from scratch after World War II, there could be no greater contrast than between British Rail's ac electric locomotive development story and that of their diesels. Diesel developments followed each other with the consistency of successive pictures in a kaleidoscope, while ac electric locomotives moved through seven related classes all with the same appearance, maximum speed and wheel arrangement.

The first five classes were offerings on the part of five manufacturers to meet a specification for a 100mph (160km/h) locomotive capable of operation on 25,000V or 6,250V 50Hz electrification systems as shown in the table.

All had frame-mounted traction motors with flexible drive. Classes "81" to "84" originally had mercury-arc rectifiers,while Class "85" was fitted with solid-state rectifiers from the start and also had rheostatic braking. In the event, the need for 6,250V operation never arose, although provision was made for it. No steam heating boilers were fitted as electrically-heated sets were provided for all the regular trains on the electrified lines. Separate steam-heating vans were provided for occasions when stock not fitted with electric heaters was hauled by electric locomotives in the winter.

When the complete electric service from London to Birmingham, Manchester and Liverpool was introduced in 1965-67, a further 100 locomotives were supplied. These were Class "AL6", later Class "86", which had solid-state silicon rectifiers, rheostatic braking as the prime braking system and—one major simplification—nose-suspended traction motors geared direct to the axles. Not surprisingly, this simple answer was too hard on the permanent way for such dense high-speed traffic and the class is now divided up as follows:

Class "86.0" in original condition, but with multiple-unit capability added ▶

Below: British Railways' class 87 Bo-Bo standard electric locomotive design. Note a single pantograph current collector.

Above: The Royal Train headed by class 87 Bo-Bo *Royal Sovereign* at Norton Bridge between Stafford and Crewe, 1980.

▶ on some and an 80mph (130km/h) speed limit imposed. Used only for freight traffic. Total 20 locomotives.

Class "86.1", rebuilt 1972 with new bogies with ASEA hollow axle flexible drive. Prototypes for Class "87". Total 3 locomotives.

Classes "86.2" and "86.3" modified to permit 100mph (160km/h) running to continue. Fitted with resilient rail wheels and (86.2 only) modified bogie springing. Total 58 of Class "86.2" and 19 of Class "86.3".

The 36 locomotives of Class "87" were supplied for the extension of electric working from Crewe to Glasgow. They were built at BR's Crewe Works with electrical equipment by GEC Traction, into which AEI, English Electric, Metropolitan Vickers and British Thompson-Houston had by now been amalgamated. Power rating had been increased 56 per cent over that of Class "81" for a 4 per cent increase of weight. The ASEA hollow-axle flexible drive, tried out on Class "86.1", was used, and multiple-unit capability was provided. At long last it had not been thought necessary to provide an exhauster for working vacuum-braked trains. All the class carry names, mostly of distinguished people living or dead, and this pleasant practice has now spilled over on to examples of Class "86".

The latest improvement is application of thyristor control, fitted to a Class "87" locomotive re-designated Class "87.1". No. 87101 carries the honoured name of *Stephenson* and no doubt, when the present pause in British electric locomotive development is over, more will be heard of this significant step in traction technology.

In May 1984, the maximum permitted line speed for the class was increased to 110mph (176km/h), and certain London to Glasgow trains were accelerated. As regards performance and reliability, it perhaps says enough that this can be entirely taken for granted with these locomotives. Ample power can be drawn from the contact wire for maintaining the maximum permitted speed with the usual loads, while the same locomotives are also suitable for heavier and slower freight trains.

Above, right: British Railways' Class 87 Bo-Bo *Thane of Fife* takes an express train through Stafford station in June 1981.

Right, below: Class 87 No. 87004 *Britannia* takes an express passenger train through the northern hills towards Glasgow.

Below: A British Railways' class 87 Bo-Bo electric locomotive at speed on the electrified West Coast main line.

Class 381 Nine-car train

Origin: Japanese National Railways (JNR). **Type:** Electric express passenger multiple-unit trainset with tilting mechanism. **Gauge:** 3ft 6in (1,067mm). **Propulsion:** Direct current at 1,500V or alternating current at 20,000V, 50 or 60Hz, fed from overhead catenary to six motor cars, each with four 160hp (100kW) traction motors geared to the axles. **Weight:** 515,760lb (234t) adhesive, 753,802lb (342t) total. **Axleload:** 21,490lb (9.75t). **Overall length:** 628ft 11in (191,700mm). **Max speed:** 75mph (120km/h). **Service entry:** 1973.

The concept of a tilting train arises from the fact that suitably designed trains can safely run round curves at much higher speeds than are normally comfortable for the passengers. This takes into account the superelevation (otherwise known as "cant" or "banking") applied to the track. The idea was born that a calculated amount of tilt could be added to the cant by servo-mechanisms on the train, and in this way trains could be run much faster, safely and comfortably, without the expensive need to build a new railway. The proposition is so attractive that many railway administrations have acquired experimental tilting trains or coaches but so far only one, Japanese National Railways, has any running in significant numbers.

The Japanese tilting trains (Class "381") are not for high-speed operation, intended to run, say, at 90mph (144km/h) where normal trains run at 75mph (120km/h), but instead to hold 60mph (96km/h) where a normal train would be limited to 50mph (80km/h). The tilt is limited to 5°, compared with the 9° of Britain's APT project, and it is applied when the cars' sensors feel a certain transverse acceleration. Being intended for lines with gradients up to 1-in-40 (2.5 per cent), ample power is provided with two out of every three cars motored. One out of every two motor cars is a power car with pantographs and control/conversion equipment to cover operation on dc and 50 or 60Hz ac. The normal formation is nine cars, with driving trailers at each end. A nine-car train has 3,200hp

Above: The tilting abilities of the class 381 multiple-unit express trains are used to best advantage on mountain lines.

(2,400kW) available and this is sufficient to produce 50mph (80km/h) up a 1-in-50 (2 per cent) gradient. Dynamic braking is available for the descent. The combination of higher uphill speeds and higher speeds on sharp curves both uphill and downhill produces worthwhile savings in overall running times. Operation of the original units has been sufficiently successful for JNR's fleet of tilting cars to have risen to over 150 during the last 10 years.

Below: The blunt nose and driver's conning tower are prominent features of the Japanese class 381 tilting train.

Class 1044 B₀-B₀

Origin: Austrian Federal Railways (OBB). **Type:** Electric express passenger locomotive. **Gauge:** 4ft 8½in (1,435mm). **Propulsion:** Low-frequency alternating current at 15,000V 16⅔Hz fed via overhead catenary, step-down transformer, and a thyristor control system to four 1,765hp (1,317kW) traction motors driving the axles through Brown Boveri spring drives and gearing. **Weight:** 185,140lb (84t). **Axleload:** 46,285lb (21t). **Overall length:** 52ft 6in (16,000mm). **Tractive effort:** 70,600lb (314kN). **Max speed:** 100mph (160km/h). **Service entry:** 1974.

Austrian locomotives were in the past distinctive almost to the point of quaintness, whether steam or electric. But since the German occupation, during which standard German types were imposed, the Federal Railways locomotives have been capable but otherwise as conventional as could be. Only one-sixth of the 406 electric locomotives supplied since the war were not Bo-Bos, and of these 50 were Co-Cos and the others rod-drive switchers.

Most of the 406 also came from the Austrian state-owned locomotive-building firm of Simmering-Graz-Pauker (SGP) of Vienna and Graz, but an exception was a batch of 10 thyristor-controlled locomotives (Class "1043") imported from Sweden between 1971 and 1973. Satisfactory experience with these led to the thought that Austrians had been building electric locomotives a lot longer than these northerners. The result was this Class "1044", of which two prototypes were completed by SGP in 1974. Orders for a further 96 have followed.

Their high-speed capability is only relevant to a tiny proportion of the Austrian rail network, but high tractive effort and surefootedness, the key

Below: An Austrian Federal Railways' class 1044 Bo-Bo with the *Transalpine* Vienna to Basle express train at Innsbruck.

to operations in the mountains, are special features. Accordingly the new locomotives were designed to complement the stepless thyristor control with other measures, to bring adhesion up to values that only a very few years ago were thought beyond the bounds of possibility.

One measure taken is to provide linkage so that the tractive effort from each bogie is transmitted to the body as near to rail level as possible. This avoids weight transfer from one wheelset to another when either bogie applies tractive force to the body. Transverse forces imposed on the bogies by constant changes of curvature in the mountains are ameliorated by giving the axles spring-controlled sideplay.

Although some problems have arisen, leading to a temporary cessation of production, their effectiveness means that one of these locomotives (and they often run in pairs) can, for example, be rostered to take 550t (605 US tons) up the 1-in-32½ (3.1 per cent) ascent to the Arlberg tunnel on the trunk route from Switzerland to Salzberg and Vienna. The amazing one-hour output of 7,057hp (5,278kW) that makes such feats possible shows how far ac traction using double-bogie four-axle locomotives has come since the New York, New Haven & Hartford Railroad put their first Baldwin-Westinghouse Bo-Bo on the rails in 1905, with a rated power output of 1,420hp (1,060kW).

Above: At Seefeld, Tirol, in 1982, an Austrian class 1044 Bo-Bo electric locomotive takes a local train out of town.

Below: With the Innsbruck locomotive depot in the foreground, a class 1044 Bo-Bo can be seen leaving the station.

Class RC4 B₀-B₀

Origin: Swedish State Railways (SJ). **Type:** Electric mixed-traffic locomotive. **Gauge:** 4ft 8½in (1,435mm). **Propulsion:** Alternating current at 15,000V 16⅔Hz, fed via overhead catenary, step-down transformer and a thyristor control system to four frame-mounted 1,206hp (900kW) traction motors, each driving one axle by gearing and ASEA hollow-axle flexible drive. **Weight:** 171,910lb (78t). **Axleload:** 42,980lb (19.5t). **Overall length:** 50ft 11in (15,520mm). **Tractive effort:** 65,200lb (290kN). **Max speed:** 84mph (135km/h). **Service entry:** 1975.

The "Rc" family of electric locomotives, developed by the Allmanna Svenska Elektriska Aktiebolaget (ASEA) organisation initially for Swedish State Railways, bids fair to be the world's most successful electric locomotive design. Basically intended for mixed traffic, the design has been developed on the one hand to cope with express passenger trains at 100mph (160km/h), while on the other a version has been supplied for hauling heavy iron ore trains in the Arctic regions. Abroad, such widely differing customers as Austria, Norway and the USA have ordered "Rc" derivatives.

One of the reasons for this pre-eminence is that the "Rc1" was the world's first thyristor locomotive design, put into service in 1967; ingenuity on the part of other manufacturers is no substitute for years of experience in service.

In 1969, 100 "Rc2s" followed the 20 "Rc1s", and they included improvements to the thyristor control system and more sophisticated electrical filters. These are needed to prevent harmonic ripples produced by the thyristor circuits feeding back into the rails and interfering with signalling currents (which also flow in the same rails) and communication circuits generally. The 10 "Rc3s" of 1970 were "Rc2s" geared for 100mph (160km/h) while 16 units, some of which have rheostatic braking, were supplied to Austria (Class "1043") in 1971-73.

In 1975 came the "Rc4" class, the design of which included a patent

Below: The Swedish State Railways' class Rc4 "universal" mixed-traffic Bo-Bo electric locomotive equipped with a solid-state control system using thyristor devices.

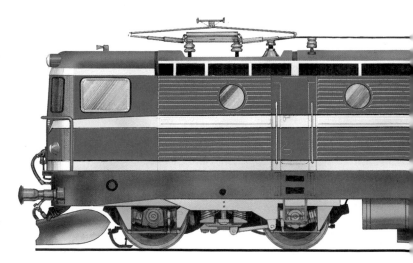

Above: A class Rc4 electric locomotive, dwarfed by the cars it is pulling, rolls a passenger train through the snow.

system developed by ASEA for countering wheelslip, which automatically reduces the current supplied to any driving motor which begins to creep faster than the others. There are also other improvements such as solid-state instead of rotary converters for power supply to auxiliary apparatus.

A total of 150 "Rc4s" have been supplied to Swedish State Railways, plus another 15 with modifications produced for Norway (Class "el.16"), but ASEA's greatest success occurred in the USA, with the fleet of "AEM7" electric locomotives supplied for Amtrak's North-East Corridor operations (qv).

Another variant was the batch of six iron-ore haulers of 1977 (Class "Rm") which had ballasting to raise the axleload to 50,700lb (23t), automatic couplers, lower gearing, rheostatic braking and multiple-unit capability, as well as better heating and more insulation in the cab.

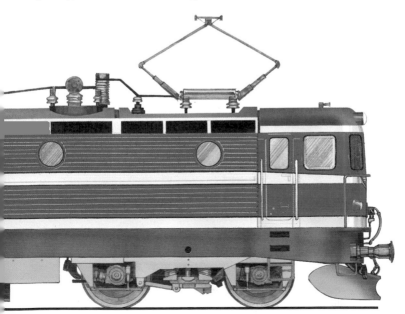

F40PH B₀-B₀

Origin: Electro-Motive Division, General Motors Corporation (EMD), USA. **Type:** Diesel-electric passenger locomotive. **Gauge:** 4ft 8½in (1,435mm). **Propulsion:** One EMD 645E3 3,000hp (2,240kW) 16-cylinder turbocharged two-stroke Vee engine and alternator supplying current through silicon rectifiers to four nose-suspended traction motors geared to the axles. **Weight:** 232,000lb (105.2t). **Axleload:** 58,000lb (26.3t). **Overall length:** 52ft 0in (15,850mm). **Tractive effort:** 68,440lb (304kN). **Max speed:** 103mph (166km/h). **Service entry:** 1976.

The last of the EMD passenger "carbody" diesels was built at the end of 1963, and with passenger traffic declining rapidly in the USA, the need for special passenger locomotives seemed to have disappeared. Both EMD and its competitors offered a train-heating steam generator as an optional extra on certain "hood" units, and this met the needs of the railroads which required replacements for ageing "E" or "F" series units.

In 1968, with the railroads' enthusiasm for high-power diesels at its climax, the Atchison,. Topeka & Santa Fe Railway proposed to buy from EMD some 20-cylinder 3,660hp (2,690kW) Co-Co locomotives geared for high speed to operate its premier passenger services. The railroad asked that the locomotives should be given a more acceptable appearance for passenger work, and that the body should have less air resistance at speed than a normal hood unit. The outcome was the "cowl", a casing shaped like an angular version of the old carbody, but differing from it in that the casing does not carry any load. The cowl extends ahead of the cab, giving the front of the cab more protection against the weather than a normal hood.

The model was designated "FP45", and was very similar in its equipment to the "SD45" road switcher. Another variant had a shorter frame resulting from the omission of the steam generator; it was designated "F45". ▶

Right: An F40PH diesel-electric locomotive on commuter service with Chicago's Regional Transportation Authority.

Below: The F40PH Bo-Bo "Cowl"-type diesel-electric unit, used by Amtrak as the standard express passenger locomotive.

In 1971 the National Railroad Passenger Corporation (Amtrak) took over most of the non-commuter passenger services in the US, and in 1973 took delivery of its first new locomotives to replace the old "E" and "F" series. By this time, enthusiasm for engines above 3,000hp had declined, so the Amtrak units were similar to the "FP45" but with a 16-cylinder 3,000hp (2,240kW) engine. A total of 150 were delivered in 1973-74. They were equipped with two steam generators mounted on skids, which could easily be replaced by two diesel-alternators when steam-heated stock was replaced by electrically-heated vehicles. In view of the similarity to the "SD40s", these locomotives were classified "SDP40F".

For a time all was well, but then an alarming series of derailments occurred to the trailing bogies of "SDP40Fs" whilst negotiating curves. No explanation could be found, but it was clear that the track had been spread or rails turned over by excessive lateral forces. The bogies were only slightly different from those of other EMD "Dash-2" three-axle bogies, but it was only part of the locomotive on which any suspicion of fault could fall.

In the meantime, for shorter-distance routes on which the coaches were already electrically-heated, Amtrak had ordered a four-axle 3,000hp (2,240kW) locomotive, with an alternator for supplying three-phase current at 60Hz for train services driven by gearing from the engine crankshaft. This model is designated "F40PH", and deliveries began in March 1976 when the problem of the "SDP40F" derailments was acute. As the well-tried Blomberg bogie fitted to the "F40PH" had given no cause for criticism, Amtrak decided that the Co-Co locomotives should be rebuilt as "F40PHs". The frame could be shortened by 16ft, as the steam generator was no longer needed. The "F40PHs" built new had a 500kW alternator, which drew a maximum of 710hp from the engine, but for the transcontinental "Superliner" trains an 800kW alternator and larger fuel tanks were needed, so that the "F40PHs" obtained by rebuilding are 4ft longer than the others.

In the fact the rebuilding was nominal, for it cost nearly 70 per cent of the price of a new locomotive, and in effect the "SDP40Fs" were scrapped when only four to five years old. Amtrak now has a fleet of 191 "F40PH" locomotives.

Many US commuter services are the responsibility of transit authorities, some of whom operate their own trains. A number of these operators bought a shortened version of the unhappy "SDP40F", in which the steam generator was replaced by an alternator. This is the

Below: A New Jersey Transit push-pull commuter train, in charge of a single F40PH unit, passes Harrison, New Jersey.

Above: A rake of striking double-deck cars of Ontario's GO Transit and headed by an F40PH unit, passes Scarborough, Ont.

"F40C", and in this application this engine is uprated to 3,200hp (2,390kW). At the moderate speeds of commuter services, no trouble has been experienced with derailments, but nevertheless when further locomotives were required the transit authorities ordered the four-axle "F40PH", in some cases with the engine uprated to 3,200hp.

Below: An F40PH Bo-Bo locomotive brings a short passenger train composed of "Amfleet" cars into Chicago's Union station.

Intercity 125 Ten-car train

Origin: British Railways (BR). **Type:** Diesel-electric high-speed train. **Gauge:** 4ft 8½in (1,435mm). **Propulsion:** One supercharged two-stroke Paxman Valenta 12RP200L Vee-type 12-cylinder engine of 2,250hp (1,680kW) with integral alternator in each of two driving motor luggage vans, each engine feeding current to sets of four traction motors mounted in the bogie frames. **Weight:** 308,560lb (140t) adhesive, 844,132lb (383t) total. **Axleload:** 38,570lb (17.5t). **Overall length:** 720ft 5in (219,584mm). **Max speed:** 125mph (200km/h). **Service entry:** 1978.

These superb diesel-electric trains, the fastest in the world with that system of propulsion, marked a great step forward in the long history of the British express passenger train and, in addition, represent the first real original and countrywide success story of Britain's nationalised rail system in the passenger field.

As with most other success stories, the main ingredient of this triumph was the technical restraint of the trains, representing as they did a development of existing equipment rather than the result of beginning with a clean sheet of paper. The disastrous experiences with the Advanced Passenger Train (qv)—a clean-sheet-of-paper design if ever there was one—are a case in point.

If, then the technology of the High-Speed Train (HST) was just an update—except possibly for bogie suspension—then so much more impressive is the somersault in operational thinking. Ever since Liverpool & Manchester days, long-distance trains had had detachable locomotives, not only beause the locomotives were liable to need more frequent (and messier) attention than the carriages, but also because they could then haul more than one type of train at different times of the day. The argument was that if the obvious disadvantages of self-propelled trains with fixed formation could be accepted, then the problems of giving them the ability to run at 125mph (200km/h) were much reduced. The power units themselves were simplified, since the need to haul other types of trains was non-existent. Things like vacuum brake equipment, slow running gear and much else were just not required and their space, cost and weight would all be saved.

As well as disadvantages, self-propelled trains have advantages. For example, HSTs can run into a London terminus and leave again after a minimum interval for servicing. At the same time there is no question of trapping its locomotive against the buffer stops until another locomotive is attached at the opposite end. Annual mileages in the quarter-million region can be the rule rather than the exception. And to counter the ▶

Above: A British Railways' express passenger train formed of an Intercity 125 diesel-electric ten-car set leaves town.

Below: The driving-motor-baggage van power cars which are placed at either end of each Intercity 125 ten-car set.

Above: An Intercity 125 train, made up temporarily to eleven cars, raises snow dust on an East Coast Main Line working.

Above, right: An Intercity 125 diesel-electric set forming a Paddington to Bristol express train, passes Reading in 1977.

Below, right: A diverted Edinburgh-London Intercity 125 express stands unexpectedly under the wires at Carlisle, 1981.

▶ argument that the locomotives that handled the day trains would be needed for sleeping car expresses at night, there is still the point that, for example, now that Newcastle to London is only a 3-hour ride, the need for sleeping car accommodation is much reduced.

The plan was originally for 132 HST trains intended to cover the principal non-electrified routes of British Railways with a network of 125mph (200km/h) trains. The routes in question were those between London (Paddington and King's Cross) and the West of England, South Wales, Yorkshire, the North East, Edinburgh and Aberdeen, as well as the North-East to South-West cross-country axis via Sheffield, Derby and Birmingham. Modifications to the plan since it was first drawn up have reduced this number to 95, providing a dense and comprehensive service of high speed diesel trains, now christened Inter-City 125, which has no precedent nor as yet any imitators worldwide. By 1985, the need to squeeze the maximum revenue-earning potential from these trainsets had seen them extended to the London to Sheffield route, and to other important destinations on a once-daily basis.

The improvement in running time over routes where there is an adequate mileage available for running at maximum speed can approach as much as 20 per cent. For example, the shortest journey time for the 268 miles (428km) from King's Cross to Newcastle is 2hr 53min (in 1985) compared with the 3hr 35min applicable during 1977 for trains hauled by the celebrated "Deltic" diesel locomotives (qv). Coupled with a

substantial improvement in passenger comfort, this acceleration has led to a gratifyingly increased level of patronage. A particular point is that the HSTs are not first-class only, or extra-fare trains, but available to all at the standard fare.

The design of the train was based on a pair of lightweight Paxman Valenta V-12 diesel engines each rated at 2,250hp (1,680kW) and located in a motor-baggage car at each end of the train. The specific weight of these engines is about half that of other conventional diesel engines in use on BR and the design is very compact. This led to the motor cars of the units being built within 154,000lb (70t) overall weight, and it was also possible to provide baggage accommodation within the vehicle's 58ft 4in (17,792mm) length. Compare this with the "Peak" (Class "44") diesel locomotives of 20 years earlier (already described), where a unit of similar power output was so heavy it needed *eight* axles to carry it. The lower axle loads of the HST trains were also important because raising the speed of trains has a progressively destructive effect on the track.

The MkIII carriages of the trains were the result of some 10 years development from British Railways' MkI stock, standard since the 1950s. In spite of the addition of air-conditioning, sophisticated bogies, soundproofing, automatic corridor doors, and a degree of luxury hardly ever before offered to second-class passengers, the weight per seat *fell* by around 40 per cent. One factor was adoption of open plan seating—allowing four comfortable seats across the coach instead of three—and ▶

191

▶ another was the increase in length from a standard of around 64ft (19,507mm) to 75ft 6in (23,000mm). This represented two additional bays of seating.

Particularly noticeable to the passenger is the superb ride at very high speeds over track whose quality is inevitably sometimes only fair. This is the result of the application of some sophisticated hardware evolved for the APT train, using air suspension. Including refreshment vehicles, some of the HST trains have seven passenger cars and others eight. For a period some of those on the East Coast route had nine, but this was only a temporary expedient, as maintenance installations had been designed around the standard formations.

The concept of the HST was to provide a super train service on the existing railway, without rebuilding, replacing or even electrifying it. This meant being able to stop when required at signals within the warning distances which were built into existing signalling systems. Accordingly, the braking—with disc brakes on all wheels—includes sophisticated

Above: Unaffected by the poor visibility implicit in this wintry scene is this Intercity 125 (or class 254) train set.

wheelslip correction equipment.

A price has literally had to be paid for these advantages, however. There have been hideous maintenance costs, and many technical problems have had to be solved expensively, despite the fact that a complete prototype train was built and tested. This train reached 143mph (230km/h) on one occasion, a world record for diesel traction. EVen so, there were aggravating problems with the production trains when they first went into service. Two things, however, mitigated the effects; first, a failure of one power car still left the other to drive the train at a more modest but still respectable pace. The second factor was the will to win through at all levels on the part of the staff, engendered by the possession of a tool which was not only a world-beater in railway terms but capable of beating airliners and motor cars as well.

193

Class 9E C₀-C₀

Origin: South African Railways (SAR). **Type:** Electric mineral-hauling locomotive. **Gauge:** 3ft 6in (1,067mm). **Propulsion:** Alternating current at 50,000V 50Hz fed via overhead catenary, step-down transformer with thyristor control to six nose-suspended 910hp (680kW) traction motors geared to the wheels. **Weight:** 370,270lb (168t). **Axleload:** 61,712lb (28t). **Overall length:** 69ft 4in (21,132mm). **Tractive effort:** 121,000lb (538kN). **Max speed:** 56mph (90km/h). **Service entry:** 1978.

It is said that the only work of man on Earth visible from the moon is the Great Wall of China, but a further likely candidate must be the 529-mile (846km) line from Sishen in the centre of South Africa to the new Atlantic port at Saldanha Bay. Not only would it have been noticed by a moon-bound earth-watcher on account of the rapidity with which it appeared, but its conspicuousness would have been enhanced by the featureless semi-desert nature of the most of the route.

Although built by the government's Iron & Steel Industrial Corporation (ISCOR) for moving iron ore for shipment, South African Transport Services operates the line, and the scale of operations is such that some unprecedented equipment has been needed. In virtually uninhabited country, electric power supplies are far apart and hence a nominal voltage twice that normally used nowadays was specified. The result is that there are only six substations for the entire route, the contact wire itself acting as a main transmission line.

The 25 locomotives built for the railway (after a period of diesel operation) were designed by GEC Traction in Great Britain but built in South Africa by Union Carriage & Wagon. They normally operate in threes, so making up a 16,350hp (12,200kW) unit capable of starting as well as hauling a 20,000t (22,000 US tons) load on the ruling gradient—against loaded trains—of 1-in-250 (0.4 per cent). They can also operate (but at reduced speed) when the voltage drops as low as 25,000, which can happen in certain conditions, say 45 miles (70km) from the nearest substation.

One delightful feature of a harsh operation in the harshest of environments is the motor scooter provided in a special cabinet below the locomotive running board. This enables someone to inspect both sides of a 200-wagon train almost 1½ miles (2.3km) long, returning reasonably quickly to the locomotive after the round trip. Other comforts provided for the crew include full air-conditioning, a toilet and a refrigerator, as well as a hotplate for cooking. The unusual appearance is due to the roof

Above: One of the remarkable 50,000-volt 5460 horse-power class 9E electric locomotives of the South African Railways.

having to be lowered to accommodate the large insulators and switchgear needed for the high voltage.

The control system is of advanced design, using thyristors. The position of the driver's main control lever is arranged to determine not external physical things such as resistance values or transformer tapping, but instead the actual value of the traction motor currents and therefore the individual torque applied to each pair of wheels. This gives a much more direct control over the movement of the train. There are five systems of braking: straight air on the locomotive, normal air braking for the train, vacuum brakes (on some units) for occasional haulage of ordinary rolling stock, a handbrake and electrical braking. The latter, which is rheostatic rather than regenerative, can hold a full 20,000t (22,000 US tons) train to 34mph (55km/h) on a 1-in-167 (0.6 per cent) downgrade. It is thought that this operation is the only one in the world where trains of this weight are worked using other than North American equipment.

Below: 16,350 horse-power moves a 20,000-tonne iron ore train on its 530 mile (345km) journey from Sishen to Salanha Bay.

Class Ge 4/4 B₀-B₀

Origin: Furka-Oberalp Railway (FOB), Switzerland. **Type:** Electric mixed-traffic mountain locomotive. **Gauge:** 3ft 3⅜in (1,000mm). **Propulsion:** Low-frequency alternating current at 11,000V 16⅔Hz fed via overhead catenary and step-down transformer with thyristor control to four 570hp (425kW) traction motors with both series and independent field windings. Connection to the wheels is through gearing and Brown Boveri spring drives. **Weight:** 110,220lb (50t). **Axleload:** 27,550lb (12.5t). **Overall length:** 42ft 6½in (12,960mm). **Tractive effort:** 40,040lb (178kN). **Max speed:** 56mph (90km/h). **Service entry:** 1979.

'To The Clouds By Rail' wrote Cecil J. Allen, King of railway journalists, referring to Switzerland's remarkable mountain railways. Nearer the clouds than most of those which crossed Alpine passes was the Furka-Oberalp Railway reaching, with rack-and-pinion assistance on 1-in-9 (11 per cent) gradients, 7,085ft (2,160m) at the Furka tunnel and 6,668ft (2,033m) at Oberalp Passhoehe. The ascents to the former were a little too close to the clouds in winter, when through running had to be suspended. These neat locomotives, with such remarkable properties for their size, were acquired in connection with an amazing project to convert the line into an all-weather route open all year round.

The project was construction of a 9¾ mile (15.5km) Furka base tunnel running from Oberwald (4,480ft—1,366m) to Realp (5,045ft—1,538m) to avoid the difficult summit section. These stations were the termini of the winter shuttle services from Brig and Andermatt respectively. Work started in 1973 and traffic began to pass on June 25, 1982; the estimates were overrun by three times in cost and one-and-a-half times in construction time.

There were to be motor-car shuttle trains through the tunnel as well as additional trains coming up from Brig. To work this traffic the FO management wondered whether the extra expense of rack-equipped motive power could be avoided, by working with adhesion on the rack sections concerned which had a lesser gradient of 1-in-11 (9 per cent). They were encouraged in this by the performance of four-axle locomotives (Class "Ge 4/4 II") recently supplied to the connecting Rhaetian Railway. On test they had produced 50 per cent adhesion, that is

Above: A rack-and-adhesion motor luggage van, class De4/4, used for climbing 1-in-9 gradients on the Furka-Oberalp line.

a drawbar pull of 25t, and in addition they could manage the equally unprecedented speed for the Swiss metre-gauge of 56mph (90km/h). This would be useful now that the FO at last had acquired straight track in the tunnel—the only possible place for high speed on its 62½ miles (100km) of route. Hence Nos.81 *Uri* and 82 *Wallis*, supplied in 1979, and lent to the Rhaetian Railway until the tunnel was ready.

Adhesion, that all important quantity for a rack-less mountain railway, was maximised on these locomotives by step-less thyristor control and low-level traction bars connecting the bogies to the body, as in the Austrian Class "1044". In addition, to minimise the effect of drawbar pull causing weight transfer from the front to the rear bogie, there is an electrically-controlled compensation system with two stages of adjustment. Wheel-creep, indicating the imminence of slipping, is also detected automatically and the appropriate motor current adjusted to correct the situation. Friction (and wear) is reduced by a flange-lubricating system ▶

Below: The class Ge6/6 adhesion-only Bo-Bo locomotive used for working motor car trains through the new Furka Tunnel.

▶ and, in addition, rheostatic braking is provided. Finally, it is a pleasure to find accompanying all this superb technology provision of retractable rail brushes for clearing and cleaning the rail heads of leaves and other detritus.

The locomotives can haul loaded car trains weighing 350t (385 US tons) on the 1-in-37 (2.7 per cent) grade in the tunnel. On 1-in-11 (9 per cent) grades, on which other motive power uses the rack for traction, some 75 t (88 US tons) could in principle be hauled by adhesion alone. This does not sound a lot, but lightweight FO carriages weigh a mere 12t empty although carrying up to 48 passengers.

Although trains are worked by adhesion alone on gradients as steep as 1-in11 (9 per cent) on other mountain railways in Switzerland, for the moment it seems that this will not occur on the Furka-Oberalp. The fleet of "De4/4" rack-and-adhesion motorluggage vans has been increased to cater for the increase in regular traffic as a result of opening the new tunnel and providing year-round service.

Right: A Ge6/6 locomotive provides motive power to take a motor car shuttle train through the new Furka Base Tunnel.

Fairlie B-B

Origin: Festiniog Railway (FR), Wales. **Type:** Steam locomotive for tourist railway. **Gauge:** 1ft 11¾in (600mm). **Propulsion:** Atomised oil fuel burnt in two fireboxes within a single boiler shell, generating steam at 1,600psi (10.6kg/cm^2) which is fed to twin 9x14in (229x356mm) cylinders on each of two bogies, the wheels of which are driven directly by connecting and coupling rods. **Weight:** 88,640lb (40t). **Axleload:** 22,040lb (10t). **Overall length:** 30ft 6in (9,297mm). **Tractive effort:** 9,140lb (41kN). **Max speed:** 25mph (40km/h). **Service entry:** 1979.

The majority of railway power units in the world run on two four-wheel bogies with all four axles driven. No exception to the rule is this Fairlie steam locomotive built in 1979 by an historic narrow-gauge tourist line in North Wales, called the Festiniog Railway. In fact, back in the mid-19 Century, Fairlie steam locomotives were the first to use this now almost universal B-B wheel arrangement. Also very unusual nowadays is the fact that the locomotive was built "in-house" at the railway's own Boston Lodge Works. The end result is a modernised version of the last one built there in 1879, 100 years before.

Although the line is operated for pleasure travellers rather than for serious customers, the specification is a severe one. Trains of up to 12 cars seating 500 passengers need to be hauled up gradients of 1-in-80 (1.25 per cent), with curves as steep as 2¼ chains (45m) radius, and all within a 22,040lb (10t) axleload limitation.

The use of oil as fuel for a steam locomotive might seem an extravagance, but a high proportion of that used is obtained cheaply as waste and residues. There had been problems with coal-burning as sparks sometimes set fire to forest plantations, while the use of steam propulsion in this day and age is essential because of the customer-drawing qualities of steam locomotives. The waste oil happily gives the authentic "'coaly" smell demanded by the public.

The Fairlie design involves raising steam in a patent double boiler with twin fireboxes and smokeboxes at both ends. The steam is then fed via two throttles—arranged so that the two handles can be moved either together or singly—and two main steam pipes complete with flexible joints to the two motor bogies. The driver and fireman have to stand in restricted space, one each side of the boiler.

A drawback of the Fairlie design is the complexity of the boiler. But

Above: A new steam locomotive on a new railway! Fairlie *Merddyn Emrys* brings a tourist train from Porthmadog into the new station at Blaenau Ffestiniog. Note the vintage slate-miners' carriage and the slate tip in the background.

once this is accepted, the advantages of being able to run out the power bogies easily from under the locomotive for repair or attention are considerable. Some concession is made on *Iarll Merionnydd (Earl of Merioneth)*—one of the titles of the Duke of Edinburgh—to the approaching 21st Century, with an electronic speedometer in the cab. An electric headlamp at each end is also a welcome innovation.

Class 120 B₀-B₀

Origin: German Federal Railway (DB). **Type:** Mixed-traffic electric locomotive. **Gauge:** 4ft 8½in (1,435mm). **Propulsion:** Alternating current at 15,000V 16⅔Hz from overhead wires rectified by thyristors and then inverted by thyristors to variable-frequency three-phase ac for supply to four 1,880 (1,400kW) induction traction motors with spring drive. **Weight:** 185,140lb (84t). **Axleload:** 46,280lb (21t). **Overall length:** 63ft 0in. (19,200mm). **Tractive effort:** 76,440lb (340kN). **Max speed:** 100mph (160km/h). **Service entry:** 1979.

The relative merits of the three types of traction motors, dc, single-phase ac and three-phase ac, were well understood at the turn of the century, but the choice of motor in early electrification schemes was determined more by considerations of supply and control than by the characteristics of the motors. The commutator motors (dc and single-phase ac) proved to be the most adaptable to the control equipment available, and three-phase motors were little used. Recently, however, new control systems using thyristors have revived the three-phase motor, because it is now possible to exploit efficiently and economically its inherent qualities.

Three-phase motors are of two types: synchronous, in which the frequency is directly tied to the supply frequency, and asynchronous or induction motors. It is the latter which have excellent traction characteristics. In this motor, three-phase current is supplied to poles located round the inside of the stator, producing a "rotating" magnetic field. The rotor carries closed turns of conductors, and as the magnetic field rotates relative to the rotor, currents are induced in the rotor conductors. Due to these currents, forces act on the conductors (the normal "motor" effect), and these cause the rotor to turn. The torque thereby exerted on the rotor shaft depends upon the difference between the rotor speed and the speed of rotation of the field. This difference is expressed as the "slip" (not to be confused with normal wheelslip).

It can be shown that the speed of the rotor is proportional to the frequency of the current supplied to the motor, to the slip, and inversely to the number of poles. Under steady running conditions, slip is only one or two per cent of the speed, so varying the slip does not offer much scope for speed control. In early three-phase systems, the frequency of the supply to the motor was the frequency of the mains supply, and was fixed. The only way of varying the speed of the motor was thus by changing the number of poles. Even by regrouping the poles by different connections, it was only possible to get three or four steady running speeds. It was this limitation control which hindered development of three-phase traction.

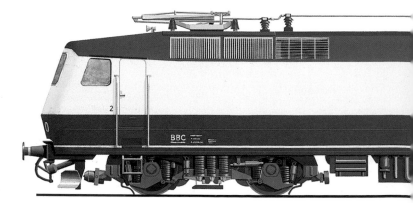

Above: The class 120 Bo-Bo electric locomotive of the German Federal Railways is intended to work all types of traffic.

It was only possible to vary the frequency of the current supplied to the motors by the use of rotating machinery. This was done in several installations by a rotary converter, but the advantages of the three-phase motor were then offset by the disadvantages of an additional heavy rotating machine.

The development of thyristors opened up a new future for the induction motor. By their ability to switch current on and off quickly and very precisely, thyristors can be used to "invert" dc to ac by interrupting a dc supply. By inverting three circuits with an interval of one third of a "cycle" between each, a three-phase ac supply can be produced, and it is relatively simple to vary the frequency of this supply within wide limits. This is the key to controlling the speed of an induction motor by varying the frequency of the current supplied to it. Furthermore, this variation can be "stepless", that is, it can be varied gradually without any discontinuities.

In any motor control system the effects of "steps" or sudden changes in motor current are important because they can institute wheelslip. With thyristor control, three-phase motors can be worked much nearer to the limit of adhesion than can other types because not only is wheelslip less ▶

Below: The German Federal Railways' class 120 design represents a fundamental step forward in locomotive control.

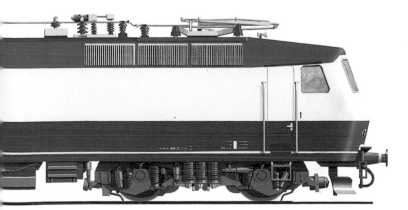

▶ likely to develop, but also it is self-correcting. If a pair of wheels loses its grip on the rail, it accelerates slightly, thereby reducing the slip, and, in turn, reducing the torque it transmits. This reduces the tendency for the wheels to lose their grip, so that wheelslip is self-correcting.

If the train begins to accelerate on a down gradient, the rotor accelerates, and "overtakes" the speed of the rotating field. Motor slip changes direction, and the motor exerts a braking rather than a driving torque, that is, the motor becomes a three-phase alternator. If provision is made for the current generated to be fed back into the overhead line, or to resistances, the induction motor provides electric braking quite simply.

Various experiments with induction motors were made in Europe in the 1960s and 1970s, both for electric locomotives and for diesel-electrics. Although all the systems had the common aim of supplying variable-frequency three-phase current to the traction motors by the use of thyristors, the circuitry varies between manufacturers.

In 1971, the West German locomotive builder Henschel completed, as a private venture, three 2,500hp (1,865kW) diesel locomotives with induction motors, using an electrical system produced by Brown Boveri (BBC). The basis of the BBC system is that the incoming supply is first changed to direct current at 2,800V, this voltage being closely controlled. This dc supply is fed into the inverter circuits, which feed variable-frequency three-phase ac to the traction motors. Deutsche Bundesbahn acquired the locomotives, and they were extensively tested and then put into regular service. In 1974 one of them had its diesel engine removed and replaced by ballast, and the locomotive was coupled permanently to an electric test coach equipped with pantograph, transformer and rectifier, from which direct current at 2,800V was supplied to the inverters on the locomotive.

Experience with this experimental unit encouraged DB to order five four-axle locomotives using equipment developed from the experimental work, and they appeared in 1979. The specification called for the locomotive to haul passenger trains of 700t at 100mph (160km/h), fast freights of 1,500t at 62mph (100km/h), and heavy freights of 2,700t at 50mph (80km/h); this performance was achieved in a locomotive weighing only 84t. Full advantage was taken of the good adhesion of the induction motors, for the continuous rating is 7,500hp (5,600kW), making them the most powerful four-axle locomotives in the world. The

omission of commutators and brushes from the motors enables their weight to be reduced, and in these locomotives the motors are 65 per cent lighter than corresponding DB single-phase motors. Maintenance is also simplified. The single-phase supply from the overhead is rectified to dc at 2,800V, and is then inverted to three-phase ac at a frequency which can vary from zero to 125Hz.

Early testing revealed a number of problems, and particular attention had to be given to the effect of the inverter circuits on signalling and telephone systems, and the general effect of thyristor control on the overhead supply (technically, the "harmonics" caused). Extensive tuning of the circuitry was necessary.

With these problems under control, the locomotives were tested on trains of various loads, and one of them was also subjected to high-speed trials hauling a test coach. It reached 143.5mph (231km/h), thus beating the previous world record for induction motor traction set up in 1903 in the Zossen-Marienfelde trials in Germany with high speed motor coaches.

In their original condition the locomotives suffered unacceptably frequent failures of various electrical components, and during 1982 each of them had a major rebuild to improve reliability and simplify some of the circuitry. The locomotives were tested over a range of loads, speeds and gradients, and their performance was outstanding. At one extreme they proved capable of starting greater loads on steep gradients than the heavier Class "151" Co-Co freight locomotives, while at the other extreme they established a world record for three-phase traction of 164.6mph (256km/h)

By 1984 DB had concluded that three-phase locomotives could exploit their adhesive weight more fully and run at higher speeds than existing units, and that they were extremely efficient and easy to maintain. Approval was given for a production batch of 44, intended to be the forerunners of a large fleet.

Below, left: A head-on view of the advanced and electrically very sophisticated German class 120 Bo-Bo locomotive design.

Below, right: One of the prototype class 120 electric locomotives at the head of a German Federal Railways express.

Class AEM7 B₀-B₀

Origin: National Railroad Passenger Corporation (Amtrak), USA. **Type:** Electric locomotive for high-speed passenger trains. **Gauge:** 4ft 8½in (1,435mm). **Propulsion:** Alternating current at 12,500V 25Hz or 60Hz, or at 25,000V 60Hz supplied via overhead catenary, a thyristor control and rectification system to four traction motors geared to each axle using ASEA hollow-shaft flexible drive. **Weight:** 199,500lb (90.6t). **Axleload:** 53,300lb (24t). **Overall length:** 51ft 5¾in (15,700mm). **Tractive effort:** 53,300lb (236kN). **Max speed:** 125mph (200km/h). **Service entry:** 1980.

The US National Railroad Passenger Corporation (better known as Amtrak) had the problem of finding motive power to replace the superb but ageing "GG1" class of 1934. New locomotives were required for use on the New York-Philadelphia-Washington main line, electrified at 11,000V 25Hz.Various substitutes fielded by US industry (which had built very few high-speed electric locomotives since the "GG1s") and one from France were disappointing, but a modified Swedish "Rc4" (qv) sent over on trial—'our little Volvo' Amtrak's motive-power men called her—proved to be just what the doctor ordered. Accordingly, a fleet of 47 was proposed.

Rather than fight the 'Buy American' lobby in the USA, ASEA sensibly licensed General Motors Electro-Motive Division to build, using some ASEA parts, what are now known as Class "AEM7". The "AEM7s" have stronger bodies, 25 per cent more power than the demonstrator, and multi-current capability to cope with conversions to 25,000V 60Hz, with a certain amount of 12,500V 60Hz.

Maximum speed is much higher at 125mph (200km/h), while the weight has risen by 17 per cent. This is no detriment, since very high axleloads are catered for in the USA by the use of heavy rail, closely-spaced sleepers and deep ballast. Vast sums have recently been expended by Amtrak to bring the North-East Corridor tracks, on which the "AEM7s" are used, up to first-class standards. The performance delivered by the "AEM7s" is what one might expect of a locomotive that can develop three times the power of Amtrak's contemporary "F40PH" diesels.

Above: The impressive front end of the standard Amtrak US-built but Swedish-designed class AEM7 electric locomotive.

Below: An AEM7 electric locomotive rolls an Amtrak express train under the wires of the North-East Corridor tracks.

XPT Eight-car train

Origin: New South Wales Public Transport Commission. **Type:** High-speed diesel-electric passenger train. **Gauge:** 4ft 8½in (1,435mm). **Propulsion:** Paxman 2,000hp (1,490kW) Valenta 12-cylinder Vee diesel engine and alternator supplying through solid-state rectifiers to four dc traction motors geared to the axles with hollow-axle flexible drive. **Weight:** 156,485lb (71t) adhesive, 826,500lb (375t) total. **Axleload:** 9,675lb (18t). **Overall length:** 590ft 2in (179,870mm). **Max speed:** 100mph (160km/h). **Service entry:** 1981.

The Inter-City 125 development in Britain (already described) is so successful and remarkable that one wonders whether others might not consider adopting it. One organisation that has done just this is the railway administration of the Australian State of New South Wales. Their Express Passenger Train or "XPT", however, has certain differences to take account of conditions 'down under'. First, there are only five passenger cars per train instead of seven or eight in Britain. Although the Paxman Valenta engines are down-rated by 10 per cent, the overall power-to-weight ratio is increased and this, combined with lower gearing (a 125mph maximum speed would be meaningless on Australian alignments), gives increased acceleration to recover from stops and slacks. Preliminary experiments led to bogie modifications to suit rather different permanent way and there are improvements to the ventilation systems to cater for a hotter and dustier external environment. The passenger cars are built of corrugated stainless steel, matching other modern Australian passenger stock, notably that of the "Indian-Pacific" Trans-Australian Sydney to Perth express.

The new train silenced many critics by pulverising the Australian speed record with 114mph (183km/h) attained near Wagga-Wagga in August 1981. Early in 1982, the XPTs went into service with a daily trip on three routes out of Sydney. Best time-saving achieved was that of 1hr 46min over the 315 miles (504km) between Sydney and Kempsey.

It says enough of the experience gained that an initial order for 10 power cars and 20 trailers to make up four five-car trains (with two spare power cars) was augmented in 1982 by an order for four power cars and 16 trailers to form six eight-car trains. In addition, Victorian Railways decided in 1982 to purchase three "XPT" sets for the Melbourne-Sydney service.

Above and below: The XPT express passenger train of the New South Wales Public Transport Commission. The overall concept and the design of the power cars as well as that of the bogies is based closely on that of the British Intercity 125 sets but the coach bodies are of Australian origin.

TGV Ten-car trainset

Origin: French National Railways (SNCF). **Type:** High-speed articulated multiple-unit electric train. **Gauge:** 4ft 8½in (1,435mm). **Propulsion:** In each of two motor coaches, current taken from overhead wires at either 1,500V dc or 25,000V 50Hz (or, in a few cases 15,000V 16⅔Hz) supplied through rectifiers and/or chopper control to six 704hp (525kW) traction motors mounted on the coach body and geared to the axles through spring drive; two motors on each bogie of the power car and two on the adjoining end bogie of the articulated set. **Weight:** 427,575lb (194t) adhesive, 841,465lb (381.9t) total. **Axleload:** 35,480lb (16.1t). **Overall length:** 656ft 9½in (200,190mm). **Max speed:** 162mph (260km/h) initially, 186mph (300km/h) ultimately. **Service entry:** 1981.

When, in 1955, two French electric locomotives separately established a world record of 205.7mph (331km/h) in the course of tests to measure various parameters on the locomotive and track,it seemed an esoteric exercise, far removed from everyday train running, which at that time was limited in France to 87mph (140km/h). But 21 years later two French test trains had between them exceeded 186mph (300km/h) on 233 test runs, and construction had commenced of 235 miles (380km) of new railway laid out for 300km/h running.

The main line of the former PLM railway connects the three largest cities in France, and has the heaviest long-distance passenger traffic in the country. Post-war electrification increased traffic still further, and by the 1960s congestion was severe. In an effort to overcome the problem of interleaving fast passenger trains and slower freights, traffic was arranged in "flights", with a succession of passenger trains at certain times of day and a succession of freights at others. The case for additional line capacity was very strong, and in 1966 serious study of a possible new route began. This line would not only relieve the existing route, but by taking advantage of French research into higher speeds,it would win traffic from air and road.

It was clear that a great advantage would accrue if the line could be dedicated solely to passenger traffic. The canting of curves on a line carrying mixed traffic at different speeds is always a compromise, and technology had reached a stage at which considerable increases in passenger train speeds were possible, but not those of freight trains. The axleloads of freight vehicles reach 20t and those of electric locomotives 23t, but if the axleloading on the new line could be limited to about 17t,it would be much easier to maintain the track in a suitable condition for very high speeds.

One outcome of the 1955 test running was that in 1967 limited running at 124mph (200km/h) was introduced on the Paris-Bordeaux line of the South Western Region, and further testing beyond that speed was made

Above: Two TGV (*Train à Grande Vitesse* or High-speed Train) ten-car sets await departure from Paris' Gare de Lyon station.

by railcar sets. The first experimental gas turbine train (qv) was run up to 147mph (236km/h), and one of the production gas turbine sets made 10 runs above 155mph (250km/h), but it was the experimental very-high-speed gas turbine set which pointed the way ahead. Designated at first TGV001 (but later change to TGS when TGV was applied to the electric version), this was the first French train specifically designed to run at 186mph (300km/h), and it made 175 runs in which 300km/h was exceeded, with a maximum of 197mph (317km/h). A special high-speed electric motor coach was also built, and this reached 192mph (309km/h).

The project for a new line (known as Paris-Sud-Est) to relieve traffic on the Paris-Lyons section was initially based on using gas turbine trains similar to TGV001. To avoid the tremendous expense of a new entry into Paris, the existing route from Paris Gare de Lyon would be used for 18.6 miles (30km), and from there to the outskirts of Lyons there would be a completely new line, connected to existing lines at two intermediate points to give access to Dijon and to routes to Lausanne and Geneva in Switzerland. Substantial state aid would be needed to finance the project, but it was predicted that both SNCF and the state would reap a satisfactory return on the investment.

Before the project received ministerial approval, the oil crisis of 1973 caused a radical change of plan, and gas turbine propulsion was abandoned in favour of electrification at 25,000V 50Hz. As the new route ▶

Below: A power car of a TGV train. All wheels, including those of the adjacent bogie of the next coach, are powered.

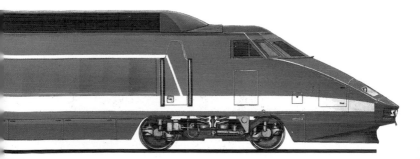

would be used solely by very fast passenger trains, it was possible to have much steeper gradients than on a conventional railway. The "kinetic energy" or energy of movement of a vehicle depends on the *square* of the speed, and the faster a train is travelling, the smaller is the loss of speed due to "rushing" a given gradient. On the new line, maximum gradient is 1-in-28.5 (3.5 per cent), or four times as steep as the gradients on the existing route. By adoption of steep gradients the cost of the line was reduced by about 30 per cent compared with a conventional railway. The longest gradient on the new line will reduce speed from 162mph (260km/h) to 137mph (220km/h).

Orders for the electric version of the TGV *(Train à Grande Vitesse)* were placed in 1976, and delivery began two years later. Although the design of the train follows that of the gas turbine version, the equipment is completely different, but it incorporates well-proven parts wherever possible. Each train comprises two end power cars flanking an eight-car articulated rake of trailers; that is, the adjoining ends of coaches are carried on a common bogie. To transmit the maximum power of 8,450hp (6,300kW) requires 12 motored axles, so in addition to the four axles of the motor coach, the end bogie of the articulated set also has motors. As the existing lines on which the trains work are electrified at 1,500V dc, the sets can operate on this system also, and six are equipped to work on 15,000V 16²/₃Hz in Switzerland. For ac working there is one transformer in each motor coach, with a separate thyristor rectifier for each motor, to reduce the risk of more than one motor being out of action at once. The same thyristors work as choppers for control of the motor voltage on dc.

The sets have a new type of bogie developed directly from that of the gas turbine train. As the new line is used only by "TGVs", the curves are canted to suit these trains, and no tilting of the coach bodies on curves is needed. The traction motors are mounted on the body of the motor coach, with a flexible drive to the axles. By this means the unsprung mass of the bogie is unusually low, and the forces exerted on the track at 300km/h are less than with an electric locomotive at 200km/h.

There are no lineside signals on the new line, the driver receiving signal indications in the cab. The permitted speed is displayed continuously in front of the driver, and he sets his controller to the speed required. The control system maintains speed automatically. There are three braking systems, all of which are controlled by the one driver's brake valve: dynamic, disc and wheel tread. The dynamic brake uses the traction motors as generators, feeding energy into resistances. During braking the motors are excited from a battery, so that failure of the overhead supply does not affect the braking. The dynamic brake is effective from full speed down to 3km/h. In normal service applications the disc brakes are half applied, and wheel tread brakes are applied lightly to clean the wheel treads. For emergency braking all systems are used fully. The braking distance from 162mph (260km/h) is 3,500m.

The trains were built by Alsthom, the motor coaches at Belfort and the trailers at La Rochelle. Initial testing was done on the Strasbourg-Belfort

Below: Tilting at speed, the TGV gives a comfortable ride.

210

Above: The French TGVs are permitted to run at 162mph and offer start-to-stop speeds over 130mph, both world records.

line, where 260km/h was possible over a distance. As soon as the first part of the new line was ready, testing was transferred, and one of the sets was fitted with larger wheels than standard to allow tests above the normal speeds. On February 26, 1981 a new world record of 236mph (380km/h) was established.

Services over the southern section of the new line began in September 1981, and passenger carryings soon showed an increase of 70 per cent. The northern section was opened in September 1983, with a scheduled time of 2 hours for the 266 miles (426km) from Paris to Lyons. In 1983 also the maximum speed was raised from 260km/h to 270km/h (168mph).

Apart from some trouble with damage to the overhead wires at maximum speed the new trains have worked very well. Riding on the new line is very good, but the sets are not so smooth when running on conventional lines.

The Paris-Sud-Est line is a remarkable achievement, for which the detailed planning and construction required only 10 years, and was completed to schedule. As a result of its immediate success in attracting new business, approval was given in 1984 for construction of a second, but slightly less ambitious, high-speed line. This is the TGV-Atlantique, which will improve services between Paris and Atlantic coast destinations. The 186 mile (300km) route will be Y-shaped with one arm running to Le Mans (for Brittany services) and the other to near Tours (for Bordeaux and the south-west). Services are expected to start in 1989-90.

SD-50 C₀-C₀

Origin: Electro-Motive Division, General Motors Corporation (EMD), USA. **Type:** High-power multi-purpose diesel-electric locomotive. **Gauge:** 4ft 8½in (1,435mm). **Propulsion:** One EMD 645F3 3,800bhp (2,840kW) 16-cylinder turbocharged two-stroke Vee diesel engine supplying current through silicon rectifiers to six nose-suspended traction motors geared to the axles. **Weight:** 368,000lb (167t). **Axleload:** 61,340lb (27.9t). **Overall length:** 71ft 2in (21,692mm). **Max speed:** 70mph (112km/h). **Service entry:** 1981.

The most prolific locomotive manufacturer the world has ever known? Well, it will not be long now, because although Baldwin produced almost 60,000 in 125 years of locomotive building, General Motors' Electro-Motive Division's score even in 1982 stood just beyond the 50,000 mark. Of course, EMD is well ahead as regards horsepower, while Baldwin certainly offered greater variety with steam of many wheel arrangements, rack-and-pinion and turbine, as well as straight electric and diesel-electric locomotives of the two normal Bo-Bo and Co-Co types, amongst others. EMD is not only the main supplier in the USA, having built some 70 per cent of locomotives now running on US Class I railroads, but also the biggest exporter. Most countries outside the communist world, except for those few with a domestic industry to protect, use General Motors' locomotives.

For just three years the "SD-50" 3,800hp (2,840kW) unit, driven by the 16-cylinder series 645F3 engine, was king of the EMD range. This engine is an improved version of that fitted to the "SD40-2" locomotive already described. The "SD40-2" series, best-seller during the 1970s, is still in the EMD range, but it appears that the "SD-45" series, which gave high horsepowers by using a 20-cylinder version of the 645 series engines, involved their users in high maintenance costs. The "SD-50" series is based on an alternative policy of strengthening and uprating the 16-cylinder engine.

The 12-wheel "SD-50" (the 'dash 2' designation, meaning modular electrics, is now taken as read) is also offered as an eight-wheeler called the "GP-50". An axleload only 6 per cent greater than that of the "SD-50" does not pose too serious a problem as regards damage to the track, but the reduced weight on the drivers means a 30 per cent lower tractive effort, so that the "GP-50" is more suited to less heavily-graded lines upon which high power output is more significant than maximum tractive effort.

Below: Model SD-50 road-switcher diesel-electric locomotives of the Kansas City Southern Railroad working in multiple.

Above: Mass coal movement is now a feature of US railroads operation. Here three SD-50s head a massive coal drag.

In this connection, EMD in 1981 introduced a considerably more sophisticated anti-wheelslip device than hitherto offered. This is known as the Super Series Adhesion Control System and uses radar to check the ground speed against the speed of revolution of individual pairs of wheels. The torque of each motor is automatically adjusted to keep the rate of wheel creep to a minimal amount. It is claimed that one-third more tractive effort can be produced by a unit which uses this device than one which does not.

In September 1984, EMD announced the "60" range of locomotives with a new 710 engine having a longer piston stroke. The new range makes a much greater use of solid-state devices (including three microprocessors) in the control system. The number of relays, for example, has come down from 51 to 15. Amongst many other advantages, the microprocessors enable engine control settings to be matched much more precisely to variable power demands. As a result of these and other improvements a 14 per cent reduction in fuel consumption compared with the "50" series is claimed, in addition to easier and less costly maintenance.

Class 370 APT-P Train

Origin: British Railways (BR). **Type:** High-speed electric passenger train. **Gauge:** 4ft 8½in (1,435mm). **Propulsion:** Alternating current at 25,000V 50Hz fed via overhead catenary, step-down transformer and thyristor-based control system to four body-mounted 1,000hp motors in two power cars, driving the wheels through longitudinal shafts and gearing. **Weight:** 297,540lb (135t) adhesive, 1,014,942lb (460.6t) total. **Axleload:** 37,248lb (16.9t). **Overall length:** 963ft 6in (293,675mm). **Max speed:** 150mph (240km/h).

Although the final outcome of this project, one of the most far-sighted and ambitious passenger train developments ever begun, is still in the future, it is fair to say that up to now it has also been one of the most painful. The saga began in the 1960s when British Railways set its much-enlarged Research Department at Derby to do a thorough study of their most fundamental problem, the riding of flanged wheels on rails. Out of this emerged the possibility of designing vehicles which could run smoothly at higher speeds than previously permitted over sharply-curved track with the usual imperfections. To keep the passengers comfortable, the trains would tilt automatically when negotiating curves which would have to stay canted or banked only for normal speeds.

Below: During trial public running, a shortened prototype Advanced Passenger Train set enters Euston station, London.

Several railways have done or are doing this, notably those of Japan, Italy and Canada. The Canadian LRC train (qv) is the only one which approaches the ambitiousness of the British scheme—in the others the body tilt is purely a passive response to the sideways forces encountered. In the APT, body-tilting is achieved in a much more sophisticated and positive manner, each coach adjusting its tilt response to curvature by sensing movement of the coach ahead. The amount of body tilt can rise to as much as 9°, which means that at full tilt one side of the car can be 16in (400mm) higher than the other. The result would be a train which could provide the high average speeds that the future would seem to demand if railways are to remain in business for journeys over 200 miles, without the huge capital investment involved in building new lines for them. For example, 105mph (167km/h) or 3h 50min between London and Glasgow is very close to 103mph (165km/h) envisaged in France over a similar distance from Paris to Marseilles, using the new purpose-built railway between Paris and Lyons. Put another way, the British solution—if it had succeeded—would have equalled the French for a cost of only one-fifth.

At this point one must say that the body-tilting is only part of this advanced concept—a new and fundamentally improved suspension system with self-steering bogies contributed even more to a package which looked like being a winner. A formal submission for funds to develop the project was made in December 1967. In 1973, after some delay, a four-car experimental prototype powered by a gas turbine was authorised and in 1975 was brought out into the world after early testing in secret on BR's test track near Nottingham. APT-E as it was called managed 151mph (242km/h) running between Reading and Swindon ▶

▶ and, more impressive, ran from London to Leicester (99 miles—158km) in just under the hour. These favourable experiences led to the authorising of three 14-car "production prototype" trains, the two central cars of each train being non-tilting and non-driving power cars, providing 8,000hp (5,970kW) for traction. The two halves of the train were isolated from one another and each had to have its own buffet/restaurant car; 72 first-class and 195 second-class seats were provided in each half.

Electric propulsion was chosen because there was no diesel engine available with a suitable power-to-weight ratio, and gas turbine was now considered too extravagant in fuel consumption after the then recent trebling in the price of oil. Moreover, the envisaged first use for APT trains was now on the longer electric journeys out of Euston to Glasgow, Liverpool and Manchester. One innovation was the solution to the problem of braking from very high speeds above 155mph (250km/h). The hydro-kinetic (water turbine) brake was adopted, giving a reasonable braking distance of 2,500yd (2,2290m) from full speed, with 2,000yd (1,839m) possible in emergency. Disc brakes provided braking force at speeds too low for the hydro-kinetic brakes to be effective.

The first APT-P train was completed in 1978, but there was a series of tiresome small defects including one that caused a derailment at over 100mph (160km/h). This meant that, although the 4hr 15min Glasgow to London service (average speed 94mph—151km/h), which it was intended to provide at first, had been printed in the public timetables for several years, it was not until late-1981 that public service actually began. Even then, only one complete Glasgow-to-London and back public run was made. A combination of further small defects, unprecedently severe weather and impending serious industrial action, led BR to take the train out of advertised public service, although tests have continued. It all happened in a blaze of unfortunate publicity, which mattered less than the fact that authorisation of a series-production version (APT-S) was deferred indefinitely.

In 1985, four years after this debacle, it appears that nothing so radical as a final decision has yet been taken, but the idea of completing the development of the self-propelled APT seems to have been abandoned. The current proposal, known as IC225, involves separate non-tilting

Above: British Rail's Advanced Passenger Train demonstrates its celebrated tilting capability during test running in 1981.

Bo-Bo electric locomotives (provisionally designated Class 91) which would haul or propel non-articulated coaches with (or possibly without) a tilting mechanism at speeds up to 140mph (225km/h). The most recent announcement at the time of writing indicates that trains operating on the West Coast routes would be tilting and those for the East Coast would be non-tilting.

Below: BR's Advanced Passenger Train was intended to run on existing lines faster than normal trains with no tilting devices.

Class 26 2-D-2

Origin: South African Transport Services (SATS). **Type:** Mixed-traffic steam locomotive. **Gauge:** 3ft 6in (1,067mm). **Propulsion:** Coal-fired gas-producer firebox with grate area of 70sq ft (6.5m²) generating superheated steam at 225psi (15.7kg/cm²) in a fire-tube boiler and supplying it to two 24x28in (610x711mm) cylinders, driving the four main axles direct by means of connecting and coupling rods. **Weight:** 167,505lb (76t) adhesive, 506,920lb (230t) total. **Axleload:** 43,640lb (19.8t). **Overall length:** 91ft 6½in (27,904mm). **Tractive effort:** 47,025lb (209kN). **Max speed:** 60mph (96km/h). **Service entry:** 1982.

Many people regard steam locomotives as the only proper motive power, any other kind being *ersatz* to some degree. Yet at the same time we are aware of steam's drawbacks—its low thermal efficiency, its labour-intensiveness and its dirtiness. Of course, the low thermal efficiency can be countered by use of less costly fuels—in some countries oil costs four (or more) times coal for the same heat content and this more than cancels out the better efficiency of diesel vis-a-vis steam. At the same time the amount of fuel wasted by a steam locomotive can be reduced by relatively small improvements, and since the dirt connected with steam operation represents waste, less waste automatically means less pollution too.

This "Red Devil" of Class "26" (named *L.D. Porta* after the Argentinian engineer who was responsible for the basics of the system) is an attempt to produce a steam locomotive for the 21st Century by rebuilding a "25NC" 4-8-4, a class built by Henschel and North British in 1953. The principal change is in the method of burning the coal, which is now gasified before being burnt; the other alterations are more in the nature of fine tuning. All were carried out in South African Transport Services' Salt River Workshops at Cape Town, at very modest cost.

The first big change is that now less than half the air needed for combustion enters the firebox through the fire itself, the amount of reduction being set by smaller and exactly calculated openings between the bars of the grate. This change cuts down waste by eliminating fire-throwing when the locomotive is working hard.

Steam is also fed into the hot firebed from the sides. This comes from the auxiliaries and from the exhaust side of the main cylinders. It reacts chemically with the hot coal to produce cleanly combustible water gas, while at the same time the reaction is one which absorbs rather than produces heat. So the temperature of the firebed does not reach the level at which fusion takes place and clinker forms. The air passing through the hot (but not too hot) firebed makes producer gas and it is this mixture of gases which burns cleanly, using the air entering through openings in the side of the firebox. The existing mechanical stoker is retained; the hard labour of running steam power is reduced both when putting the fuel in and when taking the residues out.

Other improvements made include increased superheat (with conse-

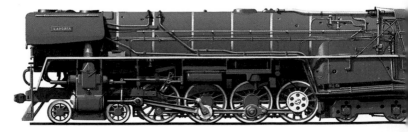

Above: Too Late? The South African Railways' "Red Devil", Steam's eleventh-hour answer, to the diesel-electric onslaught.

quent provision of improved cylinder lubrication), better draughting and a feed-water heater, all of which contribute to a further improvement in thermal efficiency. Adding this to the contribution made by the avoidance of unburnt fuel in the residues of combustion gives the startling result of one-third less fuel burnt for a given output. The maximum power output is increased, whilst both the quantity and the difficulty of disposal of the residues is considerably reduced. The result is a machine that can really look its diesel brethren in the eye in respect of such important matters as availability and cleanliness, and really wipe the floor with them when it comes to fuel costs in South African conditions.

Unfortunately, the current recession in South Africa has left the railways there with ample diesel-electric motive power for their non-electrified lines, and this situation leaves SATS understandably reluctant to undertake a major restoration of steam traction. However, these simple and cheap transformations of existing steam locomotives are being considered by a number of administrations, notably China and Zimbabwe, and have been undertaken by others, most recently by the famous Festiniog Railway in Wales.

Below: The new South African Railways' steam locomotive with gas-producer firebox. It was rebuilt from a class 25 4-8-4.

Bo-Bo

Origin: Via Rail Canada (Via). **Type:** High-speed diesel-electric locomotive for matching train with tilting mechanism. **Gauge:** 4ft 8½in (1,435mm). **Propulsion:** Alco Type 251 16-cylinder 3,900hp (2,910kW) turbocharged four-stroke diesel engine and alternator feeding via rectifiers four nose-suspended direct current traction motors geared to the axles. **Weight:** 185,135lb (84t). **Axleload:** 46,285lb (21t). **Overall length:** 66ft 5in (202,692mm). **Max speed:** 125mph (200km/h), but limited to 80mph (128km/h) by track conditions. **Service entry:** 1982.

Having as its designation carefully chosen letters that read the same in English or French—Light, Rapid, Comfortable or *Leger, Rapide Confortable* respectively—the designers had to have pointed out to them the letter L might in French just as well stand for *Lourd* or 'heavy'! The fact that an LRC passenger car weighs "only" 57 per cent more than, for example an HST car of the same capacity in Britain does lend some sharpness to the point made. Similarly the LRC locomotive weighs 20 per cent more than the HST power car. Even so, LRC is an impressive creation, although the many years which have passed in development have seen as many (or more) setbacks and premature entries into service as Britain's APT. Even so, the new trains were due to go into service between Montreal and Toronto in September 1981. A scheduled time of 3hr 40min was originally intended for the 337 miles (539km), 45 minutes better than that offered by their best predecessors, the lightweight "Turbo-trains" in the late-1970s. But by July 1982 the best offered in the timetable was 4hr 25min, with an ominous note "Timings subject to alterations, journeys may be extended by up to 55 minutes", indicating a possible need to substitute conventional equipment. In 1984, the best time was eased further to 4hr 30min, but the footnote has vanished.

This note reflected the fact that the LRC trains had to be withdrawn during the Canadian winter of 1981-82, having suffered from fine dry powdery snow getting inside sophisticated equipment. That the improvement in timings has been so relatively modest is due to the effects of heavy freight traffic on the existing track and the speed limits consequently imposed on the LRC. Two sets leased by the USA operator Amtrak have also not given satisfaction, and they were returned to the makers. Since then, problems have continued with maintenance of these trains during the four years they have been service, resulting in availability as low as 50 per cent.

Even so, LRC is a well thought out concept with a fourteen-year period of development behind it. An "active" tilting system allowing 8½° of tilt, ½° less than BR's APT, is combined with an advanced level of comfort for passengers. Ample power is available from the locomotives (which,

Above: The head end of a Via Rail Canada diesel-electric locomotive for the LRC (Light, Rapid, Comfortable) train.

incidentally, do not tilt) for both traction and substantial heating/air-conditioning requirements. One unique detail is the provision of outside loudspeakers so that announcements can be made to intending passengers on station platforms. ▶

Below: The Canadian-built LRC Bo-Bo diesel-electric locomotive decked out in the handsome livery adopted by Via Rail Canada for hauling these futuristic tilting trains.

One of Via Rail Canada's LRC tilting trains at speed with a Montreal to Toronto high-speed express passenger working.

Class 58 C_o-C_o

Origin: British Railways (BR). **Type:** Diesel-electric freight locomotive. **Gauge:** 4ft 8½in (1,435mm). **Propulsion:** One GE (Ruston) RK3ACT 3,300hp (2,460kW) 12-cylinder four-stroke turbocharged Vee engine and alternator, generating three-phase current which is supplied through rectifiers to six nose-suspended traction motors geared to the axles. **Weight:** 286,520lb (130t). **Axleload:** 47,750lb (21.7t). **Overall length:** 62ft 9in (19,130mm). **Tractive effort:** 59,100lb (263kN). **Max speed:** 80mph (129km/h). **Service entry:** 1982.

Dieselisation of the non-electrified lines of British Railways was completed in 1968, and from then onwards no new diesel locomotives were needed until, in 1973, BR was warned to expect a large increase in coal traffic due to the oil crisis. Work began forthwith on designing a new class of locomotive, to be more powerful than the existing 2,580hp (1,925kW) Class "47", and with a maximum speed of 80mph (129km/h) to give much better performance on heavy freight trains at low speeds than the 95mph (153km/h) Class "47".

The most common diesel engines on BR are the family derived from the pre-war English Electric shunter. This engine first appeared as a main line unit in 1947, developing 1,600hp (1,190kW) from 16 cylinders., By 1973 the engine had been uprated to 3,520hp (2,626kW), although for reliability BR decided to rate it at 3,250hp (2,425kW).

As BR could not produce a new design from its own resources in the time available, a contract was placed with Brush Electrical Machines to design a locomotive based on that builder's Class "47", but incorporating the English Electric-type engine and ac transmission. This work was done jointly by Brush and Electroputere of Romania, with whom Brush had an agreement for technical co-operation. As Electroputere could deliver the locomotives sooner than BR's Doncaster Works, the first 30 were ordered from Romania.

The first of these locomotives, designated Class "56", appeared in 1976. BR regarded them as an interim design, produced with the minimum of new design work to meet an urgent need, and it was soon decided that only 135 would be built. Further construction would be to a completely new design, Class "58", to be capable of hauling 1,000t on the level at 80mph (129km/h).

Below: The prototype British Railways' class 58 Co-Co diesel-electric locomotive for the haulage of freight trains.

Above: A batch of class 58 Co-Co diesel-electric locomotives being erected in a British Rail Engineering works. They have GEC-Ruston engines and GEC Traction electrical equipment.

Class "58" was much influenced by design work which had been done by BR on a 2,500 hp (1,865kW) locomotive which BR's workshop subsidiary, British Rail Engineering, hoped to sell abroad. Great emphasis had been laid on reducing the cost of this locomotive, and in its severely restricted financial condition BR was glad to have a locomotive cheaper than a Class "56".

The most obvious change in Class "58" is that it is a "hood" unit, with the structural strength in the underframe (Class "56" has a stressed bodyshell inherited from Class "47"). The massive underframe should have an indefinite life, whereas the thin panels of the stressed body corrode easily. The hood construction gives easier access to equipment and simplifies the division of the body into airtight compartments. Most of the equipment is in sub-assemblies which are bolted to the underframe, and can be replaced from stock. The cabs are self-contained, and can be disconnected, unbolted, and replaced in a few days, whereas on earlier BR diesels repairs to a damaged cab can take months. Access is from a cross-passage between the cab and the machinery compartments, so that the cab has no outside door to admit draughts.The layout of the controls is new for BR, and they can be operated whilst the driver is leaning out of the cab window.

The engine is a new model in the long line descended from the English Electric units of 1947. Compared with the engine in Class "56", the speed has been increased from 900rpm to 1,000rpm, and a new and simpler turbocharger is fitted. As a result it has been possible to reduce the number of cylinders from 16 to 12, and yet to rate the engine 50hp higher than the Class "56" engine, at 3,300hp (2,460kW).

Amongst other duties, these locomotives are used on "merry-go- ▶

▶ round" coal trains which discharge their loads at power stations whilst in motion, and for this purpose they are fitted with an automatic slow-speed control to hold the speed accurately at 1mph (1.6km/h).

Simplification in the design has produced a reduction of about 13 per cent in the cost of a Class "58" compared with a Class "56", and further economies will result from reduced maintenance costs. An initial order for 30 was placed with BREL's Doncaster Works, and the first was delivered in December 1982, wearing new colours based on the current livery of BR "Speedlink" freight wagons.

Manufacturing problems slowed delivery of the locomotives, and teething troubles were soon experienced with surging of the super-charger under certain conditions. Trouble was also encountered with excessive wheelslip, leading to a reduction in permitted loads. At starting, the drawbar pull of a locomotive causes the transfer of weight from the leading to the trailing bogie. On the "58s", this is compensated for electrically, so successfully that all axles slip simultaneously. The wheelslip detection gear, however, depends on detecting one axle accelerating *relative to the others*, and is therefore ineffective when all axles slip together. Rectification of these faults delayed production still further, but by 1984 orders had been approved for 50 of the class.

Right: One of the class 58 Co-Co diesel-electric locomotives in service. Note the provision of a driving cab at each end.

No. 12 B-B

Origin: Romney, Hythe & Dymchurch Railway (RH&DR), Great Britain.
Type: Locomotive for local passenger haulage. **Gauge:** 1ft 3in (381mm).
Propulsion: Perkins Type 6.3544 120hp (90kW) diesel engine driving all four axles direct via two-speed bi-directional gearbox and torque converter, drop-down gearbox, longitudinal cardan shafts and gearing.
Weight: 13,225lb (6t). **Axleload:** 3,310lb (1.5t). **Overall length:** 21ft 0in (6,400mm). **Tractive effort:** 6,000lb (27kN). **Max speed:** 25mph (40km/h). **Service entry:** 1983.

This minute locomotive plays a vital role in local light rail transport and may well play a bigger one in the future. Ever since it was opened in 1927, the 13 mile (21km) Romney, Hythe & Dymchurch Railway has claimed the title of "Smallest Public Railway in the World". A few years ago the claim became a degree firmer when a contract was obtained from local government to carry some 200 pupils to and from school each day.

Steam traction—however attractive as part of the RH&DR's normal tourist-railway operations—was quite uneconomic for the school train. Accordingly, with the assistance of a local government grant, a diesel locomotive was designed and built for the railway by the firm of TMA Engineering of Birmingham.

Sufficient tractive effort to handle a 200-passenger train was required and to obtain this a major ingredient was the Twin-Disc transmission. This was based on that used for many years on British Railways' diesel-mechanical trains and therefore,hopefully, the long build-up of experience so gained will lead to reliability. The shape of the locomotive has been designed to give the driver a good look-out both ways, as well as protection in the event of a level-crossing collision. The cab is heated, sound-proofed, equipped with radio for signalling purposes, and has reversible seats with duplicate instrumentation for each direction. Vacuum brake equipment is provided to work the train brakes,using an off-the-shelf exhauster and other fittings of automotive origin.

To some,of course, the introduction of diesel traction to this famous piece of railway showbiz is as if the *Folies Bergére* decided to dress its

Above: The 15in-gauge Romney Hythe & Dymchurch Railway's B-B diesel-mechanical locomotive No. 12 on a passenger train.

equally famous girls in denim overalls So to that extent a question mark must stand over the use of this acquisition. But perhaps the most interesting thing about it is that a combination of this locomotive and a rake of standard RH&DR light-alloy passenger carriages could now offer a way of providing a low-key rapid-transit system.

Such a system might bear a similar relationship to what is now called LRT (Light Rapid Transit) as LRT does to a full metro system. An LRT—effectively what used to be called trams, but mainly, or wholly confined to reserved tracks—has perhaps one-third the capacity of a hypothetical metro and achieves half the average speed, but only costs one-seventh of its grander rival. A Romney-style VLRT (Very Light Rail Transit) might provide half the capacity, and a very little lower speed, all for one-quarter the cost of LRT.

GF6C C₀-C₀

Origin: British Columbia Railway (BCR), Canada. **Type:** Heavy duty mineral-hauling electric locomotive for Arctic use. **Gauge:** 4ft 8½in (1,435mm). **Propulsion:** Alternating current at 50,000V 60Hz fed via overhead catenary and thyristor control system to six traction motors geared to the axles. **Weight:** 330,000lb (150t). **Axleload:** 82,500lb (37.5t). **Overall length:** 68ft 10in (20,980mm). **Tractive effort:** 95,180lb (421kN). **Max speed:** 68mph (109km/h). **Service entry:** 1983.

The early-1980s were years when the nuts-and-bolts of North American railroading were undergoing few physical changes. For many lines it was not a case of how many new diesel units to order but how many to put away in storage lines. There were even rumours that General Motors Electro-Motive Division's main plant at La Grange, Illinois, would have to shut down for a time. Of course, when it came to placing locomotives in store, it was the interesting and unusual ones that were put away.

However, significant moves that had been distant dreams or mere ideas in the 1970s were in the 1980s becoming possibilities. If any were to happen, the technical face of railroading in North America would change almost overnight and almost out of recognition, just as its commercial and political aspects have so recently done. Behind all these possibilities lies the huge change in the relative cost of energy obtained from coal compared with energy from oil. And the message is—put railroads under the wires because electrification is the best way to use coal for transportation power. ▶

Below: A 50,000-volt GF6C Co-Co electric locomotive of the British Columbia Railway's new Tumbler Ridge line on test.

Above: Three of these GF6C Co-Co electric locomotives are intended to be used in multiple on massive 98-car coal trains.

▶ All sorts of other conditions might also be favourable to electrification. First, government assistance might even be made available. The Department of Transportation has been issuing tentative construction timetables and schedules for suitable electrification projects. Secondly, the main locomotive builders—not surprisingly since diesel can reasonably be regarded as electric locos of the self-generating type—are able to supply suitable power. Thirdly, the risk that heavy additional local taxes might have to be paid on the fixed electrical equipment seems no longer to be valid. Fourthly, the rationalisation which is following the mega-mergers and relaxation of other restraints means there is freedom to concentrate flows of traffic on fewer routes—and electrification needs dense traffic to justify the cost of fixed equipment. Fifthly, with profitability improving, schemes involving big capital investment might no longer be so difficult to finance. Lastly, there is now no argument as to the type of electric current to be supplied to moving trains—that is, it should be the same single-phase 60Hz alternating current that we are supplied with in our own houses.

So far, it is true, electrification has been the biggest non-event in American railroad history. The USSR, for example, works nearly 60 per

Above: Tumbler Ridge line electrically-hauled coal train hauled by two class GF6C electric locomotives. Eventually trains requiring three of these powerful machines will be run.

cent of its tonne-km electrically,whereas the figure for the USA is only 0.1or even 0.01 per cent. Even 80 years ago,one could read almost the same arguments as appear above. But coming events cast their shadow before, and one notes with pleasure that General Motors (Canada) has supplied a batch of ac electric locomotives, designated "GF6C" for an 80-mile (129km,) branch of the British Columbia Railway opened for traffic in 1983. This has been built to bring out coal from a place called Tumbler Ridge in the north-eastern corner of the Province,far into the depths of the Canadian north.It is the first main-line electric railway in Canada outside the suburbs of Montreal.

The "GF6C" locomotive has a similar chassis and bogies to a standard diesel-electric road-switcher. There is a full width carbody with a depressed roof in the centre to accommodate the 50kV switchgear, and a transformer and thyristor control system replace the diesel engine and generator assembly. Three locomotives are used on each 98-car train.

ACE 3000 4-8-2

Origin: American Coal Enterprises Inc, USA. **Type:** Coal-burning freight locomotive. **Gauge:** 4ft 8½in (1,435mm). **Propulsion:** Coal-fired gas-producer firebox generating superheated steam at 300psi (21.1kg/cm²) in a fire-tube boiler and supplying it first to two high-pressure and then to two low-pressure cylinders, driving the four main axles direct by means of connecting and coupling rods. **Adhesive weight:** 240,000lb (109t). **Axleload:** 60,000lb (27.25t). **Overall length:** 458ft 6in (48,312mm). **Max speed:** 70mph (112km/h).

A most startling change in railroad motive power could be just around the corner—steam itself might be on the way back. Of course, most electric railroading is in a sense steam traction, because generators in power stations—even nuclear ones—are usually driven by steam, but the project in question is for a real steam locomotive burning coal directly. The key to the idea is the relative cost of different energy sources. In the 1940s and 1950s, when US railroads changed from steam traction to diesel, diesel fuel cost around one-fifteenth of today's price. Coal, on the other hand, then cost only about a quarter of what it does today. Put another way, a dollar spent on coal now buys nearly four times as much energy as the same sum spent on diesel fuel. It is granted that the steam locomotive will be less thermally-efficient, but there will still be a handsome margin of saving.

The idea that steam traction might have substantially lower costs than diesel is one that takes a little getting used to. Even the most rabid steam fan never claims more than that the diesel takeover battle was a much closer one than the victors ever admit. The big hurdle is to produce a machine that is less labour-intensive and polluting than its predecessors, but which at the same time retains the simplicity and reliability which was steam's greatest asset.

The original proposer of the "ACE 3000" project (ACE stands for American Coal Enterprises) was a man named Ross E. Rowland. He and his design team have borne all these things well and truly in mind because Rowland, a commodities broker, has had experience in running conventional steam locomotives on diesel-worked railroads. He was the man who put a Nickel Plate 2-8-4, a Reading 4-8-4 and a Chesapeake & Ohio 4-8-4 back on the rails, and naturally most of the original features of the new project are orientated towards solving the problems of servicing. For example, run-of-the-mine coal used as fuel would be supplied ready

Picture Credits

GF Allen: p17. AMTRAK: p4-5, 85, 132, 133, 204-5. ASEA: p205. ATSF: p25. H Ballantyne: p74-5, 100-1, 104-5, 113, 115 (both), 129 (top), 152-3, 156, 175, 177 (top), 189, 192-3, 214-5, 225. R Bastin: p51, 59, 107, 159, 160, 177, 191 (both). J Benson: p45, 97. British Columbia Rwy: p228, 229, 230-1. British Rail: p216-7, 224. Colour-rail: p36 (Swain), 43 (Hill), 49 (Quinn), 68-9 (Bell), 73, 103 (Hughes), 157, 197, 219, 227 (top Whitelaw). Colourviews: p35, 57, 58, 62, 102 (PJH), 171 (PJH), 186 (PJH). P Cook: p46-7, 67, 110, 127. D Cross: p37, 55, 108. DB: p149, 201, 202, 203, B endpapers. G Drury: p95, 143. FOB: p199 (top). C Gammell: p12-13, 22-3, 32, 70-1, 81, 112-3, 116, 144, 145, 154-5. General Electric: p134, 135. General Motors-EMD: p2-3, 212, 213. R Gillard: p80. Dr Hedley: p77. Hollingsworth: p8-9 (Gulash), 96, 199 (btm). J Jarvis: p19, 33, 38, 39, 48, 79, 93. H Kawai: p137 (both), 139,

packaged in 11-ton modules. The locomotive-type boiler and direct-drive compound double-acting cylinders correspond to conventional principles, although the layout proposed has not previously been successful.

An important technical feature is one that has been developed in Argentina and more recently in South Africa. The coal is to be converted to a mixture of water and producer gas before being burnt, by introducing steam into the firebed. The reaction takes place at a modest temperature; consequently clinker does not form. There are two advantages. First, the coal is consumed more thoroughly and so the process is more efficient. Secondly, since the air for combustion is introduced above the firebed, unpleasant emissions of unburnt fuel in the form of smoke and ash are virtually eliminated, thereby making steam traction acceptable to people who object to black smoke.

To give the machine a long range between water stops, a bulky condensing tender is planned. A sophisticated electronic control system would enable the locomotive to run in multiple with diesel locomotives or another "ACE 3000", and it could be driven from a cab at either end or from another "ACE 3000". The four driving axles are rigidly mounted on the same chassis; the two inner ones have crankshafts and are coupled together by a pair of internal connecting rods. This arrangement allows for perfect balance to be achieved.

A totally new feature is that a microprocessor will look after combustion of the fuel as well as setting the precise steam thrust on the pistons at every point during each revolution of the wheels. This would cover dynamic braking as well as normal traction, thereby opening a totally new concept of locomotive control. Trials of the computer equipment have been carried out on the preserved Chesepeake & Ohio Greenbriar 4-8-4 No.614, owned and adapted by Rowland to test his theories. This locomotive hauled 3,500-tone coal trains on Chessie System's line between Huntington and Hinton, West Virginia, in January 1985.

Finance has now been raised to construct a pair of "ACE 3000" prototypes, to be tried out on the Chessie System, during 1986. Substantial savings are possibly in prospect for any railroad that adopts "new steam", and for that and every other reason the appearance of actual hardware is eagerly awaited. One reservation must be that, in contrast to the elegant simplicity of the alternative scheme arising out of the South African Class "26", this design involves much complexity, and complexity has never mixed well with steam traction.

Below: This is how the steam loco of the future could look, if ever the visionary American COALS project reaches fruition.

PRINTED IN BELGIUM BY